bibliography index

REFORM OF LOCAL GOVERNMENT STRUCTURES IN THE UNITED STATES: 1945–1971

Edited by
THOMAS J. MICHALAK
Columbia University Libraries

and

ROBERT U. GOEHLERT
Indiana University Library

Published by **JAI PRESS**
(A division of Johnson Associates Inc.)
321 Greenwich Avenue, Greenwich, Conn. 06830

Copyright © JAI Press, 1976

Printed in the United States of America
Library of Congress Cataloging in Publication Data
ISBN 0-89232-037-0

TABLE OF CONTENTS

	PAGES
INTRODUCTION	i-iv
PERMISSIONS	v
ACKNOWLEDGEMENTS	vi-viii
BIBLIOGRAPHY	1-190
INDEX	191-273

INTRODUCTION

The growth of urbanism after World War II was accomplished by strains on the traditional fabric and structure of local governments. As citizen demands for new, improved or extended governmental services increased, along with demands for greater efficiency, accountability and responsiveness, local governments, state legislatures, the Federal government, citizens groups, research institutions and individual scholars began to reexamine the governmental structures of cities, towns, and regions. A common theme in the literature of local government during the period 1945 to 1970 is the inadequacy of contemporary governmental organizations for solving the problems and meeting the needs of an increasingly urbanized and interdependent America. Structural solutions to the problems confronting local governments were numerous. Proposals for local government reform range from annexation, consolidations, creation of special districts and authorities, urban counties and townships, councils of governments, improvements in home rule, charter revision, and city-county agencies on the one hand; to decentralization, deannexation, mini-governments, and neighborhood or community control, on the other.

The documentation on changes in local government structures, whether proposed or implemented, is widely scattered, difficult to identify, and sometimes impossible to obtain. Reports of special commissions or citizens panels have often become dispered or lost after such groups disband. When proposals fail, the documentation surrounding the proposal is often lost. As a large proportion of the literature of local government reform are documents, the usual problems facing the researcher utilizing state and local documents confront the student of local government reform.

In responding to the continuing exigencies of urban governmental problems, such documentation has value for the scholar and student of local government, as well as officials and citizens attempting to find ways to improve and reform local governments. The literature of local government reform has taken on an increasing importance in view of recent emphasis

REFORM OF LOCAL GOVERNMENT STRUCTURES IN THE UNITED STATES: 1945-1971.

on citizen participation, community development, and institutional responsiveness in the American political process.

This bibliography focuses on those governmental changes which have had a significant impact or which have been adopted by other governmental units. Emphasis is on governmental units which have, or may serve, as models for others. The literature identified in this bibliography includes legislative studies, reports of special commissions instituted to solve governmental problems in specific cities, states, or regions; analyses and studies by citizens' groups and public service groups; publications from research institutes in universities and colleges; and administrative reports and documents of governmental agencies at all levels which have been identified as significant in the history of the reform or local government structures. Included as well, are more general surveys of local governments on a state, regional or municipal basis which provides useful background for the study of local governments in specific geographic areas.

There are a number of exclusions in this bibliography. First, material published before 1945 and after 1970 is excluded. Secondly, for the most part, commercially published monographs are excluded. Some exceptions have been made in the case of monographs which, while commercially published, are studies commissioned by or undertaken for municipalities or other public bodies. Third, periodical articles are excluded. Fourth, documents which deal with the delivery of specific governmental services, e.g. police, sewage treatment, public welfare, even though some governmental change may be involved, are not included. The majority of items in the bibliography can be considered documents. The bibliography is not intended to be exhaustive, but reflects a selection of material which documents the history of the reform of local government structures. More exhaustive bibliographies such as <u>Metropolitan Communities: A Bibliography with Special Emphasis upon Government and Politics</u> (Chicago: Public Administration Service, 1952/55-1968/70, 5 volumes), or some of the bibliographies

INTRODUCTION

published by the Council of Planning Librarians, should be consulted for a more complete identification of the literature relevant to the subject.

The bibliography is intended to serve as a source guide to the collection "Reform of Local Government Structures in the United States: 1945-1971; A Microfiche Library". The number assigned to each of the 836 documents contained in the collection is a location device for finding the item in the microfiche collection. The bibliography is arranged alphabetically by main entry. Each bibliographic entry contains the following elements of information, if applicable: Document Number, Entry, Title, Author (s), Place, Publisher, Date of Publication, Pagination, Series, and a list of Subject Descriptors which have been assigned to the document. As many subject descriptors needed to fully describe the content of the document have been assigned.

Following the bibliography is a dictionary index of the subject descriptors, geographic descriptors, corporate authors, personal authors, and institutions or groups affiliated with specific studies. Geographic descriptors have been assigned wherever possible to reflect the municipality, county, state, and region discussed in each document. Thus a document dealing with a specific city is indexed under the city as well as the state in which the city is located. Counties and/or regions are also included when identifiable and relevant.

Besides each personal and corporate author or editor, each individual author within a collection or edited work is listed separately. Personal authors included in symposia, conferences, and hearings are analysed as well. Individuals or groups providing public testimony at hearings are indexed, but statements submitted for the record are not. The latter are not indexed because of the high correlation between public testimony and statements submitted for the record, and to include them would add unnecessary bulk to the index.

REFORM OF LOCAL GOVERNMENT STRUCTURES IN THE UNITED STATES: 1945-1971.

In the preparation of a bibliography of this kind, many editorial decisions must be made regarding the inclusion or exclusion of specific documents and the assignment of specific subject and geographic descriptors. Responsibility for these decisions rests with the editors. It will be appreciated if any errors which may have occurred would be brought to our attention.

                                              Thomas J. Michalak
                                              Robert U. Goehlert

PERMISSIONS

Permission to reprint documents in this collection "The Reform of Local Government Structures in the United States: 1945-1971; A Microfiche Library", is gratefully acknowledged of the following: Bureau of Public Administration, University of Alabama; Chamber of Commerce of the United States, Urban Strategy Center; Citizens Research Council of Michigan; University of Colorado; Iola O. Hessler Silberstein, Institute of Governmental Research, University of Cincinnati; Institute of Government and Public Affairs, University of California, Los Angeles; Center for Research in Urban Government, Loyola University of Chicago; Bureau of Governmental Research, University of Maryland; Metropolitan Fund, Detroit; University of Michigan Law School; Bureau of Governmental Research, University of Mississippi; National League of Cities; National Municipal League; Division of Government Research, University of New Mexico; Department of Community Affairs, Commonwealth of Pennsylvania; Regional Plan Association; Southern Methodist University Press; Lyndon B. Johnson School of Public Affairs, University of Texas at Austin; Tulane University; Warren J. Wicker, Institute of Government, University of North Carolina; and Joseph V. Zimmerman, State University of New York at Albany.

REFORM OF LOCAL GOVERNMENT STRUCTURES IN THE UNITED STATES: 1945-1971.

Invaluable assistance in the preparation of the index was provided by Mr. Robb Wardrop. Individuals at many institutions graciously assisted in the many problems encountered in identifying and gathering materials for the bibliography and the collection. Staff members of the Indiana University Library's Interlibrary Loan Department and the Reference Department was especially helpful. In addition, assistance was provided by individuals in the following libraries and organizations.

Alameda County Public Library, Hayward, California

Albuquerque Public Library, Albuquerque, New Mexico

Aurora Public Library, Aurora, Colorado

Bureau of Governmental Research and Service, University of Oregon, Eugene, Oregon

Carnegie Free Library of Pittsburgh, Pittsburgh, Pennslyvania

Center for Economic Development and Community Services, University of Utah, Salt Lake City, Utah

Chapel Hill Public Library, Chapel Hill, North Carolina

Charleston Public Library, Charleston, South Carolina

Chattanooga Public Library, Chattanooga, Tennessee

Citizens Union Research Foundation, New York, New York

College of William and Mary Library, Williamsburg, Virginia

Contra Costa County Library System, Pleasant Hill, California

Dayton and Montgomery County Public Library, Dayton, Ohio

DeKalb County Library System, Decatur, Georgia

Fairfax County Public Library, Fairfax, Virginia

Fresno County Free Library, Fresno, California

Governmental Research Center, University of Kansas, Lawrence, Kansas

Grand Rapids Public Library, Grand Rapids, Michigan

Greensboro Public Library, Greensboro, North Carolina

Hartford Public Library, Hartford, Connecticut

Institute for Social and Environmental Studies, University of Kansas, Lawrence, Kansas

Jacksonville Public Library, Jacksonville, Florida

Janesville Public Library, Janesville, Wisconsin

Jersey City Public Library, Jersey City, New Jersey

ACKNOWLEDGEMENTS

Kalamazoo Library System, Kalamazoo, Michigan
Library Association of Portland Oregon
Long Beach Public Library, Long Beach, California
Los Angeles Municipal Reference Library, Los Angeles, California
Marin County Free Library, San Rafael, California
Metropolitan Washington Council of Governments, Washington, D.C.
Milwaukee Public Library, Milwaukee, Wisconsin
Muskegon County Library, Muskegon, Michigan
New York Public Library, New York, New York
North Bend Public Library, North Bend, Oregon
Oakland Public Library, Oakland, California
Orlando Public Library, Orlando, Florida
Park College Library, Parkville, Missouri
Park Ridge Public Library, Park Ridge, Illinois
Pennsylvania Economy League, Philadelphia, Pennsylvania
Penrose Public Library, Colorado Springs, Colorado
Pomona Public Library, Pomona, California
Public Library of Knoxville and Knox County, Knoxville, Tennessee
Public Library of Nashville and Davidson County, Nashville, Tennessee
Richmond Public Library, Richmond, California
Richmond Public Library, Richmond, Virginia
Rollins College, Winter Park, Florida
Sacramento City-County Library System, Sacramento, California
Saint Louis Public Library, St. Louis, Missouri
Salem Public Library, Salem, Oregon
Salt Lake City Public Library, Salt Lake City, Utah
San Antonio Public Library, San Antonio, Texas
San Diego Public Library, San Diego, California
San Luis Obispo City-County Library, San Luis Obispo, California
Santa Rosa-Sonoma County Free Library, Santa Rosa, California
Savannah Public and Chatham Effingham Liberty Regional Library, Savannah, Georgia
Silver Spring Library, Silver Spring. Maryland
Stanislaus County Free Library, Modesto, California

REFORM OF LOCAL GOVERNMENT STRUCTURES IN THE UNITED STATES: 1945-1971.

Syracuse Public Library, Syracuse, New York
University of Illinois, Urbana, Illinois
Utah State Library Commission, Salt Lake City, Utah
Walla Walla Public Library, Walla Walla, Washington
Wichita Public Library, Wichita, Kansas
Wichita State University Library, Wichita, Kansas

BIBLIOGRAPHY

Document No. 001

ACKERMAN, DUKE R.
    Incorporation? Annexation?: A Study to Investigate the Governmental Possibilities Available to the Brisbane Area. San Francisco: Coro Foundation, 1960. 31p., (1) leaf of plates. (Under the Sponsorship of the Brisbane Improvement Association).

    Descriptors: Annexation and Boundary Changes
                   Governmental Consolidation

Document No. 002

ALDERFER, HAROLD F.
    A Citizen's Guide to Pennsylvania Local Government. Harrisburg: Commonwealth of Pennsylvania, Department of Internal Affairs, 1967. 86p.

    Descriptors: Citizen Participation
                   Political Leadership

Document No. 003

AMERICAN BAR ASSOCIATION. SECTION OF LOCAL GOVERNMENT LAW.
    Proposed Recommendation of Committee on Metropolitan Area Problems Concerning Structure of Local Government in Metropolitan Areas. Chicago: American Bar Association, Section of Local Government Law, 1965. 12p.

    Descriptors: Administrative Reorganization
                   Home Rule
                   Municipal Government

Document No. 004

AMERICAN SOCIETY OF PLANNING OFFICIALS.
    Extraterritorial Zoning. Chicago: American Society of Planning Officials, 1952. 34p., (Information Report No. 42).

    Descriptor: Annexation and Boundary Changes

Document No. 005

ANCHORAGE, ALASKA. CHARTER.
    City of Anchorage, Alaska Municipal Charter. Anchorage, Alaska: City Bank of Anchorage, 1959. 36p.

    Descriptor: Charters

REFORM OF LOCAL GOVERNMENT STRUCTURES IN THE UNITED STATES: 1945-1971.

Document No. 006

ANDERSON, ROBERT T.
    Past, Present and Future of Contract Services. (s.l.):
    (s.n.), 1960. 14p., (3) (Keynote Address to the First
    Annual Seminar of California Contract Cities, Palm Springs,
    California, April 29, 1960).

    Descriptors: Decentralization
                    Governmental Consolidation
                    Incorporation

Document No. 007

ANTON, THOMAS J.
    The Northeastern Illinois Metropolitan Planning Commission.
    Urbana, Illinois: Institute of Government and Public Affairs,
    University of Illinois, 1964. 20p., (Commission Papers of
    the Institute of Government and Public Affairs).

    Descriptors: Planning Commissions
                    Policy Planning
                  Regional Agencies

Document No. 008

ARKANSAS. LEGISLATIVE COUNCIL. RESEARCH DEPARTMENT.
    Annexation by Arkansas Municipalities of Territory in
    Adjoining Counties. Research Department, Arkansas
    Legislative Council. Little Rock, Arkansas: Arkansas
    Legislative Council, Research Department, 1964. 9p.,
    (Research Report No. 128).

    Descriptor: Annexation and Boundary Changes

Document No. 009

ARONSON, STEPHEN.
    The Legal Powers of Town Councils in Rhode Island.
    Kingston, Rhode Island: Bureau of Government Research,
    University of Rhode Island, 1966, 53p., (Research Series
    No. 10).

    Descriptors: Council Government
                    Home Rule

BIBLIOGRAPHY

Document No. 010

ASSEMBLY ON ILLINOIS LOCAL GOVERNMENT, MONTICELLO, ILLINOIS. 1961.
    Illinois Local Government: Final Report and Background
    Papers. Urbana, Illinois: Institute of Government and
    Public Affairs, University of Illinois, 1965. 83p.,
    (University of Illinois Bulletin, Volume 62, No. 92).

    Descriptors: County Government
                    Home Rule
                    Intergovernmental Cooperation

Document No. 011

ASSOCIATION OF BAY AREA GOVERNMENTS.
    Response Analysis Study: Analysis of the Response to the
    Preliminary Regional Plan. Berkeley, California: Associ-
    ation of Bay Area Governments, 1970. 42p., (Supplemental
    Report p. 249 1.0).

    Descriptors: Citizen Participation
                    Council of Governments
                    Planning Commissions
                    Policy Planning
                    Regional Agencies

Document No. 012

BAIN, CHESTER W.
    Annexation in Virginia: The Use of the Judicial Process
    for Readjusting City-County Boundaries. Charlottesville,
    Virginia: University of Virginia Press, 1966. xiv, 258p.

    Descriptor: Annexation and Boundary Changes

Document No. 013

BAIN, CHESTER W.
    "A Body Incorporate": The Evolution of City-County
    Separation in Virginia. Charlottesville, Virginia:
    University of Virginia Press, 1967. 142p.

    Descriptors: District Government
                    Municipal Corporations
                    Policy Planning
                    Regional Agencies
                    Special Districts and Authorities

REFORM OF LOCAL GOVERNMENT STRUCTURES IN THE UNITED STATES: 1945-1971.

Document No. 014

BAIN, HENRY.
    The Development District: A Governmental Institution for the Better Organization of the Urban Development Process in the Bi-County Region. Washington, D.C.: Washington Center for Metropolitan Studies, 1968. viii, 204p., (Working Paper No. 5).

    Descriptors: Governmental Separation
                      Incorporation

Document No. 015

BAKER, BENJAMIN.
    Municipal Charter Revision in New Jersey. New Brunswick, New Jersey: Rutgers University Press, 1953. vii, 27p.

    Descriptors: Charters
                      Council - Manager Government
                      Mayor - Council Government

Document No. 016

BANKS, JOHN C.
    Colorado Law of Cities and Counties. Denver: Sage Books, 1959, 316p.

    Descriptors: Charters
                      Citizen Participation
                      Incorporation
                      Municipal Corporations
                      Special Districts and Authorities

Document No. 017

BANOVETZ, JAMES M.
    Leadership, Localism and Urbanism: Components in Search of a System. James Banovetz, Peter J. Fugiel, Paul Mandy, Richard B. Ogilvie, Gene H. Graves. Chicago: Center for Research in Urban Government, Loyola University, 1968. 39p., (No. 10, A Collection of Ideas From Loyola University's Urban Policy Seminars 1966-67).

    Descriptors: County Government
                      Political Leadership

BIBLIOGRAPHY

Document No. 018

BANOVETZ, JAMES M.
    Perspectives on the Future of Government in Metropolitan Areas. Chicago: Center for Research in Urban Government, Loyola University, 1967. 52p., (No. 11).

    Descriptors: Council of Governments
                  Governmental Consolidation
                  Intergovernmental Cooperation
                  Special Districts and Authorities

Document No. 019

BARNES, PHILIP W.
    Metropolitan Coalitions: A Study of Councils of Governments in Texas. Austin, Texas: Institute of Public Affairs, University of Texas, 1969. 113p., (1) fold. leaf of plates. (Public Affairs Series No. 76).

    Descriptors: Councils of Governments
                  Policy Planning
                  Regional Agencies

Document No. 020

BEMIS, GEORGE W.
    Los Angeles County as an Agency of Municipal Government. George W. Bemis and Nancy Basche. Los Angeles: Haynes Foundation, 1946. xv, 105p.

    Descriptors: Advisory Councils
                  Community Control
                  County Government
                  Decentralization
                  District Government

Document No. 021

BERNARD, WILLIAM CHARLES.
    Metro Denver: Mile High Government (Revised). William Charles Bernard; edited by Mrs. Ashley Baker Nugent. Boulder, Colorado: Bureau of Governmental Research and Service, University of Colorado, 1970. ix, 69p.

    Descriptors: Annexation and Boundary Changes
                  Council of Governments
                  District Government
                  Regional Agencies
                  Speical Districts and Authorities

REFORM OF LOCAL GOVERNMENT STRUCTURES IN THE UNITED STATES: 1945-1971.

Document No. 023

BILLS (FRANK J.) AND ASSOCIATES.
    The Urban Services Crisis of Local Government Jurisdictions in Clark County, Nevada: A Report on the Feasibility of Alternative Courses of Action. Las Vegas, Nevada: Franklin J. Bills and Associates, 1968. 15p.

    Descriptors: County Government
                    Governmental Consolidation
                    Intergovernmental Cooperation

Document No. 024

BINGHAM, DAVID A.
    Constitutional Municipal Home Rule in Arizona. Tucson, Arizona: Bureau of Business and Public Research, University of Arizona, 1960. v, 66p., (Special Studies No. 16).

    Descriptors: Charters
                    Home Rule

Document No. 025

BINGHAM, DAVID A.
    Government in Arizona's Metropolitan Areas. David A. Bingham and Dean E. Mann. Tucson, Arizona: Bureau of Business and Public Research, University of Arizona, 1959. 48p., (Reprinted from Arizona Review of Business and Public Administration, Volume 8, Nos. 11 and 12, November and December, 1959).

    Descriptors: Annexation and Boundary Changes
                    County Government
                    Incorporation
                    Intergovernmental Cooperation
                    Municipal Government
                    Special Districts and Authorities

Document No. 026

BIRD, FREDERICK L.
    Local Special Districts and Authorities in Rhode Island: A Report Prepared for the State of Rhode Island and Providence Plantations by the Institute of Public Administration. Kingston, Rhode Island: Bureau of Government Research, University of Rhode Island, 1962. 38p., (Research Series No. 4)

    Descriptors: Advisory Councils
                    Special Districts and Authorities

BIBLIOGRAPHY

Document No. 027

BIRKHEAD, GUTHERIE S.
Metropolitan Issues: Social, Governmental, Fiscal. Gutherie S. Birkhead, editor; Harvey E. Brazer, Scott Greer, York Willbern. Syracuse, New York: Maxwell Graduate School of Citizenship and Public Affairs, Syracuse University, 1962. 84p. (Background papers prepared for the Third Annual Faculty Seminar on Metropolitan Research, August 20-30, 1961).

Descriptors: Municipal Corporations
              Municipal Government
              Special Districts and Authorities

Document No. 028

BLACK, GUY.
The Decentralization of Urban Government: A Systems Approach. Washington, D.C.: Program of Policy Studies in Science and Technology, George Washington University, 1968. 30p., (Staff Discussion Paper 102).

Descriptors: Administrative Reorganization
              Decentralization

Document No. 029

BLAIR, GEORGE S.
Interjurisdictional Agreements in Southeastern Pennsylvania. Philadelphia: Fels Institute of Local and State Government, University of Pennsylvania, 1961. vi, 136p.

Descriptors: Intergovernmental Cooperation
              Regional Agencies
              Special Districts and Authorities

Document No. 030

BLUE EARTH COUNTY COUNCIL ON INTERGOVERNMENTAL RELATIONS (MINNESOTA).
A Progess Report of the Blue Earth County Experiment. Mankato, Minnesota: Blue Earth County Council on Intergovernmental Relations, 1945. 35p.

Descriptor: Intergovernmental Cooperation

Document No. 031

BOLLENS, JOHN.
A Study of the Los Angeles City Charter: A Report of the Municipal and County Government Section of Town Hall. Los Angeles: Town Hall, 1963. 215p.

Descriptors: Charters
              Mayor - Council Government
              Political Leadership

REFORM OF LOCAL GOVERNMENT STRUCTURES IN THE UNITED STATES: 1945-1971.

Document No. 032

BOOTH, DAVID A.
    The Community Setting. Boston: Bureau of Public Affairs, Boston College: Bureau of Government Research, University of Massachusetts, 1965. 36p., (Part I in a Series on Modernizing Local Government in Massachusetts).

    Descriptors: County Government
                    Special Districts and Authorities

Document No. 033

BOOTH, DAVID A.
    Metropolitics: The Nashville Consolidation. East Lansing, Michigan: Institute for Community Development and Services, Michigan State University, 1963. viii, 108p.

    Descriptors: Annexation and Boundary Changes
                    Governmental Consolidation
                    Political Leadership

Document No. 034

BOWEN, DON L.
    Local Government in Maryland. Don L. Bowen and Robert S. Friedman. College Park, Maryland: Bureau of Government Research, College of Business and Public Administration, University of Maryland, 1955. v, 143p., (1) fold. leaf of plates.

    Descriptors: County Government
                    Municipal Government
                    Special Districts and Authorities

Document No. 035

BRIDGE, FRANKLIN M.
    Metro Denver: Mile-High Government. Boulder, Colorado. Bureau of Governmental Research and Service, University of Colorado, 1963. 77p., (5) transparencies, (1) leaf of plates.

    Descriptors: County Government
                    Governmental Consolidation
                  Mayor - Council Government
                  Regional Agencies
                  Special Districts and Authorities

BIBLIOGRAPHY

Document No. 036

BRILEY, BEVERLY.
    The Davidson County Story. Nashville, Tennessee: County Government Institute, 1964. (5).

    Descriptors: Charters
                  Governmental Consolidation

Document No. 037

BROMAGE, ARTHUR W.
    Constitutional Aspects of State-local Relationships - I: Municipal and County Home Rule for Michigan. Detroit: Citizens Research Council of Michigan, 1961. 28p., (Con-Con Research Paper No. 3, Memorandum No. 203).

    Descriptors: County Government
                  Home Rule
                  Municipal Government

Document No. 038

BROMAGE, ARTHUR W.
    Manager Plan Abandonments: Why 51 Communities Shelved Council-Manager Government. 4th ed. New York: National Municipal League, 1954. 40p.

    Descriptors: Charters
                  Council - Manager Government

Document No. 039

BROWN, BERNARD G.
    A Case Study of Urban Expansion and Annexation, Harris County, Texas. Bernard G. Brown and Harvey Shapiro. Washington: U.S. Department of Agriculture, Economic Research Service; in cooperation with University of Houston, 1965. iv, 50p., (Agricultural Economic Report No. 86).

    Descriptor: Annexation and Boundary Changes

Document No. 040

BUECHE, KENNETH G.
    Incorporation Laws: One Aspect of the Urban Problem. Boulder, Colorado: Bureau of Governmental Research and Services, University of Colorado, 1963. 24p.

    Descriptor: Incorporation

REFORM OF LOCAL GOVERNMENT STRUCTURES IN THE UNITED STATES: 1945-1971.

Document No. 041

BUECHNER, JOHN C.
    City Managers and Councils: Charter Provisions in Colorado Home Rule Cities. Boulder, Colorado: Bureau of Governmental Research and Service, University of Colorado, 1964. vii, 37p.

    Descriptors: Charters
                          Council - Manager Government
                          Home Rule

Document No. 042

BUECHNER, JOHN C.
    Differences in Role Perceptions in Colorado Council-Manager Cities. Boulder, Colorado: Bureau of Governmental Research and Service, University of Colorado, 1965. vii, 62p.

    Descriptor: Council - Manager Government

Document No. 043

BUREAU OF MUNICIPAL RESEARCH (SYRACUSE, NEW YORK).
    Nottingham-Tecumseh Area Annexation: Financial Considerations to the City of Syracuse. Syracuse, New York: Bureau of Municipal Research, 1957. 33p., (1).

    Descriptor: Annexation and Boundary Changes

Document No. 044

BURGESS, JR., JAMES V.
    A Study of Intergovernmental Cooperation in Georgia: Legal Basis. James V. Burgess and George A. Bell, Jr. Athens, Georgia: Institute of Community and Area Development and Institute of Law and Government, University of Georgia, 1963. iii, 20p.

    Descriptors: Intergovernmental Cooperation
                          Special Districts and Authorities

Document No. 045

CALIFORNIA. COORDINATING COUNCIL ON URBAN POLICY.
    California Urban Policy for Intergovernmental Action: First Report of the Coordinating Council on Urban Policy. Sacramento: Coordinating Council on Urban Policy, 1965. 27p.

    Descriptors: Federation
                          Intergovernmental Cooperation
                          Policy Planning

BIBLIOGRAPHY

Document No. 046

CALIFORNIA. COUNCIL ON INTERGOVERNMENTAL RELATIONS.
Allocation of Public Service Responsibilities in California: Part I, A Report of the California Council on Intergovernmental Relations. Sacramento: California Council on Intergovernmental Relations. 1970. 29p.

Descriptors: Intergovernmental Cooperation
Policy Planning
Special Districts and Authorities

Document No. 047

CALIFORNIA. GOVERNOR'S COMMISSION OF METROPOLITAN AREA PROBLEMS.
Metropolitan California: Papers Prepared for the Governor's Commission on Metropolitan Area Problems. edited by Ernest A. Engelbert. Sacramento: Governor's Commission on Metropolitan Area Problems. 1961. x, 185p.

Descriptors: Annexation and Boundary Changes
Federation
Intergovernmental Cooperation
Planning Commissions
Regional Agencies

Document No. 048

CALIFORNIA. INTERGOVERNMENTAL COUNCIL ON URBAN GROWTH.
A Report on a Survey of Local Agency Formation Commissions, 1966. Intergovernmental Council on Urban Policy. Sacramento: The Council, 1966. 39p.

Descriptors: Commission Government
Intergovernmental Cooperation
Planning Commissions
Policy Planning
Regional Agencies

Document No. 049

CALIFORNIA. INTERGOVERNMENTAL COUNCIL ON URBAN GROWTH.
Summary of Council Activities and Accomplishments. Sacramento: Intergovernmental Council on Urban Growth. 1967. 5p.

Descriptors: Federation
Intergovernmental Cooperation
Planning Commissions
Regional Agencies

REFORM OF LOCAL GOVERNMENT STRUCTURES IN THE UNITED STATES: 1945-1971.

Document No. 050

CALIFORNIA. LEGISLATURE. ASSEMBLY. INTERIM COMMITTEE ON
CONSERVATION, PLANNING AND PUBLIC WORKS. SUBCOMMITTE ON PLANNING.
    A Metropolitan Multipurpose District for California: Report
of the Subcommittee on Planning. Report Prepared by Pacific
Planning and Research. Sacramento: Assembly of the State of
California, 1959. 101p., (Assembly Interim Committee Reports,
Volume 13, No. 24, 1957-1959).

    Descriptors: District Government
                Policy Planning
                Special Districts and Authorities

Document No. 051

CALIFORNIA. LEGISLATURE. ASSEMBLY. INTERIM COMMITTEE ON
MUNICIPAL AND COUNTY GOVERNMENT.
    Annexation and Related Incorporation Problems in the State of
California: Final Report of the Assembly Interim Committee on
Municipal and County Government, House Resolution No. 326.16.
Sacramento: Assembly of the State of California, 1959. 63p.,
(Assembly Interim Committee Reports, Volume 6, No. 16, 1959-1961).

    Descriptors: Annexation and Boundary Changes
                Government Consolidation
                Incorporation

Document No. 052

CALIFORNIA. LEGISLATURE. ASSEMBLY. INTERIM COMMITTEE ON
MUNICIPAL AND COUNTY GOVERNMENT.
    City and County Functional Consolidation, City and County
Retirement Problems: Final Report of the Assembly Interim
Committee on Municipal and County Government, House Resolution
No. 203, 1955. Sacramento: Assembly of the State of California,
1955. 15p., (Assembly Interim Committee Reports, Volume 6, No. 5,
1955-1957).

    Descriptors: Governmental Consolidation
                Intergovernmental Cooperation

Document No. 053

CALIFORNIA. LEGISLATURE. ASSEMBLY. INTERIM COMMITTEE ON MUNICIPAL
AND COUNTY GOVERNMENT.
    Financing Local Government in Los Angeles County. Sacramento:
Assembly of the State of California, 1953. 119p.

    Descriptors: County Government
                Intergovernmental Cooperation
                Policy Planning

BIBLIOGRAPHY

Document No. 054

CALIFORNIA. LEGISLATURE. ASSEMBLY. INTERIM COMMITTEE ON MUNICIPAL AND COUNTY GOVERNMENT.
    Functional Consolidation of Local Government: Final Report of the Assembly Interim Committee on Municipal and County Government, House Resolution No. 277, 1957. Sacramento: Assembly of the State of California, 1957. 27p., (Assembly Interim Committee Reports, Volume 6, No. 10, 1957-1959).

    Descriptors: Citizen Participation
                     Governmental Consolidation
                     Intergovernmental Cooperation

Document No. 055

CALIFORNIA. LEGISLATURE. ASSEMBLY. INTERIM COMMITTEE ON MUNICIPAL AND COUNTY GOVERNMENT.
    Incorporation Practices: Final Report of the Assembly Interim Committee on Municipal and County Government, House Resolution No. 277, 1957. Sacramento: Assembly of the State of California, 1957. 22p., (Assembly Interim Committee Reports, Volume 6, No.11, 1757-1959).

    Descriptors: Annexation and Boundary Changes
                     Home Rule
                     Incorporation

Document No. 056

CALIFORNIA. LEGISLATURE. ASSEMBLY. INTERIM COMMITTEE ON MUNICIPAL AND COUNTY GOVERNMENT.
    Multipurpose Districts: Final Report of the Assembly Interim Committee on Municipal and County Government, House Resolution No. 361.16. Sacramento: Assembly of the State of California, 1962. 95p., (Assembly Interim Committee Reports, Volume 6, No.19, 1961-1963).

    Descriptors: Intergovernmental Cooperation
                     Policy Planning
                     Regional Agencies
                     Special Districts and Authorities

Document No. 057

CALIFORNIA. LEGISLATURE. ASSEMBLY. INTERIM COMMITTEE ON MUNICIPAL AND COUNTY GOVERNMENT.
    Supervisorial Redistricting and Consolidation of Special Taxing Districts: Final Report of the Assembly Interim Committee on Municipal and County Government, House Resolution No. 361.16. Sacramento: Assembly of the State of California, 1962. 26p. (Assembly Interim Committee Reports, Volume 6, No.18, 1961-1963).

    Descriptors: Annexation and Boundary Changes
                     Special Districts and Authorities

REFORM OF LOCAL GOVERNMENT STRUCTURES IN THE UNITED STATES: 1945-1971.

Document No. 058

CALIFORNIA. LEGISLATURE. ASSEMBLY. INTERIM COMMITTEE ON MUNICIPAL AND COUNTY GOVERNMENT.
    Transcript of Proceedings. Sacramento: The Committee, 1962. 80p.

    Descriptors: Annexation and Boundary Changes
                  Special Districts and Authorities

Document No. 059

CALIFORNIA. LEGISLATURE. ASSEMBLY. INTERIM COMMITTEE ON MUNICIPAL AND COUNTY GOVERNMENT.
    Transcript of Proceedings: Annexation and Related Incorporation Problems. Sacramento: The Committee, 1960. 77p.

    Descriptors: Annexation and Boundary Changes
                  Incorporation

Document No. 060

CALIFORNIA. LEGISLATURE. ASSEMBLY. INTERIM COMMITTEE ON MUNICIPAL AND COUNTY GOVERNMENT.
    Transcript of Proceedings on the Subject of Cooperative Metropolitan Services, Los Angeles, California, November 13, 1962. Sacramento: Assembly of the State of California, 1962. 77p.

    Descriptors: Intergovernmental Cooperation
                  Policy Planning
                  Regional Agencies
                  Special Districts and Authorities

Document No. 061

CALIFORNIA. LEGISLATURE. ASSEMBLY. MUNICIPAL AND COUNTY GOVERNMENT COMMITTEE.
    City Annexations Across County Lines: Legislative Ramifications: Staff Memo to the Municipal and Government Committee. Thomas H. Willoughby and Kathleen Bowden. Sacramento: The Committee, 1968. 47p.

    Descriptor: Annexations and Boundary Changes

BIBLIOGRAPHY

Document No. 062

CALIFORNIA. LEGISLATURE. JOINT COMMITTEE ON BAY AREA REGIONAL ORGANIZATION.
    Public Hearings - A Summary. San Francisco: The Committee. 1968, iv, 26p.

    Descriptors: Council of Governments
                  Planning Commissions
                  Policy Planning
                  Regional Agencies

Document No. 063

CALIFORNIA. LEGISLATURE. SENATE. COMMITTEE OF GOVERNMENTAL EFFICIENCY.
    Regional Government and Resource Preservation in the San Francisco Bay Area: A Staff Appraisal. Prepared by the Staff of the Committee on Government Efficiency. Sacramento: The Committee, 1969. 155p.

    Descriptors: Planning Commissions
                  Policy Planning
                  Regional Agencies

Document No. 064

CALIFORNIA. LEGISLATURE. SENATE. COMMITTEE ON LOCAL GOVERNMENT.
    Public Hearing: Local Government: Prospectus for 1969. Sacramento: The Committee, 1968. ii, 271p., (1).

    Descriptors: Annexation and Boundary Changes
                  Special Districts and Authorities

Document No. 065

CALIFORNIA. LEGISLATURE. SENATE. SUBCOMMITTEE OF THE SENATE COMMITTEE ON LOCAL GOVERNMENT.
    Public Hearing: County Service Areas. Sacramento: The Committee, 1967. i, 56p.

    Descriptors: Annexation and Boundary Changes
                  County Government
                  Incorporation

REFORM OF LOCAL GOVERNMENT STRUCTURES IN THE UNITED STATES: 1945-1971.

Document No. 066

CALIFORNIA. LEGISLATURE. SENATE. FACT FINDING COMMITTE ON LOCAL GOVERNMENT.
    Report to the Legislature, 1961 Regular Session. Fact Finding Committee on Local Government. Sacramento: Senate of the State of California, 1961. 82p.

    Descriptors: Councils of Government
                  Governmental Consolidation
                  Intergovernmental Cooperation

Document No. 067

CALIFORNIA. LEGISLATURE. SENATE. INTERIM COMMITTEE ON BAY AREA PROBLEMS.
    Final Report: Senate Interim Committee on Bay Area Problems: Recommending the Creation of a Golden Gate Authority in the San Francisco Bay Area. Sacramento: Senate of the State of California, 1959. 146p.

    Descriptor: Special Districts and Authorities

Document No. 068

CALIFORNIA MUNICIPAL SEMINAR, 3rd, PALM SPRINGS, CALIFORNIA.
    Proceedings: Third Annual Municipal Seminar. Pico Rivera, California: California Contract Cities Association, 1962. iv, 94p.

    Descriptors: Councils of Government
                  Home Rule
                  Intergovernmental Cooperation

Document No. 069

CAMPBELL, ERNEST HOWARD.
    County Government in the State of Washington: Effect of Adoption on Proposed County Home Rule Constitutional Amendment. Ernest Howard Campbell and Herbert H. Legg, Jr. Seattle: Bureau of Governmental Research and Services, University of Washington, 1948. 36p., (Report No. 93).

    Descriptors: County Government
                  Home Rule

BIBLIOGRAPHY

Document No. 070

CAMPBELL, ERNEST H.
    Intergovernmental Relations: Existing Authority for Intergovernmental Relations of Cities and Towns by Contract or Otherwise. Seattle: Association of Washington Cities; in cooperation with the Bureau of Governmental Research and Services, 1964, 29p., (Information Bulletin No. 265).

    Descriptors: Intergovernmental Cooperation
                    Municipal Cooperation
                    Special Districts and Authorities

Document No. 071

CAPE, WILLIAM H.
    County Government in Kansas. Lawrence, Kansas: Governmental Research Center, University of Kansas, 1958. 35p., (Citizen's Pamphlet Series No. 23).

    Descriptors: Commission Government
                    County Government

Document No. 072

CAPE, WILLIAM H.
    The Emerging Patterns of County Executives. Lawrence, Kansas: Governmental Research Center, University of Kansas, 1967. 123p., (Governmental Research Series No. 35).

    Descriptors: Council - Manager Government
                    County Government
                    Political Leadership

Document No. 073

CAPE, WILLIAM H.
    Government by Special Districts. William H. Cape, Leon B. Graves, Burton M. Michaels. Lawrence, Kansas: Governmental Research Center, University of Kansas, 1969. 240p., (Governmental Research Series No. 37).

    Descriptors: Planning Commissions
                    Special Districts and Authorities

REFORM OF LOCAL GOVERNMENT STRUCTURES IN THE UNITED STATES: 1945-1971.

Document No. 074

CAPE, WILLIAM H.
    Toward Home Rule in South Dakota. Vermillion, South Dakota: Governmental Research Bureau, University of South Dakota, 1956. v, 42p., (Report No. 36).

    Descriptors: Charters
                    Home Rule

Document No. 075

CASSELLA, JR., WILLIAM N.
    Constitutional Aspects of State-Local Relationships - II: Metropolitan Government. Detroit: Citizens Research Council of Michigan, 1961. v, 36p., (Con-Con Research Paper No.5. Memorandum No. 205).

    Descriptors: Home Rule
                    Governmental Consolidation
                    Governmental Separation

Document No. 076

CECIL COUNTY, MARYLAND. GOVERNMENTAL STUDY COMMISSION.
    Report and Proposed Home Rule Charter. Elkton, Maryland: Cecil County Government Study Commission. 1966, vi, 87p.

    Descriptors: Charters
                    Council - Manager Government
                    County Government
                    Home Rule

Document No. 077

CHAMBER OF COMMERCE OF THE UNITED STATES.
    Jacksonville, Florida, Merges City and County Government. Washington, D.C.: Chamber of Commerce of the United States, 1968. 20p., (Urban Action Clearinghouse Case Study No. 4).

    Descriptor: Governmental Consolidation

BIBLIOGRAPHY

Document No. 078

CHAMBERLIN, JOSEPH E.
    A Factual Report on Annexation for the Metropolitan Area of Colorado Springs. Colorado Springs: City of Colorado Springs, Office of the City Manager, 1950. ix, 92, xxp.

    Descriptor: Annexation and Boundary Changes

Document No. 079

CHANDLER, L.E.
    A Study of Parish Government in Louisiana. Hammond, Louisiana: Southeastern Louisiana College, 1960. 27p., (College Bulletin Volume XVII, No. 2).

    Descriptors: Commission Government
                County Government
                Special Districts and Authorities

Document No. 080

CHARLESTON, SOUTH CAROLINA. UNIFICATION STUDY BOARD.
    A Report of the Charleston Unification Study Board to the Mayor and Aldermen of the City of Charleston, South Carolina, November, 1956. Charleston, South Carolina: Charleston Unification Study Board, 1956. 56p.

    Descriptors: Governmental Consolidation
                Special Districts and Authorities

Document No. 081

CHARLESTON COUNTY, SOUTH CAROLINA. CHARTER COMMISSION.
    Proposed Charter for Consolidated Government for Charleston County, South Carolina. Charleston, South Carolina: Charleston County Charter Commission, 1970. 48p., (15).

    Descriptors: Charters
                County Government
                Governmental Consolidation

REFORM OF LOCAL GOVERNMENT STRUCTURES IN THE UNITED STATES: 1945-1971.

Document No. 082

CHARLESTON COUNTY, SOUTH CAROLINA. CHARTER COMMISSION.
    Proposed Home Rule Charter for Charleston County, South Carolina.
    Charleston, South Carolina: (s.n.), 1970. 47p., (4).

    Descriptors: Charters
                    County Government
                    Home Rule

Document No. 083

CHATHAM COUNTY GEORGIA. LOCAL GOVERNMENT STUDY COMMISSION.
    Plan of Improvement for the Governments of Savannah and
    Chatham County Georgia: Report and Recommendations of the
    Local Government Study Commission of Chatham County.
    Savannah, Georgia: Local Government Study Commission, 1961.
    ii, 97p.

    Descriptors: County Government
                    Governmental Consolidation
                    Intergovernmental Cooperation

Document No. 084

CHILDS, RICHARD S.
    The Charter Problem of Metropolitan Cities. New York: Citizen's
    Union Research Foundation, 1960. 19p.

    Descriptor: Charters

Document No. 085

CHO, YONG H.
    Final Report: Administrative Organization for the City of
    Akron, Ohio: Recommendations for Reorganization and Proposed
    Administrative Code. Yong H. Cho, Edward Hanten, Frank Simonetti.
    Akron, Ohio: Center for Urban Studies, University of Ohio, 1969.
    122p., (Prepared for the Mayor's Administrative Code Revision
    Committee).

    Descriptors: Administrative Reorganization
                    Municipal Government

BIBLIOGRAPHY

Document No. 086

CINCINNATI BUREAU OF GOVERNMENTAL RESEARCH.
    Legal Aspects of the Metropolitan Area Problem. Cincinnati: Cincinnati Bureau of Governmental Research, 1953. 40p., (Prepared for The Committee on Metropolitan Area Problems, Report No. 115).

    Descriptors: Home Rule
                    Governmental Consolidation

Document No. 087

CITIZENS COMMITTEE FOR METROPOLITAN GOVERNMENT (NASHVILLE, TENNESSEE).
    You and Metropolitan Government. Prepared by Citizens Committee for Metropolitan Government. Nashville, Tennessee: The Committee, (1960). 15p.

    Descriptor: Charters

Document No. 088

CITIZENS' CONFERENCE FOR GOVERNMENTAL COOPERATION (OREGON).
    Final Report 1958-1959. Salem, Oregon: Citizens' Conference for Government Cooperation, 1959. (310), (10) fold. leaves of plates.

    Descriptors: Advisory Councils
                    Citizen Participation
                    Home Rule
                    Intergovernmental Cooperation

Document No. 089

CITIZEN'S COUNCIL ON CITY PLANNING.
    Regional Citizens' Organization Study. Philadelphia: Citizens' Council on City Planning, 1960. a-e, 42p., (Prepared for Pennsylvania - New Jersey - Delaware Metropolitan Project, Inc.).

    Descriptor: Citizen Participation

REFORM OF LOCAL GOVERNMENT STRUCTURES IN THE UNITED STATES: 1945-1971

Document No. 090

CITIZENS LEAGUE (MINNESOTA).
    Citizens League Report: A Metropolitan Council for the Twin Cities Area. Minneapolis: Citizens League, 1967. 50p.

    Descriptors: Council Government
                   Decentralization

Document No. 091

CITIZENS LEAGUE (MINNEAPOLIS, MINNESOTA).
    Metropolitan Policy and Metropolitan Development: A Proposal for Government in the Twin Cities Area. Prepared by the Metropolitan Development Guide Committee. Minneapolis: Citizens League, 1968. iv, 51p.

    Descriptors: Council Government
                   Decentralization

Document No. 092

CITIZENS LEAGUE OF MINNEAPOLIS AND HENNEPIN COUNTY.
    An Analysis of Minneapolis City Government With Some Suggestions for its Reorganization. Minneaplis: Citizens League of Minneapolis and Hennepin County, 1956. 38, (2), 3 leaves of plates.

    Descriptors: Administrative Reorganization
                   Charters
                   Citizen Participation

Document No. 093

CITIZENS LEAGUE OF MINNEAPOLIS AND HENNEPIN COUNTY.
    1959 Local Government School, 2nd Session: Minneapolis Charter Progress. Minneapolis: Citizens League of Minneapolis and Hennepin County, 1959. 22p. in various pagings.

    Descriptors: Charters
                   Municipal Government

BIBLIOGRAPHY

Document No. 094

CITIZENS RESEARCH COUNCIL OF MICHIGAN.
    Annexation of Ecorse Township: An Appraisal Conducted for the City of Wyandotte. Detroit: Citizens Research Council of Michigan, 1956. ii, 18p., (Report No. 187).

    Descriptor: Annexation and Boundary Changes

Document No. 095

CITIZENS RESEARCH COUNCIL OF MICHIGAN.
    Consolidation of the Cities of Grosse Pointe, Grosse Pointe Park, and Grosse Pointe Farms. Detroit: Citizens Research Council of Michigan, 1958. x, 44p., (Report No. 192).

    Descriptors: Administrative Reorganization
                    Governmental Consolidation
                    Intergovernmental Cooperation

Document No. 096

CITIZENS RESEARCH COUNCIL OF MICHIGAN.
    Five Examples of Governmental Cooperation in the Southeast Michigan Six-County Region. Detroit: Metropolitan Fund, 1967, ix, 104p., (A Research Project by Metropolitan Fund, Inc.).

    Descriptors: Intergovernmental Cooperation
                    Policy Planning
                    Regional Agencies

Document No. 097

CITIZENS RESEARCH COUNCIL OF MICHIGAN.
    Governmental Organization in the Greater Midland Area. Detroit: Citizens Research Council of Michigan, 1970. x, 63p., vii. (Report No. 238).

    Descriptors: Annexation and Boundary Changes
                    Home Rule
                    Incorporation

REFORM OF LOCAL GOVERNMENT STRUCTURES IN THE UNITED STATES: 1945-1971.

Document No. 098

CITIZENS RESEARCH COUNCIL OF MICHIGAN.
    Home Rule for Michigan Counties. Detroit: Citizens Research Council of Michigan, 1958. 19 (9).

    Descriptor: Home Rule

Document No. 099

CITIZENS RESEARCH COUNCIL OF MICHIGAN.
    Local Government Organization and Services in the Greater Port Huron Area. Detroit: Citizens Research Council of Michigan, 1966. v, 115p., (3). (Report No. 226).

    Descriptors: Governmental Consolidation
                Incorporation

Document No. 100

CITIZENS RESEARCH COUNCIL OF MICHIGAN.
    Metropolitan Area Unification in the Battle Creek Urban Area. Detroit: Citizens Research Council of Michigan, 1966. viii, 67p., (Report No. 225).

    Descriptor: Governmental Consolidation

Document No. 101

CITIZENS RESEARCH COUNCIL OF MICHIGAN.
    Municipal Consolidation in the Jackson Community. Detroit: Citizens Research Council of Michigan, 1966. xii, 79p., (2). (Report No. 223).

    Descriptor: Governmental Consolidation

Document No. 102

CITIZENS RESEARCH COUNCIL OF MICHIGAN.
    Staff Papers on Governmental Organization for Metropolitan Southeast Michigan. Detroit: Citizens Research Council of Michigan, 1965. 239 pp. in various pagings. (Report No. 218).

    Descriptors: Annexation and Boundary Changes
                Home Rule
                Incorporation
                Intergovernmental Cooperation
                Planning Commissions
                Regional Agencies
                Special Districts and Authorities

BIBLIOGRAPHY

Document No. 103

CITIZENS RESEARCH COUNCIL OF MICHIGAN.
    Warren Woods: A Study of Reorganization Alternatives.
    Detroit: Citizens Research Council of Michigan, 1960.
    vii, 35p., (Report No. 205).

    Descriptors: Annexation and Boundary Changes
                    Governmental Consolidation
                    Special Districts and Authorities

Document No. 104

CITIZENS SEMINARS ON THE FISCAL, ECONOMIC AND POLITICAL PROBLEMS OF BOSTON AND THE METROPOLITAN COMMUNITY, BOSTON COLLEGE, 1959.
    Proceedings....Boston: College of Business Administration.

    Descriptors: Citizen Participation
                    Planning Commissions
                    Regional Agencies

Document No. 105

CITIZENS UNION RESEARCH FOUNDATION.
    Community Administration Within New York City: Home Town in
    the Big City. New York: Citizens Union Research Foundation,
    1962. 18p., (1) fold. leaf of plates.

    Descriptors: Citizen Participation
                    Community Control
                    Decentralization
                    District Government
                    Neighborhood Control
                    Planning Commissions

Document No. 106

CITY CLUB OF PORTLAND.
    Report on Portland City Government. Portland, Oregon: City
    Club of Portland, 1961. (45)., (Portland City Club Bulletin,
    Volume 41, No. 51).

    Descriptors: Commission Government
                    Mayor - Council Government

REFORM OF LOCAL GOVERNMENT STRUCTURES IN THE UNITED STATES: 1945-1971.

Document No. 107

CITY-COUNTY CHARTER COMMITTEE, ALBUQUERQUE, NEW MEXICO.
    Proposed Charter for the City-County of Albuquerque.
    Albuquerque, New Mexico: City-County Charter Committee,
    1958. 12p.

    Descriptors: Charters
                     Incorporation

Document No. 108

CLARK, JAMES L.
    Cross-County Annexation by Municipal Corporations in
    California. James L. Clark and Louis F. Weschler. Davis,
    California: Institute of Governmental Affairs, University
    of California, Davis, 1965. 59p., (California Government
    Series No. 8).

    Descriptors: Annexation and Boundary Changes
                     Municipal Corporations

Document No. 109

CLAUNCH, JOHN M.
    The Government of Dallas County, Texas. Dallas: Southern
    Methodist University Press, 1954. xii, 217p., (Arnold
    Foundation Studies, Volume V, New Series).

    Descriptors: Commission Government
                     County Government
                     Intergovernmental Cooperation

Document No. 110

CLEVELAND BUREAU OF GOVERNMENTAL RESEARCH.
    Development of the Administrative Officer in Cuyahoga
    County: A Report to the Board of County Commissioners
    of Guyahoga County. Bureau of Governmental Research.
    Cleveland: The Bureau, 1954. 28p., (2) leaves of plates.

    Descriptors: Administrative Reorganization
                     County Government
                     Political Leadership

BIBLIOGRAPHY

Document No. 111

CLEVELAND BUREAU OF GOVERNMENTAL RESEARCH.
    Intergovernmental Problems in the Chagrin Falls Area: A Case Study. Cleveland: Cleveland Bureau of Governmental Research, 1960. 39p., (5) leaves of plates.

    Descriptors: Governmental Consolidation
                    Intergovernmental Cooperation

Document No. 112

CLEVELAND BUREAU OF GOVERNMENTAL RESEARCH.
    Proposed Consolidation of Parkview and Fairview Park: An Analysis Made at the Request of the Mayors and Councils of the Village of Parkview and the City of Fairview Park. Cleveland: Cleveland Bureau of Governmental Research, 1961. 56p.

    Descriptors: Annexation and Boundary Changes
                    Governmental Consolidation

Document No. 113

CLEVELAND METROPOLITAN SERVICES COMMISSION.
    Prologue to Progress. Cleveland: Cleveland Metropolitan Services Commissions, 1959. 77p.

    Descriptors: County Government
                    Planning Commissions
                    Regional Agencies

Document No. 114

CLEVELAND METROPOLITAN SERVICES COMMISSION. STUDY GROUP ON GOVERNMENTAL ORGANIZATION.
    Government Organization for Metropolitan Cleveland. Cleveland: Cleveland Metropolitan Services Commission, 1959. vi, 17p.

    Descriptors: Advisory Councils
                    Citizen Participation
                  Council Government
                  County Government

REFORM OF LOCAL GOVERNMENT STRUCTURES IN THE UNITED STATES: 1945-1971.

Document No. 115

CLEVELAND METROPOLITAN SERVICES COMMISSION. STUDY GROUP ON LAND USE AND DEVELOPMENT.
    Land Use Planning and Control in Metropolitan Cleveland. Cleveland: Cleveland Metropolitan Services Commission, 1959, v, 29p.

    Descriptors: Planning Commissions
                    Policy Planning

Document No. 116

COHN, RUBIN G.
    Chicago's Government: An Interpretive Summary of the Report of the Chicago Home Rule Commission. Rubin G. Cohn and Gilbert Y. Steiner. Urbana, Illinois: Institute of Government and Public Affairs, University of Illinois, 1954. v, 12p.

    Descriptors: Administrative Reorganization
                    Home Rule

Document No. 117

COKE, JAMES G.
    Planning in the Penjerdel Region. James G. Coke and Thomas J. Anton. Philadelphia: Pennsylvania - New Jersey - Delaware Metropolitan Project, (1961). iv, 38p.

    Descriptors: Planning Commissions
                    Policy Planning
                    Regional Agencies

Document No. 118

COLLIER, JAMES M.
    County Government in New Jersey. New Brunswick, New Jersey: Rutgers University Press, 1952. 64p., (1) leaf of plates.

    Descriptors: Commission Government
                    County Government

BIBLIOGRAPHY

Document No. 119

COLMAN, WILLIAM G.
    Organization and Structure of Municipal Government in the
    United States. (s.l.): (s.n.), 1960. 26p., (Prepared for
    VIIIth Inter-American Municipal Congress, San Diego,
    California, October 16-22, 1960).

    Descriptors: Commission Government
                    Council - Manager Government
                    Federation
                    Home Rule
                    Mayor - Council Government

Document No. 120

COLORADO. DIVISION OF LOCAL GOVERNMENT.
    Problems of Local Government in Colorado. Denver:
    State of Colorado, Division of Local Government, 1968.
    iii, 28p.

    Descriptors: Administrative Reorganization
                    Councils of Government
                    County Government
                    Model Cities
                    Planning Commissions
                    Regional Agencies

Document No. 121

COLORADO. GOVERNOR'S LOCAL AFFAIRS STUDY COMMISSION.
    Local Government in Colorado: Findings and Recommendations:
    Final Report of the Governor's Local Affairs Study Commission.
    Denver: Governor's Local Affairs Study Commission, 1966.
    xv, 140p.

    Descriptors: County Government
                    District Government
                    Home Rule
                    Intergovernmental Cooperation
                    Municipal Government
                    Special Districts and Authorities

REFORM OF LOCAL GOVERNMENT STRUCTURES IN THE UNITED STATES: 1945-1971.

Document No. 122

COLORADO. GOVERNOR'S LOCAL AFFAIRS STUDY COMMISSION.
　　　Metropolitan Problems in Colorado: Findings and Recommendations: An Interim Report of the Local Affairs Study Commission. Denver: Governor's Local Affairs Study Commission, 1965. x, 110p., (Government Report No. 2).

　　　Descriptors:　County Government
　　　　　　　　　　Governmental Consolidation
　　　　　　　　　　Home Rule

Document No. 123

COLORADO CONFERENCE FOR THE STUDY OF URBAN AND COMMUNITY PROBLEMS.
　　　A Study Proposal for Governmental Reorganization in Colorado Urban Areas. Compiled by the Colorado State Planning Division. Denver: Colorado State Planning Division, 1959. 23p., (5).

　　　Descriptors:　County Government
　　　　　　　　　　Special Districts and Authorities

Document No. 124

COLQUITT COUNTY ON INTERGOVERNMENTAL RELATIONS (GEORGIA).
　　　Colquitt County, Georgia: A Field Laboratory for Study and Experiment in Intergovernmental Relations. Moultrie, Georgia: Colquitt County Council on Intergovernmental Relations, 1947. 69p.

　　　Descriptors:　Advisory Councils
　　　　　　　　　　Citizen Participation
　　　　　　　　　　Federation
　　　　　　　　　　Intergovernmental Cooperation

Document No. 125

COMMITTEE FOR ECONOMIC DEVELOPMENT.
　　　Guiding Metropolitan Growth. by the Research and Policy Committee for Economic Development. New York: The Committee, 1960. 47p., (3).

　　　Descriptors:　Community Control
　　　　　　　　　　Federation
　　　　　　　　　　Policy Planning

BIBLIOGRAPHY

Document No. 126

COMMITTEE FOR ECONOMIC DEVELOPMENT.
    Modernizing Local Government to Secure A Balanced Federalism. by the Research and Policy Committee, Committee for Economic Development. New York: The Committee, 1966. 77p.

    Descriptors: Administrative Reorganization
                      Citizen Participation
                      Federation

Document No. 127

COMMITTEE FOR ECONOMIC DEVELOPMENT.
    Reshaping Government in Metropolitan Areas. by the Research and Policy Committee, Committee for Economic Development. New York: The Committee, 1970. 83p.

    Descriptors: Community Control
                      Decentralization
                      Federation
                      Intergovernmental Cooperation

Document No. 128

COMMITTEE OF ONE HUNDRED.
    Final Report of the Committee of One Hundred: A Proposal for a Voluntary Council of Governments in Southeast Michigan. Detroit: Committee of One Hundred, 1966. 37p.

    Descriptors: Council of Governments
                      Intergovernmental Cooperation
                      Planning Commissions
                      Regional Agencies

Document No. 129

COMMITTEE OF 100 FOR PULASKI COUNTY. GOVERNMENT OPERATIONS COMMITTEE.
    A Program of Unity for Progress in Metropolitan Pulaski County: Report of the Government Operations Committee of the Urban Services Survey for Pulaski County. Little Rock, Arkansas: Committee of One Hundred for Pulaski County, 1964, 82 pp. in various, (3) leaves of plates (1 fold.).

    Descriptors: Annexation and Boundary Changes
                      County Government
                      Special Districts and Authorities

REFORM OF LOCAL GOVERNMENT STRUCTURES IN THE UNITED STATES: 1945-1971.

Document No. 130

COMMUNITY RESEARCH (DAYTON).
Annexation: The Alternatives in Sugarcreek Township. Dayton, Ohio: Community Research, 1969. 88p., (Fifth in a series of studies on annexation).

Descriptors: Annexation and Boundary Changes
              Incorporation

Document No. 131

COMMUNITY RESEARCH (DAYTON).
Annexation and Selected Neighborhoods: Costs, Services, and Selected Levels. Dayton, Ohio: Community Research, 1965. vii, 302p., (Second in a series of studies on annexation and the City of Dayton).

Descriptor: Annexation and Boundary Changes

Document No. 132

COMMUNITY RESEARCH (DAYTON).
City-County Health Services: A Study of Possible Cooperation or Consolidation. Dayton, Ohio: Community Research, 1966. 43p.

Descriptor: Governmental Consolidation

Document No. 133

COMMUNITY RESEARCH (DAYTON).
Cooperation: Possibilities and Practice. Dayton, Ohio: Community Research, 1966. xi, 24p., (Prepared as Background Material for the Governmental Cooperation Conference, October 29, 1966).

Descriptors: Annexation and Boundary Changes
              Councils of Government
              Federation
              Governmental Consolidation
              Governmental Separation
              Intergovernmental Cooperation
              Special Districts and Authorities

BIBLIOGRAPHY

Document No. 134

COMMUNITY RESEARCH (DAYTON).
    Cooperation: Present Status. Dayton, Ohio: Community Research, 1966. ix, 10p., (Prepared as Background for the Governmental Cooperation Conference, April 29, 1966).

    Descriptors: Advisory Councils
                       Planning Commissions
                       Regional Agencies

Document No. 135

COMMUNITY RESEARCH (DAYTON).
    A Council of Governments for the Miami Valley Area. Prepared by the Montgomery County Mayors and City Manager's Association, Executive Committee and Community Research. Dayton, Ohio: Community Research, 1967. vi, 61p.

    Descriptors: Council of Governments
                       Intergovernmental Cooperation

Document No. 136

COMMUNITY RESEARCH (DAYTON).
    The Kind of Charter Needed for Montgomery County, Ohio. Dayton, Ohio: Community Research, 1961. 38p.

    Descriptors: Administrative Reorganization
                     Charters
                     Commission Government

Document No. 137

COMMUNITY SERVICE.
    Bottom-up Democracy: The Affiliation of Small Democratic Units for Common Service. Yellow Springs, Ohio: Community Service, 1954. 64p.

    Descriptors: Citizen Participation
                     Community Control
                     Intergovernmental Cooperation

REFORM OF LOCAL GOVERNMENT STRUCTURES IN THE UNITED STATES: 1945-1971.

Document No. 138

COMMUNITY SERVICES COMMISSION FOR DAVIDSON COUNTY AND THE CITY OF NASHVILLE (TENNESSEE).
    A Future for Nashville: A Report of the Community Services Commission for Davidson County and the City of Nashville. Nashville, Tennessee: Community Services Commission for Davidson County and the City of Nashville, 1952. x, 201p.

    Descriptors: Annexation and Boundary Changes
                          Home Rule
                          Planning Commissions

Document No. 139

COMMUNITY STUDIES (KANSAS CITY, MISSOURI).
    Johnson County, Kansas: An Analysis of its Governmental Organization. Kansas City, Missouri: Community Studies, 1958. v, 105p., 13 leaves of plates (12 fold.), (Publication 121).

    Descriptors: Advisory Councils
                          Commission Government
                          Governmental Consolidation
                          Special Districts and Authorities

Document No. 140

CONDON, GEORGE A.
    Governing Washington's Cities. Pullman, Washington: Division of Governmental Studies and Services, Washington State University, 1968. 28p.

    Descriptors: Commission Government
                          County Government

Document No. 141

CONFERENCE OF METROPOLITAN AREA PROBLEMS, EMORY UNIVERSITY, 1961.
    Metropolitan Area Problems. Atlanta, Georgia: Institute of Citizenship, Emory University, 1961. vii, 118p., (Addresses and Discussion at the Conference in Metropolitan Area Problems, a program of the Institute of Citizenship at Emory University, Atlanta, Georgia, April 10-12, 1961).

    Descriptors: Citizen Participation
                          Municipal Government
                          Policy Planning

BIBLIOGRAPHY

Document No. 142

CONFERENCE ON BAY AREA REGIONAL ORGANIZATION, 1970.
    Adapting Government to Regional Needs. Stanley Scott and Harriet Nathan, editors. Berkeley, California: Institute of Governmental Studies, University of California, 1971. xv, 306p.

    Descriptors: Council of Government
                       Home Rule
                       Regional Agencies

Document No. 143

CONFERENCES ON COMMUNITY PLANNING, 1967-1968.
    Adapting Local Government to Urban Growth Problems: Proceedings....Edited by Lowell W. Culver, Ruth Ihner. Tacoma, Washington: Urban Affairs Program, Pacific Lutheran University, 1969. xiv, 121p., (Sponsored by Pacific Lutheran University; in cooperation with Planning and Community Affairs Agency of the State of Washington).

    Descriptors: Councils of Government
                       Governmental Consolidation
                       Intergovernmental Cooperation

Document No. 144

CONFERENCE ON CURRENT GOVERNMENTAL PROBLEMS, 10th, UNIVERSITY OF MASSACHUSETTS, 1950.
    Intermunicipal Cooperation in Massachusetts. George Goodwin, Jr., editor. Amherst, Massachusetts: Bureau of Public Administration, University of Massachusetts, 1950. 43p., (Talks presented at the Tenth Annual Conference on Current Governmental Problems, April 21, 1950).

    Descriptors: Intergovernmental Cooperation
                       Special Districts and Authorities

Document No. 145

CONFERENCE ON GOVERNMENT OF METROPOLITAN AREAS, UNIVERSITY OF PENNSYLVANIA, 1957.
    The Government of Metropolitan Areas. Philadelphia: Institute of Local and State Government, University of Pennsylvania, 1957. (42p.).

    Descriptors: Federation
                       Special Districts and Authorities

REFORM OF LOCAL GOVERNMENT STRUCTURES IN THE UNITED STATES: 1945-1971.

Document No. 146

CONFERENCE ON INTERGOVERNMENTAL RELATIONS, BERKELEY, CALIFORNIA, 1966.
    Where Governments Meet: Emerging Patterns of Intergovernmental Relations. Willis D. Hawley, editor. Berkeley, California: Institute of Governmental Studies, University of California, 1967. vii, 116p.

    Descriptors: Councils of Government
                    Federation
                    Intergovernmental Cooperation
                    Regional Agencies

Document No. 147

CONNECTICUT. COMMISSION TO STUDY THE NECESSITY AND FEASIBILITY OF METROPOLITAN GOVERNMENT.
    The States Biggest Business - Local and Regional Problems. Hartford, Connecticut: Connecticut Commission to Study the Necessity and Feasibility of Metropolitan Government, 1967. 59p., (2), (Report of the Connecticut Commission to Study the Necessity and Feasibility of Metropolitan Government).

    Descriptors: Advisory Councils
                    Regional Agencies
                    Special Districts and Authorities

Document No. 148

CONNECTICUT. UNIVERSITY. INSTITUTE OF PUBLIC SERVICES.
    The Future of Local Government in the Lower Naugatuck Valley: An Overview of Governmental Alternatives for the Lower Naugatuck Valley Region with Appended Selective Background Material. Prepared by the Institute of Public Services for the Lower Naugatuck Valley Chamber of Commerce. Storrs, Connecticut: The Institute, 1969. ix, 99p.

    Descriptors: Planning Commissions
                    Regional Agencies

Document No. 149

CONNECTICUT PUBLIC EXPENDITURE COUNCIL.
    Connecticut's Home Rule Law: An Aid to Charter Commission Members: Including Amendments by the 1961 General Assembly. Hartford, Connecticut: Connecticut Public Expenditure Council, 1962. 27p.

    Descriptors: Charters
                    Governmental Consolidation
                  Home Rule
                  Special Districts and Authorities

BIBLIOGRAPHY

Document No. 150

CONNERY, ROBERT H.
    Governmental Organization Within the City of New York.
    6th ed. New York: Institute of Public Administration,
    1960. 42p.

    Descriptors: Advisory Councils
                Mayor - Council Government
                Special Districts and Authorities

Document No. 151

CONTRA COSTA COUNTY, CALIFORNIA. OFFICE OF THE COUNTY ADMINISTRATOR.
    Some Aspects of the Special District Situation in the County
    of Contra Costa California. Rev. (Martinez, California):
    Office of the County Administrator, 1966. 9p., (Issued by the
    Office of the County Administrator Contra Costa County,
    California, November 6, 1964).

    Descriptors: Governmental Consolidation
                Governmental Separation
                Special Districts and Authorities

Document No. 152

COOPER, WELDON.
    Metropolitan County: A Survey of Government in the Birmingham
    Area. Birmingham, Alabama: Bureau of Public Administration,
    University of Alabama, 1949. viii, 165p.

    Descriptors: County Government
                Federation
                Governmental Consolidation
                Planning Commissions

Document No. 153

COUNCIL OF STATE GOVERNMENTS.
    Patterns of Intergovernmental Cooperation. Chicago: Council
    of State Governments, 1959. iii, 24p., (RM - 324).

    Descriptors: Federation
                Intergovernmental Cooperation

REFORM OF LOCAL GOVERNMENT STRUCTURES IN THE UNITED STATES: 1945-1971.

Document No. 154

COUNCIL OF STATE GOVERNMENTS.
State Responsibility in Urban Regional Development: A Report to the Governor's Conference. Chicago: Council of State Governments, 1962. xxiii, 209p., (RR - 7).

Descriptors: Annexation and Boundary Changes
Home Rule
Incorporation
Planning Commissions
Planning Policy
Regional Agencies

Document No. 155

COUNCIL OF STATE GOVERNMENTS.
The State and the Metropolitan Problem: A Report to the Governors' Conference. Chicago: Council of State Governments, 1956. x, 153p.

Descriptors: Annexation and Boundary Changes
Federation
Governmental Consolidation
Governmental Separation
Special Districts and Authorities

Document No. 156

THE COUNTY AND INTERGOVERNMENTAL RELATIONS.
Kansas City, Missouri: Governmental Research Bureau, Park College, 1968. Edited by Jerzy Hauptmann. 64p.

Descriptors: Councils of Government
County Government
Intergovernmental Cooperation
Special Districts and Authorities

Document No. 157

COUNTY COMMISSIONERS CONFERENCE, 5th, BOULDER, COLORADO, 1958.
Better County Government for Colorado Through Amendments Nos. 2 and 3. Boulder, Colorado: Bureau of State and Community Service, University of Colorado: in cooperation with Colorado State Association of County Commissioners, 1958. ii, 19p.

Descriptor: County Government

BIBLIOGRAPHY

Document No. 158

COUNTY HOME RULE CONGRESS, NEW YORK, 1962.
    An Action Program From the County Home Rule Congress; 27th Annual Conference of the National Association of Counties. Washington, D.C.: National Association of Counties, 1962. 102p.

    Descriptors: Charters
                        Home Rule
                        Special Districts and Authorities

Document No. 159

COUNTY SUPERVISORS ASSOCIATION OF CALIFORNIA.
    Local Agency Formation Commission Manual for Executive Officers. Sacramento: County Supervisors Association of California, 1965. 50p., (42) leaves of plates (4 fold.).

    Descriptors: County Government
                        Planning Commissions

Document No. 160

CRAWFORD, FRED G.
    Organizational and Administrative Development of the Government of the City of Los Angeles: During the Thirty-year Period July 1, 1925 to September 30, 1955. Los Angeles: School of Public Administration, University of Southern California, 1955. xv, 281p.

    Descriptors: Administrative Reorganization
                        Advisory Councils
                        Mayor - Council Government
                        Special Districts and Authorities

Document No. 161

CUYAHOGA COUNTY, OHIO. CHARTER COMMISSION.
    Proposed Home Rule Charter for Cuyahoga County, Ohio: To be submitted to the Electors of Cuyahoga County at the General Election on Tuesday, November 3, 1959. Cleveland: Cuyahoga County Charter Commission, 1959. 27p.

    Descriptor: Home Rule

REFORM OF LOCAL GOVERNMENT STRUCTURES IN THE UNITED STATES: 1945-1971.

Document No. 162

DADE COUNTY, FLORIDA. BUDGET DEPARTMENT.
    A Report on Administrative Improvement: Through February 1959. Miami, Florida: Metropolitan Dade County, Budget Department, 1959. 14p., (2).

    Descriptor: Administrative Reorganization

Document No. 163

DADE COUNTY, FLORIDA. CHARTER.
    The Charter of Metropolitan Dade County Florida. Miami, Florida: Metropolitan Dade County, 1957. 25p., (2).

    Descriptor: Charters

Document No. 164

DADE COUNTY, FLORIDA. HOME RULE AMENDMENT.
    The Home Rule Amendment and Charter. Miami, Florida: Metropolitan Dade County, 1963. 28p., (1).

    Descriptors: Charters
                 Home Rule

Document No. 165

DADE COUNTY, FLORIDA. METROPOLITAN DADE COUNTY PLANNING DEPARTMENT.
    A Report to the Concerned Leadership of Dade County About Its Local Planning Organization and Program. Prepared by Metropolitan Dade County Planning Department. Miami, Florida: The Department, 1959. 73p.

    Descriptors: Planning Commissions
                 Planning Policy

Document No. 166

DADE COUNTY, FLORIDA. OFFICE OF COUNTY MANAGER.
    The First Annual Report on the Progress of Metropolitan Dade County, Florida as presented to the Board of County Commissioners. O.W. Campbell. Miami, Florida: Office of County Manager, 1958. 48p., (1) fold. leaf of plates.

    Descriptors: Administrative Reorganization
                 Federation

BIBLIOGRAPHY

Document No. 167

DADE COUNTY, FLORIDA. OFFICE OF COUNTY MANAGER.
A Preliminary Report on the Transfer of Municipal Functions as Proposed by the Cities of Miami and Miami Beach. Miami, Florida: Office of County Manager, 1964. 19p., (3) leaves of plates.

Descriptor: Governmental Consolidation

Document No. 168

DADE COUNTY, FLORIDA. OFFICE OF COUNTY MANAGER.
Survey of Area-Wide Government Cooperation: Metropolitan Dade County. Miami, Florida: Office of County Manager, 1963. ii, 71p.

Descriptors: Planning Policy
Political Leadership

Document No. 169

DADE COUNTY RESEARCH FOUNDATION (FLORIDA).
A Commentary on the Proposed Metropolitan Ordinances. Miami, Florida: Dade County Research Foundation, 1957. 10p., (2) leaves of plates.

Descriptor: Administrative Reorganization

Document No. 170

DALAND, ROBERT T.
Municipal Fringe Area Problem in Alabama. Birmingham: Bureau of Public Administration, University of Alabama and the Alabama League of Municipalities, 1953. 66p., (6).

Descriptors: Annexation and Boundary Changes
Intergovernmental Cooperation

Document No. 171

DAUER, MANNING J.
Municipal Charters in Florida: Law and Drafting. Manning J. Dauer and George John Miller. Gainesville, Florida: Public Administration Clearing Service of the University of Florida, 1953. 68p., (Studies in Public Administration, No. 11; Reprinted from University of Florida Law Review, Symposium on Florida Municipal Law, Volume VI, No. 3, Fall 1953).

Descriptors: Annexation and Boundary Changes
Charters
Governmental Consolidation

REFORM OF LOCAL GOVERNMENT STRUCTURES IN THE UNITED STATES: 1945-1971.

Document No. 172

DAVIES, AUDREY M.
    Political Units in the New York Metropolitan Region. New York: Institute of Administration, 1959. 12p.

    Descriptor: Regional Agencies

Document No. 173

DAVIS, J. WILLIAM.
    Municipal and County Government. J. William Davis and William E. Oden. Dallas: Arnold Foundation, Southern Methodist University, 1961. vi, 130p., (Arnold Foundation Monograph, VIII).

    Descriptors: County Government
                 Municipal Corporations
                 Municipal Government

Document No. 174

DAVIS, RAYMOND G.
    Regional Government for Lake Tahoe: A Case Study. Davis, California: Institute of Governmental Affairs, University of California, 1970. i, 29p., (Environmental Quality Series No. 2).

    Descriptors: Planning Commissions
                 Regional Agencies

Document No. 175

DECISIONS IN SYRACUSE.
    Roscoe C. Martin, Frank J. Munger, Jesse Burkhead, Gutherie S. Birkhead, Harold Herman, Herbert Herman, Herbert M. Kago, Lewis P. Welch, Clyde J. Wingfield. Bloomington, Indiana: Indiana University Press, 1961. xvi, 368p., (Metropolitan Action Series No. 1).

    Descriptors: Administrative Reorganization
                 Community Control
                 County Government

BIBLIOGRAPHY

Document No. 176

DEKALB COUNTY, GEORGIA. LOCAL GOVERNMENT COMMISSION.
Final Report and Finding of DeKalb Local Government Commission. Decatur, Georgia: DeKalb County Local Government Commission, 1961. iii, 16, 74p., (Exhibit A: A Final Report by Public Administration Service to the Commission, Improving Local Government Services in DeKalb County, Georgia).

Descriptors: Administrative Reorganization
County Government

Document No. 177

DEKALB COUNTY, GEORGIA. LOCAL GOVERNMENT COMMISSION.
Final Report of DeKalb County Local Government Commission, November 30, 1954 and supplemented by Report on the Governments of DeKalb County and Municipalities therein: Prepared by Griffenhagen and Associates. Decatur, Georgia: DeKalb County Local Government Commission, 1954. xii, 9, ii, 114p.

Descriptors: Administrative Reorganization
County Government
Planning Policy

Document No. 178

DEKALB COUNTY, GEORGIA. LOCAL GOVERNMENT COMMISSION.
Interim Report and Finding of the DeKalb Local Government Commission as of December 1, 1959. Decatur, Georgia: DeKalb County Local Government Commission, 1960. 88, 4p., (Exhibit A: Preliminary report of Public Administration Service to Commission, Report on Local Government in DeKalb County, Georgia).

Descriptors: Administrative Reorganization
County Government

Document No. 179

DELAWARE. GOVENOR'S COMMITTEE ON REORGANIZATION OF THE GOVERNMENT OF NEW CASTLE COUNTY, DELAWARE.
Report and Proposed Legislation. Newark, Delaware: University of Delaware, 1964. iv, 123p.

Descriptors: Council - Manager Government
County Government

REFORM OF LOCAL GOVERNMENT STRUCTURES IN THE UNITED STATES: 1945-1971.

Document No. 180

DEMING, GEORGE H.
    Can We Get There From Here? New York: Conference on Metropolitan Area Problems, 1959. 6p., (A statement prepared for Panel 2, How Shall We Organize to Govern and Plan the Metropolitan Region?, Annual Conference, American Institute of Planners, Seattle, Washington, July 28, 1959).

    Descriptor: Regional Agencies

Document No. 181

DENTON, EUGENE H.
    Extension of Municipal Services to Fringe Areas (By Kansas Cities With More Than 10,000 Population). Lawrence, Kansas: Governmental Research Center, University of Kansas, 1959. 32p., (Special Report No. 93).

    Descriptors: Annexation and Boundary Changes
                  Incorporation
                  Special Districts and Authorities

Document No. 182

DEUTSCH, KARL W.
    The Confederation of Urban Governments: How Self-Controls for the American Megalopolis Can Evolve. Kark W. Deutsch and Richard L. Meier. Berkeley, California: Center for Planning and Development Research, Institute of Urban and Regional Development, University of California, 1968. iv, 51p., (Working Paper No. 77).

    Descriptors: Citizen Participation
                  Community Control
                  Councils of Government
                  Federation
                  Neighborhood Control

Document No. 183

DINERMAN, BEATRICE.
    Metropolitan Services: Studies of Allocation in a Federated Organization. Beatrice Dinerman, Ross Clayton, Richard D. Yerby. Los Angeles: Bureau of Governmental Research, University of California, 1961. v, 148p.

    Descriptor: Federation

BIBLIOGRAPHY

Document No. 184

DIXON, ROBERT G.
    Adjusting Municipal Boundaries: The Law and Practice in 48 States. Robert G. Dixon and John R. Kerstetter. Washington, D.C.: American Municipal Association, 1959. xii, 339p., (31).

    Descriptor: Annexation and Boundary Changes

Document No. 185

DONOGHUE, JAMES R.
    County Government and the Constitution: A Report to the County Government Committee of the Wisconsin Legislative Council. Madison, Wisconsin: Bureau of Government, University of Wisconsin, 1960. v, 40p.

    Descriptors: Administrative Reorganization
                  Citizen Participation
                  County Government

Document No. 186

DONOGHUE, JAMES R.
    The Local Government System of Wisconsin. Madison, Wisconsin: Institute of Governmental Affairs, University of Wisconsin, 1968. 211p., (Reprinted from the 1968 Wisconsin Blue Book).

    Descriptors: County Government
                  Municipal Government

Document No. 187

DOUGLAS, PETER.
    The Southern California Association of Governments: A Response to Federal Concern for Metropolitan Areas. Los Angeles: Institute of Government and Public Affairs, University of California, Los Angeles, 1968. 34p., (MR-112).

    Descriptors: Councils of Government
                  Planning Commissions
                  Regional Agencies

REFORM OF LOCAL GOVERNMENT STRUCTURES IN THE UNITED STATES: 1945-1971.

Document No. 188

DOVELL, J.E.
    City-County Consolidation: Its Possibilities in Florida. Gainesville, Florida: Public Administration Clearing Service of the University of Florida, 1956. 12p., (Civic Information Series, No. 22).

    Descriptor: Governmental Consolidation

Document No. 189

DOVELL, J.E.
    Florida's County Government. Gainsville, Florida: Public Administration Clearing Service of the University of Florida, 1952. 16p., (Civic Information Series, No. 13).

    Descriptor: County Government

Document No. 190

DOWLING, EDWARD T.
    Administrative Organization in Massachusetts Towns. Amherst, Massachusetts: Bureau of Governmental Research, University of Massachusetts, 1960. vi, 42p., (Public Information Series No.1).

    Descriptor: Council - Manager Government

Document No. 191

DRURY, JAMES W.
    Home Rule in Kansas. Lawrence, Kansas: 1965. 88p., (Governmental Research Series No. 31).

    Descriptor: Home Rule

Document No. 192

DUNCAN, JOHN PAUL.
    County Government - An Analysis. Oklahoma City: Oklahoma State Legislative Council, 1948. viii, 43p., (2) leaves of plates. Constitutional Studies No. 12; prepared for the Oklahoma State Legislative Council.

    Descriptors: Governmental Consolidation
                   Home Rule

BIBLIOGRAPHY

Document No. 193

DUNCAN, JOHN PAUL.
    County Government (Constitutional Data). Oklahoma City: Oklahoma State Legislative Council, 1948. 42p., (Constitutional Studies No. 13; prepared for the Oklahoma State Legislative Council).

    Descriptor: County Government

Document No. 194

DUNCAN, JOHN PAUL.
    County Government (Forms). Oklahoma City: Oklahoma State Legislative Council, 1948. 23p., (7) leaves of plates. (Constitutional Studies No. 14; prepared for the Oklahoma State Legislative Council).

    Descriptor: County Government

Document No. 195

DUNCOMBE, HERBERT SYDNEY.
    County Government in America. Washington, D.C.: National Association of Counties Research Foundation, 1966. xiii, 288p.

    Descriptor: County Government

Document No. 196

DURHAM CITY-COUNTY CHARTER COMMISSION (NORTH CAROLINA).
    Report of the Durham City-County Charter Commission. Durham, North Carolina: Durham City-County Charter Commission, 1960. 129p.

    Descriptor: Charters

Document No. 197

DURHAM CITY-COUNTY CHARTER COMMISSION (NORTH CAROLINA).
    Report of the Durham City-County Charter Commission. Durham, North Carolina: Durham City-County Charter Commission, 1960. 176p., in various pagings.

    Descriptors: Commission Government
                Governmental Consolidation

REFORM OF LOCAL GOVERNMENT STRUCTURES IN THE UNITED STATES: 1945-1971.

Document No. 198

DYERSBURG REGIONAL PLANNING COMMISSION (TENNESSEE).
  Annexation Study: Dyersburg, Tennessee. Prepared by the Dyersburg Regional Planning Commission; with the assistance of the West Tennessee Office of the Tennessee State Planning Commission. Dyersburg, Tennessee: The Commission, 1956. 38p.

  Descriptor: Annexation and Boundary Changes

Document No. 199

EAST BATON ROUGE PARISH COUNCIL.
  The Plan of Government of the Parish of East Baton Rouge and the City of Baton Rouge. Baton Rouge: (s.n.), 1948. 82p.

  Descriptor: County Government

Document No. 200

EDELMAN, SIDNEY.
  Approaches to Governmental Organization for Metropolitan Areas. (General): (WHO), 1964. 31, 5p., (World Health Organization Expert Committee on "Health and Sanitary Aspects of Metropolitan Planning, Housing and Industrialization", June, 1964, Geneva, Switzerland; Agenda Item C-2: Public Administration - Legal Factors).

  Descriptors: Advisory Councils
               Annexation and Boundary Changes
               Governmental Consolidation
               Policy Planning

Document No. 201

EFFROSS, HARRIS E.
  Adaptability of Local Government in Six Municipalities in the New Jersey Portion of the Penjerdel Region. Philadelphia: Pennsylvania-New Jersey-Delaware Metropolitan Project, 1964. xvii, 114p.

  Descriptors: Planning Commissions
               Policy Planning
               Regional Agencies

BIBLIOGRAPHY

Document No. 202

ELAZAR, DANIEL J.
    A Case Study of Failure in Attempted Metropolitan Integration: Nashville and Davidson County, Tennessee. Chicago: National Opinion Research Center, 1961. iv, 120p., (Report No. 81).

    Descriptors: Citizen Participation
                    Governmental Consolidation

Document No. 203

ELKINS, EUGENE R.
    Municipal Home Rule in West Virginia. Morgantown, West Virginia: Bureau for Government Research, West Virginia University, 1965. v, 53p.

    Descriptors: Annexation and Boundary Changes
                    Home Rule

Document No. 204

ENGELBERT, ERNEST A.
    Metropolitan California: Papers prepared for the Govenor's Commission on Metropolitan Area Problems. Edited by Ernest A. Engelbert. Sacramento: Govenor's Commission on Metropolitan Area Problems, 1961. x, 185p.

    Descriptors: Annexation and Boundary Changes
                    Federation
                    Incorporation
                    Policy Planning

Document No. 205

EURMAN, STUART.
    Report on Metropolitan Urban Functions: A Survey of Selected Cities. (s.l.): (s.n.), 1962. 27p.

    Descriptors: Annexation and Boundary Changes
                    Citizen Participation
                    Federation
                    Governmental Consolidation
                    Political Leadership
                    Regional Agencies
                    Special Districts and Authorities

REFORM OF LOCAL GOVERNMENT STRUCTURES IN THE UNITED STATES: 1945-1971.

Document No. 206

EWALD, JR., WILLIAM R.
    Recommendations for a Study to Improve Urban Services and to Guide Growth in Pulaski County. William R. Ewald and York Willbern. (s.l.): (s.n.), 1962. 20p.

    Descriptors: County Government
                     Governmental Consolidation
                     Incorporation

Document No. 207

FAIRFAX COUNTY, VIRGINIA. BOARD OF COUNTY SUPERVISORS.
    A Plan for Orderly Growth: Fairfax County 1968-72. Fairfax, Virginia: Board of County Supervisors, 1966. 25p.

    Descriptors: Planning Commissions
                     Policy Planning

Document No. 208

FAIRFAX COUNTY, VIRGINIA. COMMISSION ON URBAN COUNTY GOVERNMENT. CHARTER COMMITTEE.
    Proposed Charter for City of Fairfax. Fairfax, Virginia: Fairfax County Commission on Urban County Government, 1959. 20p.

    Descriptors: Charters
                     Council - Manager Government
                     Incorporation

Document No. 209

FEISS, CARL.
    Five Year Program of Operation for Mississippi-Arkansas-Tennessee Council of Governments-Summary Report. prepared by Carl Feiss; and associated consultants, City Planning and Architectural Associates, the INTERPLAN Corporation, The Research Group. Memphis, Tennessee: Mississippi-Arkansas-Tennessee Council of Governments, 1970. ii, 63p., (H.U.D. Project No. Tenn. P-115 (6)).

    Descriptors: Citizen Participation
                     Councils of Government
                     Policy Planning
                     Regional Agencies

BIBLIOGRAPHY

Document No. 210

FISCHER, CLAUDE S.
 The Metropolitan Experience. Berkeley, California: Institute of Urban and Regional Development, University of California, 1972. 72p., (Working Paper No. 195).

 Descriptors: Citizen Participation
       Community Control

Document No. 211

FLORIDA. LEGISLATIVE SERVICE.
 Local Government Study Commission: Recommendations Relative to Local Government in Florida. Tallahassee, Florida: Florida Legislative Service, 1967. 9p., (Special Report, August 4, 1967).

 Descriptor: Home Rule

Document No. 212

FLORIDA. STATE UNIVERSITY. BUREAU OF GOVERNMENTAL RESEARCH AND SERVICE.
 The Problem of Government in Leon County. Penrose B. Jackson, James J. Flannery and Fred Bair, Jr. Tallahassee, Florida: Bureau of Governmental Research and Service, School of Public Administration, Florida State University, 1955. 126p., (Studies in Government No. 14).

 Descriptors: County Government
       Governmental Consolidation
       Governmental Separation

Document No. 213

FORDE, KEVIN M.
 The Government of Cook County: A Study in Governmental Obsolesence. Chicago: Center for Research in Urban Government, Loyola University. 1969. 38p., (No. 13).

 Descriptors: Commission Government
       County Government

REFORM OF LOCAL GOVERNMENT STRUCTURES IN THE UNITED STATES: 1945-1971.

Document No. 214

FORDHAM, JEFFERSON B.
    Model Constitutional Provisions for Municipal Home Rule.
    Chicago: American Municipal Association, 1953. 30p.

    Descriptors: Charters
                      Home Rule
                      Incorporation

Document No. 215

FRIEDELBAUM, STANLEY H.
    Municipal Government in New Jersey. New Brunswick, New Jersey:
    Rutgers University Press, 1954. vii, 56p.

    Descriptors: Commission Government
                      Council - Manager Government
                      Mayor - Council Government
                      Municipal Government

Document No. 216

FRIEDEN, BERNARD J.
    Metropolitan America: Challenge to Federalism: Commission
    Findings and Proposals. Washington: Advisory Commission on
    Intergovernmental Relations, 1966. x, 176p.

    Descriptors: Advisory Councils
                      Annexation and Boundary Changes
                      Federation
                      Governmental Consolidation
                      Governmental Separation
                      Intergovernmental Cooperation

Document No. 217

FRIESEMA, H. PAUL.
    Communications, Coordination, and Control Among Local Governments
    in the Siouxland - A Study of Intergovernmental Relations. Iowa
    City: Institute of Public Affairs, University of Iowa, 1965.
    xiv, 63p., (Siouxland Studies No. 4).

    Descriptors: Advisory Councils
                      Intergovernmental Cooperation
                      Political Leadership

BIBLIOGRAPHY

Document No. 218

FRYE, ROBERT J.
    The City Manager System in Alabama. Robert J. Frye, John A. Dyer. Birmingham, Alabama: Bureau of Public Administration. University of Alabama, 1961. ix, 45p.

    Descriptors: Council - Manager Government
                   Political Leadership

Document No. 219

FRYER, ROBERT E.
    Analysis of Annexation in Michigan Together with a Comparison of Annexation in Other States. Ann Arbor, Michigan: Bureau of Government, Institute of Public Administration, University of Michigan, 1951. 58p., (Papers in Public Administration No. 5).

    Descriptors: Annexation and Boundary Changes
                   Home Rule

Document No. 220

FULTON COUNTY, GEORGIA. LOCAL GOVERNMENT COMMISSION.
    Local Government Commission of Fulton County: Final Report. Atlanta, Georgia: Local Government Commission of Fulton County, 1966. 45p., (94).

    Descriptors: Advisory Councils
                   Regional Agencies

Document No. 221

FULTON COUNTY, GEORGIA. LOCAL GOVERNMENT COMMISSION.
    Plan of Improvement for the Governments of Atlanta and Fulton County, Georgia: Report of the Local Government Commission of Fulton County. Atlanta, Georgia: Local Government Commission of Fulton County, 1950. viii, 104p.

    Descriptors: Administrative Reorganization
                   Governmental Consolidation
                   Incorporation

REFORM OF LOCAL GOVERNMENT STRUCTURES IN THE UNITED STATES: 1945-1971.

Document No. 222

THE FUTURE OF NORTHEASTERN ILLINOIS.
Chicago: Chicago University Press, 1962. 138p., (Proceeding of a lecture and discussion series sponsored by Downtown Center, University of Chicago and the Northeastern Illinois Area Planning Commission, October 18 - December 20, 1961).

Descriptors: Planning Commissions
              Policy Planning
              Regional Agencies

Document No. 223

GALLAGHER, JOHN F.
Supervisorial Districting in California Counties: 1960-1963. Davis, California: Institute of Governmental Affairs, University of California, 1963. 48p., (California Government Series No. 1).

Descriptors: Annexation and Boundary Changes
              Citizen Participation

Document No. 224

GALLOWAY, JAMES L.
Municipal Home Rule for Illinois: A Statement of Position. James L. Galloway and Charles B. Hetrick. Park Ridge, Illinois: City of Park Ridge, 1962. 22p.

Descriptor: Home Rule

Document No. 225

GERE, EDWIN ANDRUS.
Home Rule. Edwin Andrus Gere and Michael P. Curran, editors. Boston: Bureau of Public Affairs, Boston College; Bureau of Governmental Research, University of Massachusetts, 1969. 57p., (Part II in a Series on Modernizing Local Government in Massachusetts).

Descriptor: Home Rule

Document No. 226

GIBSON, FRANK K.
County Government in Virginia. Frank K. Gibson and Edward S. Overman. 2d edition. Charlottesville, Virginia: League of Virginia Counties and Bureau of Public Administration, University of Virginia, 1961. iv, 38p.

Descriptors: Citizen Participation
              Commission Government
              County Government
              Planning Commissions

BIBLIOGRAPHY

Document No. 227

GIBSON, FRANK K.
    Forms of City Government in Georgia. Prepared by Frank K. Gibson, Ted L. Hammock. Athens, Georgia: Bureau of Public Administration, University of Georgia, 1957. 46p., (Study No. 10).

    Descriptors: Annexation and Boundary Changes
                      Council - Manager Government
                      Governmental Consolidation
                      Home Rule
                      Incorporation
                      Mayor - Council Government
                      Municipal Government

Document No. 228

GILLESPIE, JOHN.
    Government in Metropolitan Austin. Austin, Texas: Institute of Public Affairs, University of Texas, 1956. 82p., (Public Affairs Series No. 26).

    Descriptors: Annexation and Boundary Changes
                      Governmental Consolidation
                      Special Districts and Authorities

Document No. 229

GLADFELDER, JANE.
    California's Emergent Counties. Sacramento: County Supervisors Association of California, 1968. ix, 121p.

    Descriptors: County Government
                      Planning Commissions
                      Special Districts and Authorities

Document No. 230

GOFF, CHARLES D.
    A Case Study of Council-Manager Abandonment: Marinette, Wisconsin. Milwaukee: (s.n.), 1960. i, 64p.

    Descriptor: Council - Manager Government

REFORM OF LOCAL GOVERNMENT STRUCTURES IN THE UNITED STATES: 1945-1971.

Document No. 231

GOLDEN GATE AUTHORITY COMMISSION.
    Transcript of Public Hearings: Governmental Aspects of a Regional Bay Area Authority. San Francisco: Golden Gate Authority Commission, 1960. 51p., (18).

    Descriptors: Regional Agencies
                  Special Districts and Authorities

Document No. 232

GOODWIN, GEORGE.
    Intermunicipal Relations in Massachusetts. Amherst, Massachusetts: Bureau of Government Research, University of Massachusetts, 1956. 36p., (7) leaves of plates.

    Descriptors: Annexation and Boundary Changes
                  District Government
                  Federation
                  Special Districts and Authorities

Document No. 233

GORYNSKI, JULIUSZ.
    The Functional Metropolis and Systems of Government. Juliusz Gorynski and Zygmunt Rybicki. Toronto: Bureau of Municipal Research, 1967. xi, 59p., (Paper No. 2).

    Descriptors: Decentralization
                  Policy Planning

Document No. 234

GOVE, SAMUEL K.
    The Lakewood Plan. Urbana, Illinois: Institute of Government and Public Affairs, University of Illinois, 1961. 26p., (Commission Papers of the Institute of Government and Public Affairs).

    Descriptors: Intergovernmental Cooperation
                  Incorporation

BIBLIOGRAPHY

Document No. 235

GOVERNMENT AFFAIRS FOUNDATION.
   Metropolitan Surveys: A Digest. Prepared by Government Affairs Foundation. Chicago: Public Administration Service, 1958. xvi, 256p.

   Descriptors: Annexation and Boundary Changes
               Charters
               Federation

Document No. 236

GOVERNMENT RESEARCH INSTITUTE (ST. LOUIS, MISSOURI).
   A Home Rule Charter for St. Louis County. St. Louis, Missouri: Government Research Institute, 1946. 16p.

   Descriptor: Home Rule

Document No. 237

GOVERNMENT RESEARCH INSTITUTE (ST. LOUIS, MISSOURI).
   A Report on the Proposed Consolidation of the Municipalities of Ladue, Frontenac, and Huntleigh Village, Missouri. The Institute, 1958. 36p., (Prepared at the Request of the Governing Officials of Ladue, Frontenac, and Huntleigh Village).

   Descriptor: Governmental Consolidation

Document No. 238

GOVENOR'S INTERGOVERNMENTAL RELATIONS AND REGIONAL PLANNING WORKSHOP, 4th, AUSTIN, TEXAS, 1969.
   Condensed Proceedings. Condensed and edited by Elbert V. Bowden. Austin, Texas: State of Texas, Office of the Govenor, Division of Planning Coordination, 1970. viii, 222p.

   Descriptors: Councils of Government
               Intergovernmental Cooperation
               Planning Commissions
               Regional Agencies

REFORM OF LOCAL GOVERNMENT STRUCTURES IN THE UNITED STATES: 1945-1971.

Document No. 239

GRAVES, W. BROOKE.
    Intergovernmental Relations in the United States: An Annotated Chronology of Significant Events, Developments, and Publications with Particular Reference to the Period of the Last Fifty Years. Chicago: Council of State Governments, 1958. ix, 110p., (RM 321).

    Descriptor: Intergovernmental Cooperation

Document No. 240

GRAVES, W. BROOKE.
    Interlocal Cooperation: The History and Background of Intergovernmental Agreements. Washington, D.C.: National Association of Counties Research Foundation, 1962. (9). (Information and Education Service: Report No. 23).

    Descriptors: Intergovernmental Cooperation
                 Planning Commissions
                 Regional Agencies
                 Special Districts and Authorities

Document No. 241

GREENBERG, MILTON.
    Approaches to Governmental Reorganization: A Preliminary Overview. Kalamazoo, Michigan: Kalamazoo County Citizens Study Committee on Community Services, 1966. 6p., (Staff Paper No. 7).

    Descriptors: Advisory Councils
                 Annexation and Boundary Changes
                 Governmental Consolidation
                 Governmental Separation
                 Incorporation
                 Special Districts and Authorities

Document No. 242

GREENBERG, MILTON.
    Special Districts in Ohio. Cleveland: Cleveland Metropolitan Services Commission, 1957. 30p.

    Descriptor: Special Districts and Authorities

BIBLIOGRAPHY

Document No. 243

GREENE, LEE S.
    The Problem of Government in Metropolitan Areas: A Symposium.
    Lee S. Greene, John G. Grumm, Frederick C. Irion, J. Lee Rodgers,
    and W.E. Benton. Dallas, Texas: Arnold Foundation, Southern
    Methodist University, 1958. vi, 55p., (Arnold Foundation
    Monographs III).

    Descriptor: Municipal Government

Document No. 244

GRIER, GEORGE W.
    Penjerdel: Region in Transition. Analysis and text by George W.
    Grier; based on statistics compiled by Stephen Decter and with
    the assistance of Barbara Shidler, Carolyn Nichols. Philadelphia:
    Pennsylvania - New Jersey - Delaware Metropolitan Project, 1964.
    vii, 84p.

    Descriptors: Policy Planning
                Regional Agencies

Document No. 245

GRIFFENHAGEN-KROEGER.
    Consolidation and the North Bend Taxpaper: A Report to the
    City of North Bend. Portland, Oregon: Griffenhagen-Kroeger,
    1962. 35p., (A Report to the City of North Bend).

    Descriptors: Annexation and Boundary Changes
                Incorporation

Document No. 246

GROBMAN, HULDA.
    Municipal Government Problems of Interest in Florida. Hulda
    Grobman, editor. Gainsville, Florida: Public Administration
    Clearing Service of the University of Florida, 1950. 101p.,
    (1), (Studies in Public Administration No. 4).

    Descriptors: Intergovernmental Cooperation
                Policy Planning

REFORM OF LOCAL GOVERNMENT STRUCTURES IN THE UNITED STATES: 1945-1971.

Document No. 247

GUGIN, DAVID A.
    An Enquiry into Rapid City's Rejection of Home Rule. Vermillion, South Dakota: Government Research Bureau, University of South Dakota, 1965. 7p., (Public Affairs No. 23).

    Descriptors: Home Rule
                    Political Leadership

Document No. 248

GULICK, LUTHER.
    Toward Metropolitan Governmental Action in the Tri-State Metropolitan Region. New York: Regional Plan Association, 1958. 15p.

    Descriptors: Advisory Councils
                    Regional Agencies

Document No. 249

HAAG, JAMES J.
    Forms of Municipal Government in the United States and in Maine. Bangor, Maine: Bureau of Public Administration, University of Maine at Orono, 1970. iv, 35p., (Maine Municipal Government, Charter Study Series No. 2).

    Descriptors: Commission Government
                    Council - Manager Government
                    Mayor - Council Government
                    Municipal Government

Document No. 250

HAAG, JAMES J.
    Introduction to the Charter Drafting Process. Bangor, Maine: Bureau of Public Administration, University of Maine, 1970. viii, 44p., (1) fold. leaf of plates, (Maine Municipal Government: Charter Study Series No. 1).

    Descriptors: Charters
                    Incorporation
                    Municipal Corporation

BIBLIOGRAPHY

Document No. 251

HAGENSICK, A. CLARKE.
    Municipal Autonomy of Consolidation for the City of St. Francis: A Report to the Consolidation Study Committee, St. Francis, Wisconsin. A. Clarke Hagensick and John W. Ryan. Madison, Wisconsin: Bureau of Government, University of Wisconsin, 1960. iii, 40p., (Report NS 3).

    Descriptor: Governmental Consolidation

Document No. 252

HAGENSICK, A. CLARKE.
    Municipal Home Rule in Wisconsin. Madison, Wisconsin: Bureau of Government, University of Wisconsin, 1961. ii, 25p., (Report NS 6).

    Descriptor: Home Rule

Document No. 253

HAGMAN, DONALD G.
    The Unconstitutionality of Incorporation and Boundary Change Laws as an Impetus for Needed Reform. Los Angeles: Institute of Government and Public Affairs, University of California at Los Angeles, 1970. 42p., (MR-146).

    Descriptors: Annexation and Boundary Changes
                Incorporation

Document No. 254

HAM, ELTON W.
    Kalamazoo City-Township Consolidation: A Report for the Greater Kalamazoo Home Improvement Committee. Kalamazoo (s.n.), 1951. 47, 9p.

    Descriptors: Citizen Participation
                Governmental Participation

Document No. 255

HANSON, ROYCE.
    Metropolitan Councils of Governments: An Information Report. Washington: Advisory Commission on Intergovernmental Relations, 1966. vii, 69p.

    Descriptors: Councils of Government
                Intergovernmental Cooperation

REFORM OF LOCAL GOVERNMENT STRUCTURES IN THE UNITED STATES: 1945-1971.

Document No. 256

HANSON, ROYCE.
    The Politics of Metropolitan Cooperation: Metropolitan
    Washington Council of Governments. Washington, D.C.:
    Washington Center for Metropolitan Studies, 1964. viii, 75p.

    Descriptors: Councils of Government
                    Regional Agencies

Document No. 257

HARRIS, CHARLES W.
    A Research Brief on Councils of Government and the Central
    City. Detroit: Metropolitan Fund, 1970. 45p.

    Descriptors: Citizen Participation
                    Councils of Government

Document No. 258

HARRIS COUNTY, TEXAS. HOME RULE COMMISSION.
    Metropolitan Harris County: A Report of the Harris County
    Home Rule Commission. Houston, Texas: Harris County Home
    Rule Commission, 1957. x, 103p.

    Descriptors: Annexation and Boundary Changes
                    Federation
                    Governmental Consolidation
                    Home Rule
                    Policy Planning

Document No. 259

HARTLEY, REX.
    A Voluntary Approach to Intergovernment Cooperation. (s.l.):
    (s.n.), 1961. 16p., (Presented at American Municipal Congress,
    Seattle, Washington, August 29, 1961).

    Descriptors: Advisory Councils
                    Citizen Participation
                    Intergovernmental Cooperation

BIBLIOGRAPHY

Document No. 260

HARVARD, WILLIAM C.
　　An Administrative Survey of the Greater Gulf Beaches Opposite
　　St. Petersburg. Gainsville, Florida: Public Administration
　　Clearing Service of the University of Florida, 1955. ii, 68p.,
　　(1) fold. leaf of plates, (Studies in Public Administration No. 13).

　　Descriptors:　Governmental Consolidation
　　　　　　　　　　Municipal Corporations
　　　　　　　　　　Special Districts and Authorities

Document No. 261

HAWAII. LEGISLATIVE REFERENCE BUREAU.
　　Article VII: Local Government. (Judy E. Stalling). Honolulu:
　　Legislative Reference Bureau, 1968. iv, 71p., (Hawaii Consti-
　　tutional Convention Studies No. 16).

　　Descriptors:　Charters
　　　　　　　　　　Special Districts and Authorities

Document No. 262

HAWKINS, BRETT W.
　　Nashville Metro: The Politics of City-County Consolidation.
　　Nashville, Tennessee: Vanderbilt University Press, 1966.
　　xii, 162p., (1) fold. leaf of plates.

　　Descriptors:　Annexation and Boundary Changes
　　　　　　　　　　Charters
　　　　　　　　　　Citizen Participation
　　　　　　　　　　Political Leadership

Document No. 263

HENRY COUNTY, COUNCIL ON INTERGOVERNMENTAL RELATIONS (INDIANA).
　　A Progress Report of the Henry County Demonstration. New
　　Castle, Indiana: Henry County Council on Intergovernmental
　　Relations, 1946. 48p., (1) leaf of plates.

　　Descriptors:　Advisory Councils
　　　　　　　　　　Citizen Participation
　　　　　　　　　　Intergovernmental Cooperation

REFORM OF LOCAL GOVERNMENT STRUCTURES IN THE UNITED STATES: 1945-1971.

Document No. 264

HESSLER, IOLA O.
    Hamilton County's Patchwork Quilt. Cincinnati: Institute of Governmental Research, University of Cincinnatii, 1969. 30p.

    Descriptors: Charters
                     Governmental Consolidation
                     Planning Commissions
                     Regional Agencies
                     Special Districts and Authorities

Document No. 265

HESSLER, IOLA O.
    Metropolitan Answers: The Art of the Possible in Greater Cincinnati. Cincinnati: Stephen H. Wilder Foundation, 1968. 67p., (A Report to the Stephen H. Wilder Foundation).

    Descriptors: Annexation and Boundary Changes
                     Councils of Government
                     Federation
                     Planning Commissions
                     Regional Agencies

Document No. 266

HESSLER, IOLA O.
    29 Ways to Govern a City: A Comparative Analysis of the Governments of 29 of the Largest Cities in the United States. Cincinnati: Hamilton County Research Foundation, 1966. iv, 101p.

    Descriptors: Citizen Participation
                     Council - Manager Government
                     Mayor - Council Government

Document No. 267

HETRICK, CHARLES B.
    Illinois Machinery for Local Government in Limbo: A Report to the Illinois Cities and Villages Municipal Problems Commission. Park Ridge, Illinois: Office of the City Manager, 1966. 22p.

    Descriptors: Administrative Reorganization
                     Federation

BIBLIOGRAPHY

Document No. 268

HIGHSAW, ROBERT B.
    Conflict and Change in Local Government: Patterns of
    Cooperation. Robert B. Highsaw and John A. Dyer.
    University, Alabama: University of Alabama Press, 1965.
    164p.

    Descriptors: Ingergovernmental Cooperation
                  Regional Agencies

Document No. 269

HIGHSAW, ROBERT B.
    Municipal Government in the South: A Mid-Century Appraisal.
    Robert B. Highsaw and Charles N. Fortenberry. University,
    Mississippi: Bureau of Public Administration, University of
    Mississippi, 1952. v, 22p., (Municipal Study Series, No. 14).

    Descriptors: Commission Government
                  Council - Manager Government
                  Mayor - Council Government

Document No. 270

HILLERY, JR., GEORGE A.
    The Rural-Urban Fringe and Louisiana's Agriculture: A Case
    Study of the Baton Rouge Area. Paul H. Price and George A.
    Hillery, Jr. Baton Rouge, Louisiana: Agricultural Experi-
    ment Station, Agricultural and Technical College, Louisiana
    State University, 1959. 52p., (Bulletin No. 526).

    Descriptors: Annexation and Boundary Changes
                  Citizen Participation

Document No. 271

HINDMAN, JO.
    Blame Metro...: When Urban Renewal Strikes!: When Laws
    Oppress. Cladwell, Idaho: Caxton Printers, 1966. 175p.,
    (1) fold. leaf of plates.

    Descriptors: Citizen Participation
                  Policy Planning
                  Regional Agencies

REFORM OF LOCAL GOVERNMENT STRUCTURES IN THE UNITED STATES: 1945-1971.

Document No. 272

HIRSCH, WERNER Z.
    The Urban Challenge to Governments. Los Angeles: Institute of Government and Public Affairs, University of California at Los Angeles, 1969. 25p., (MR-127).

    Descriptors: Decentralization
                   Federation
                 Governmental Consolidation

Document No. 273

HOBBS, EDWARD H.
    A Manual of Mississippi Municipal Government. Edward H. Hobbs and Donald S. Vaughan. 2d edition. University, Mississippi: Bureau of Government, University of Mississippi, 1962. 196p., (Municipal Study Series No. 20).

    Descriptors: Commission Government
                   Council - Manager Government
                 Mayor - Council Government
                 Municipal Corporations
                 Policy Planning

Document No. 274

HOLDEN, JR., MATTHEW.
    County Government In Ohio: Staff Report to Study Group on Government Organization. Cleveland: Cleveland Metropolitan Services Committee, 1958. iv, 23p.

    Descriptors: Charters
                 Commission Government
                 County Government
                 Policy Planning

Document No. 275

HOLDEN, JR., MATTHEW.
    Inter-Governmental Agreements in the Cleveland Metropolitan Area: Staff Report to Study Group on Governmental Organization. Cleveland: Cleveland Metropolitan Services Commission, 1958. 56p.

    Descriptor: Intergovernmental Cooperation

BIBLIOGRAPHY

Document No. 276

HOLLANDS, ROGER G.
    A Study of Local Government for the City of Cambridge, Maryland. College Park, Maryland: Maryland Technical Advisory Service, Bureau of Governmental Research, College of Business and Public Administration, University of Maryland, 1970. iii, 36p.

    Descriptors: Council - Manager Government
                          Intergovernmental Cooperation
                          Mayor - Council Government

Document No. 277

HOME RULE IN ACTION.
    Boston: Bureau of Public Affairs, Boston College, 1970. ix, 98, 51, 48p., (1), (Community Analysis and Action Series; Monographs No. 4. A Series of Lectures delivered at the Massachusetts Municipal Training Institute at Boston College.).

    Descriptors: Home Rule
                          Regional Agencies

Document No. 278

HOWARD, L. VAUGHAN.
    Government in Metropolitan New Orleans. L. Vaughan Howard and Robert S. Friedman. New Orleans: Tulane University, 1960. 227p., (1) fold. leaf of plates, (Tulane Studies in Political Science, Volume VI).

    Descriptors: County Government
                          Policy Planning

Document No. 279

HOWARDS, IRVING.
    Selected Aspects of State Supervision Over Local Government in Illinois: A View of State-Local Relations. Carbondale, Illinois: Public Affairs Research Bureau, Southern Illinois University, 1964. x, 109p.

    Descriptors: Intergovernmental Cooperation
                          Policy Planning

REFORM OF LOCAL GOVERNMENT STRUCTURES IN THE UNITED STATES: 1945-1971.

Document No. 280

HOYT, JR., JOHN S.
    Regional Development Systems in Minnesota. Collegeville, Minnesota: Agricultural Extension Service and Agricultural Experiment Station, Institute of Agriculture, University of Minnesota; Center for the Study of Local Government, St. John's University, 1969. viii, 306p., (1).

    Descriptors: Policy Planning
                      Regional Agencies

Document No. 281

HUNGER, JOHN M.
    Constitutional Changes Concerning the Milwaukee County Executive--1962 Referendum. John M. Hunger and Edward V. Schten. Madison, Wisconsin: Bureau of Government, University of Wisconsin, 1963. 24p., (Report NS 15).

    Descriptors: Administrative Reorganization
                      County Government

Document No. 282

HUTCHINSON, THEODORE M.
    Metropolitan Area Problems: The Role of the Federal Government. Ann Arbor, Michigan: University of Michigan Law School, 1961. v, 65p.

    Descriptors: Federation
                      Intergovernmental Cooperation

Document No. 283

IDAHO. LEGISLATIVE COUNCIL. COMMITTEE ON LOCAL GOVERNMENT.
    A Study of Local Government. Boise, Idaho: Idaho Legislative Council, 1968. xii, 142p., (Research Publication No. 14).

    Descriptors: Administrative Reorganization
                      Governmental Consolidation
                  Special Districts and Authorities

BIBLIOGRAPHY

Document No. 284

ILLINOIS. CITIES AND VILLAGES MUNICIPAL PROBLEMS COMMISSION.
1959 Illinois Municipal Problems: First Report of the Cities
and Villages Municipal Problems Commission to the Seventy-first
General Assembly of Illinois. Springfield, Illinois: Cities
and Villages Municipal Problems Commission, 1959. 32p.

　　Descriptors:　Annexation and Boundary Changes
　　　　　　　　　Policy Planning

Document No. 285

ILLINOIS. CITIES AND VILLAGES MUNICIPAL PROBLEMS COMMISSION.
1961 Illinois Municipal Problems: Second Report of the Cities
and Villages Municipal Problems Commission to the Seventy-
second General Assembly of Illinois. Springfield, Illinois:
Cities and Villages Municipal Problems Commission, 1961. 30p.

　　Descriptors:　Annexation and Boundary Changes
　　　　　　　　　Policy Planning

Document No. 286

ILLINOIS. CITIES AND VILLAGES MUNICIPAL PROBLEMS COMMISSION.
1963 Illinois Municipal Problems: Third Report of the Cities
and Villages Municipal Problems Commission to the Seventy-
third General Assembly of Illinois. Springfield, Illinois:
Cities and Villages Municipal Problems Commission, 1963. 41p.

　　Descriptors:　Annexation and Boundary Changes
　　　　　　　　　Policy Planning

Document No. 287

ILLINOIS. CITIES AND VILLAGES MUNICIPAL PROBLEMS COMMISSION.
1965 Illinois Municipal Problems: Fourth Report of the Cities
and Villages Municipal Problems Commission to the Seventy-
fourth General Assembly of Illinois. Springfield, Illinois:
Cities and Villages Municipal Problems Commission, 1965. 42p.

　　Descriptor:　Home Rule

REFORM OF LOCAL GOVERNMENT STRUCTURES IN THE UNITED STATES: 1945-1971.

Document No. 288

ILLINOIS. CITIES AND VILLAGES MUNICIPAL PROBLEMS COMMISSION.
1967 Illinois Municipal Problems: Fifth Report of the Cities and Villages Municipal Problems Commission to the Seventy-fifth General Assembly of Illinois. Springfield, Illinois: Cities and Villages Municipal Problems Commission, 1967. 43p.

Descriptor: Policy Planning

Document No. 289

ILLINOIS. CITIES AND VILLAGES MUNICIPAL PROBLEMS COMMISSION.
1969 Illinois Municipal Problems: Sixth Report of the Cities and Villages Municipal Problems Commission to the Seventy-sixth General Assembly of Illinois. Springfield, Illinois: Cities and Villages Municipal Problems Commission, 1969. 36p.

Descriptor: Policy Planning

Document No. 290

ILLINOIS. COMMISSION ON INTERGOVERNMENTAL COOPERATION.
Biennial Report to the Governor and General Assembly. State of Illinois, Commission on Intergovernmental Cooperation. Springfield, Illinois: The Commission, 1957. 25p.

Descriptors: Advisory Councils
Intergovernmental Cooperation

Document No. 291

ILLINOIS. COMMISSION ON LOCAL GOVERNMENT.
Report to Richard B. Ogilvie and Members of the 76th Illinois General Assembly. Commission on Local Government. Springfield, Illinois: The Commission, 1969. 113p.

Descriptors: Councils of Government
County Government
Municipal Government
Special Districts and Authorities

Document No. 292

ILLINOIS. COMMISSION ON URBAN AREA GOVERNMENT.
The Constitution and Urban Area Government. Chicago: Public Administration Service, 1969. ii, 35p., (Staff Paper No. 6).

Descriptors: County Government
Municipal Government
Special Districts and Authorities

BIBLIOGRAPHY

Document No. 293

ILLINOIS. COMMISSION ON URBAN AREA GOVERNMENT.
    Policy Recommendations for Constitutional Modernization.
    Springfield, Illinois: The Commission, 1970. (14).

    Descriptors: Governmental Consolidation
                    Home Rule
                    Incorporation

Document No. 294

ILLINOIS. CONSTITUTIONAL CONVENTION, 1969-1970. COMMITTEE ON LOCAL GOVERNMENT.
    Proposed Article on Local Government. Springfield, Illinois: Committee on Local Government, 1970. vi, 227p., (47).

    Descriptors: Annexation and Boundary Changes
                    Citizen Participation
                    Intergovernmental Cooperation

Document No. 295

ILLINOIS. CONSTITUTIONAL CONVENTION, 1969-1970. COMMITTEE ON LOCAL GOVERNMENT.
    Minority Proposals 1A-1M. Springfield, Illinois: Committee on Local Government, 1970. i, 79p.

    Descriptors: Annexation and Boundary Changes
                    Citizen Participation
                    Intergovernmental Cooperation

Document No. 296

ILLINOIS. CONSTITUTIONAL CONVENTION, 1969-1970. COMMITTEE ON LOCAL GOVERNMENT.
    Minority Proposal No. 1N. Springfield, Illinois: Committee on Local Government, 1970. 5p.

    Descriptors: Annexation and Boundary Changes
                    Citizen Participation
                    Intergovernmental Cooperation

Document No. 297

ILLINOIS. COUNTY PROBLEMS COMMISSION.
    Report of the County Problems Commission to Governor William G. Stratton and Members of the 71st General Assembly. Springfield, Illinois: The Commission, 1959. 17p.

    Descriptor: County Government

REFORM OF LOCAL GOVERNMENT STRUCTURES IN THE UNITED STATES: 1945-1971.

Document No. 298

ILLINOIS. COUNTY PROBLEMS COMMISSION.
Report to Governor Otto Kerner and the 73rd General Assembly of Illinois, 1963. Springfield, Illinois: The Commission, 1963. ii, 15p.

Descriptor: County Government

Document No. 299

ILLINOIS. COUNTY PROBLEMS COMMISSION.
Report to Governor Otto Kerner and to the 75th General Assembly of Illinois, 1967. Springfield, Illinois: The Commission, 1967. i, 30, 40p.

Descriptor: County Government

Document No. 300

ILLINOIS. COUNTY STUDY AND SURVEY COMMISSION.
Source Book on Illinois County Government. Carbondale, Illinois: Illinois County Study and Survey Commission; in cooperation with Local Government Center, Public Affairs Research Bureau, Southern Illinois University, 1969. x, 120p.

Descriptors: Annexation and Boundary Changes
County Government

Document No. 301

ILLINOIS. LEGISLATIVE COUNCIL.
Chicago Charter Problems. Springfield, Illinois: Illinois Legislative Council, 1954. iv, 38p., (Publication No. 119).

Descriptor: Charters

Document No. 302

ILLINOIS. LEGISLATIVE COUNCIL.
Structure of Governments in Metropolitan Areas. Springfield, Illinois: Illinois Legislative Council, 1952. v, 42p., (Publication No. 113).

Descriptors: County Government
Governmental Consolidation
Governmental Separation
Special Districts and Authorities

BIBLIOGRAPHY

Document No. 303

ILLINOIS CITY MANAGERS' ASSOCIATION. STUDY COMMITTEE ON METROPOLITAN GOVERNMENT.
    Government Structure in the Chicago Metropolitan Area: Facts and Alternatives. Study Committee on Metropolitan Government, Illinois City Managers' Association. Chicago: The Association, 1966. iv, 92p.

    Descriptors: County Government
                     Municipal Government
                     Planning Commissions
                     Regional Agencies
                     Special Districts and Authorities

Document No. 304

INDIANA. COMMISSION TO STUDY THE OVERLAPPING OF FUNCTIONS OF PUBLIC OFFICIALS AND GOVERNING BODIES IN INDIANAPOLIS AND MARION COUNTY: REPORT TO 1965 INDIANA GENERAL ASSEMBLY.
    Report of the Commission to Study Overlapping of Functions of Public Officials and Governing Bodies in Indianapolis and Marion County. Indianapolis: 1965. 27p.

    Descriptors: Citizen Participation
                     Governmental Consolidation

Document No. 305

INDIANA. DEPARTMENT OF COMMERCE. DIVISION OF PLANNING.
    Council of Governments: An Approach to Regional Problems. Indianapolis: Indiana Department of Commerce, Division of Planning, 1954. iv, 17p.

    Descriptors: Councils of Government
                     Planning Commissions
                     Regional Agencies

Document No. 306

INDIANA. DEPARTMENT OF COMMERCE. DIVISION OF PLANNING.
    Interlocal Cooperation Act of 1957. Prepared by the Class in Municipal Corporations of the Indiana School of Law, Indianapolis Division. Indianapolis: Indiana Department of Commerce, Division of Planning, 1959. 26p., (A Planning Separate No. H-59).

    Descriptors: Governmental Consolidation
                     Intergovernmental Cooperation

REFORM OF LOCAL GOVERNMENT STRUCTURES IN THE UNITED STATES: 1945-1971.

Document No. 307

INDIANA. LEGISLATIVE ADVISORY COMMISSION. MUNICIPAL PROBLEMS STUDY COMMISSION.
    Report of the Municipal Problems Study Committee. Indianapolis: Indiana Legislative Advisory Commission, Municipal Study Committee, 1960. 41p. in various pagings.

    Descriptor: Municipal Government

Document No. 308

INDIANA. METROPOLITAN AREA STUDY COMMISSION OF MARION COUNTY.
    Report and Recommendations for the Eighty-eighth Session of the General Assembly, State of Indiana: submitted by the Metropolitan Area Study Commission of Marion County. Indianapolis: Metropolitan Area Study Commission of Marion County, 1952. 58p., (7) leaves of plates (1 fold.).

    Descriptors: Administrative Reorganization
                  Annexation and Boundary Changes
                  County Government
                  Governmental Consolidation
                  Planning Commissions
                  Regional Agencies

Document No. 309

INDIANAPOLIS CHAMBER OF COMMERCE. GOVERNMENTAL AFFAIRS DEPARTMENT.
    Synopsis: Consolidated Government for Indianapolis - Marion County: 1969 Acts of Indiana. Indianapolis: The Department, 1969, 6p.

    Descriptor: Governmental Consolidation

Document No. 310

INDIANAPOLIS CHAMBER OF COMMERCE. GOVERNMENTAL RESEARCH DEPARTMENT.
    A Primer of Local Government in Marion County. 3d ed., rev. Indianapolis: Government Research Department, Indianapolis Chamber of Commerce, 1964. 85p.

    Descriptors: County Government
                  Municipal Government
                Special Districts and Authorities

BIBLIOGRAPHY

Document No. 311

INSTITUTE FOR LOCAL SELF GOVERNMENT (CALIFORNIA).
    ABAG Appraised: A Quinquennial Review of Voluntary Regional Co-Operative Action Through the Association of Bay Area Governments. Berkeley, California: Institute for Local Self Government, 1965. 60p.

    Descriptors: Councils of Government
                       Planning Commissions
                       Regional Agencies

Document No. 312

INSTITUTE FOR LOCAL SELF GOVERNMENT (CALIFORNIA).
    Special Districts or Special Dynasties?: Democracy Denied. Berkeley, California: Institute for Local Self Government, 1970. viii, 101p.

    Descriptors: Citizen Participation
                       Special Districts and Authorities

Document No. 313

INSTITUTE FOR RURAL AMERICA.
    Multi-Jurisdictional Area Development: A Model and Legislative Program. Institute for Rural America; in association with: Spindletop Research. Lexington, Kentucky: Spindletop Research, 1969. vii, 126p.

    Descriptors: Federation
                       Planning Commissions
                     Regional Agencies

Document No. 314

INTER-COUNTY REGIONAL PLANNING COMMISSION (DADE COUNTY, FLORIDA).
    Metropolitan Dade County: A Comparation with the Denver Inter-County Area. Miami, Florida: The Commission, 1960. ii, 29p.

    Descriptors: Commission Government
                       Planning Commissions
                     Special Districts and Authorites

REFORM OF LOCAL GOVERNMENT STRUCTURES IN THE UNITED STATES: 1945-1971.

Document No. 315

INTERGOVERNMENTAL CHALLENGES IN NEW ENGLAND.
Robert A. Shanley, editor. Amherst, Massachusetts: Bureau of Government Research, University of Massachusetts, 1965. 73p.

Descriptors: Federation
Planning Commissions
Regional Agencies
Special Districts and Authorities

Document No. 316

INTERGOVERNMENTAL COOPERATION COUNCIL (OREGON).
Compact of Voluntary Intergovermental Cooperation. Salem, Oregon: Intergovernmental Cooperation Council, 1959. 16p.

Descriptor: Intergovernmental Cooperation

Document No. 317

INTERGOVERNMENTAL COOPERATION COUNCIL (OREGON).
Report on Intergovernmental Cooperation, Mid-Willamette Valley of Oregon, June 1958 to June 1960. Salem, Oregon: Intergovernmental Cooperation Council, 1960. 6p.

Descriptor: Intergovernmental Cooperation

Document No. 318

IOWA. UNIVERSITY. INSTITUTE OF PUBLIC AFFAIRS.
The Development of Local Government in Iowa. Iowa City: Institute of Public Affairs, University of Iowa, 1970. iii, 33p., (Local Government in Iowa: Problems and Perspectives; Working Paper No.2).

Descriptors: County Government
Municipal Government

Document No. 319

IOWA. UNIVERSITY. INSTITUTE OF PUBLIC AFFAIRS.
1965 Iowa Laws Affecting Local Government. Iowa City: Institute of Public Affairs, University of Iowa, Iowa City; in cooperation with the League of Iowa Municipalities, 1965. 83p.

Descriptor: Intergovernmental Cooperation

BIBLIOGRAPHY

Document No. 320

IOWA. UNIVERSITY. INSTITUTE OF PUBLIC AFFAIRS.
    Legal Aspects of Local Government in Iowa. Iowa City: Institute of Public Affairs, University of Iowa, 1970. v, 65p., (Local Government in Iowa: Problems and Perspectives; Working Paper No.1).

    Descriptors: Commission Government
                    Council - Manager Government
                    Intergovernmental Cooperation
                    Mayor - Council Government
                    Special Districts and Authorities

Document No. 321

ITTNER, RUTH.
    Government in the Metropolitan Seattle Area. Ruth Ittner; in collaboration with Donald H. Webster, Ernest H. Campbell, Warren A. Bishop, Joshua H. Vogel. Seattle: Bureau of Governmental Research and Services, University of Washington, 1956. vi, 148p., (Report No.133).

    Descriptors: County Government
                    Federation
                    Special Districts and Authorities

Document No. 322

ITTNER, RUTH.
    Special Districts in the State of Washington. Seattle: Bureau of Governmental Research and Services, University of Washington, 1963. vii, 352p., (Report No. 150).

    Descriptor: Special Districts and Authorities

Document No. 323

JANOWITZ, MORRIS.
    Public Administration and the Public - Perspectives Toward Government in a Metropolitan Community. Morris Janowitz, Deil Wright, William Delany. Ann Arbor, Michigan: Bureau of Government, Institute of Public Administration, University of Michigan, 1958. vii, 140p., (Michigan Governmental Studies No. 36).

    Descriptors: Citizen Participation
                    Community Control

REFORM OF LOCAL GOVERNMENT STRUCTURES IN THE UNITED STATES: 1945-1971.

Document No. 324

JANS, RALPH T.
    The Urban Fringe Problem: Solutions Under Michigan Law.
    Ann Arbor, Michigan: Bureau of Government, Institute of
    Public Administration, University of Michigan, 1957. 57p.,
    (Michigan Pamphlets No. 26).

    Descriptors: Charters
                    Incorporation

Document No. 325

JERSEY CITY. CHARTER COMMISSION OF THE CITY OF JERSEY CITY.
    Report of the Charter Commission of the City of Jersey City.
    Jersey City, New Jersey: The Charter Commission, 1960. 77p.

    Descriptors: Charters
                    Commission Government
                    Council - Manager Government
                    Home Rule
                    Mayor - Council Government

Document No. 326

JOINER, CHARLES A.
    Organizational Analysis: Political, Sociological and
    Administrative Processes of Local Government. East Lansing,
    Michigan: Institute for Community Development and Services,
    Michigan State University, 1964. ix, 61p.

    Descriptors: Commission Government
                    Council - Manager Government
                    Planning Commissions

Document No. 327

JOINT COMMITTEE OF THE CITIZENS UNION AND CITIZENS HOUSING AND PLANNING COUNCIL OF NEW YORK CITY.
    A Program for Community Districts. New York: Citizens' Housing
    and Planning Council of New York and Citizens Union of the City of
    New York, 1964. 19p.

    Descriptors: Community Control
                    Decentralization
                    District Government
                    Little City Halls
                    Planning Commissions

BIBLIOGRAPHY

Document No. 328

JOINT COMMITTEE ON CHARTER REVIEW (MINNEAPOLIS, MINNESOTA).
    First Interim Report of the Joint Committee on Charter Review. Minneapolis, Minnesota: Joint Committee on Charter Review, 1959. 20p., (The Joint Committee on Charter Review consists of members from Citizens League of Minneapolis and Hennepin County, the Hennepin County Democratic - Farmer - Labor Committee, the Hennepin County Republican Committee, the League of Women Voters of Minneapolis, and the Minneapolis Chamber of Commerce.).

    Descriptors: Charters
                       Mayor - Council Government

Document No. 329

JOINT COMMITTEE ON METROPOLITAN GROWTH OF THE LEAGUE OF WOMEN VOTERS OF ATLANTA AND OF DEKALB COUNTY.
    Metropolitan Atlanta: 5 Counties, 50 Governments! Atlanta: League of Women Voters of Atlanta and of DeKalb County, 1962. 52p.

    Descriptors: Annexation and Boundary Changes
                       Federation
                       Governmental Consolidation

Document No. 330

KALAMAZOO COUNTY CITIZENS STUDY COMMITTEE ON COMMUNITY SERVICES.
    The Future of Governmental Services in Kalamazoo County: A Report to the Chamber of Commerce and the Citizens. Kalamazoo, Michigan: The Committee, 1967. v, 18p.

    Descriptors: Citizen Participation
                       County Government

Document No. 331

KALAMAZOO COUNTY CITIZENS STUDY COMMITTEE ON COMMUNITY SERVICES. SUBCOMMITTEE ON ALTERNATIVE FORMS OF GOVERNMENT.
    Report of the Subcommittee on Alternative Forms of Government to the Committee of the Whole. Kalamazoo, Michigan: Kalamazoo County Citizens Study Committee, 1967. 10p.

    Descriptors: Advisory Councils
                       Federation
                     Governmental Consolidation
                     Home Rule
                     Special Districts and Authorities

REFORM OF LOCAL GOVERNMENT STRUCTURES IN THE UNITED STATES: 1945-1971.

Document No. 332

KALAMAZOO COUNTY CITIZENS STUDY COMMITTEE ON COMMUNITY SERVICES.
SUBCOMMITTEE ON MERGER.
    Report of the Subcommittee on Merger to the Committee of the
    Whole. Kalamazoo, Michigan: Kalamazoo County Citizens Study
    Committee on Community Services, 1967. 12p.

    Descriptors: Annexation and Boundary Changes
                  County Government
                  Governmental Consolidation

Document No. 333

KAMMERER, GLADYS M.
    The Changing Urban County. Gainsville, Florida: Public
    Administration Clearing Services, University of Florida,
    1963. 32p., (Civic Information Series No. 41).

    Descriptors: Administrative Reorganization
                  Federation
                  Governmental Consolidation
                  Home Rule

Document No. 334

KELSO, PAUL.
    A Decade of Council - Manager Government in Phoenix, Arizona.
    Tucson, Arizona: Council of the City of Tucson, 1960. 66p.

    Descriptors: Administrative Reorganization
                  Citizen Participation
                  Council - Manager Government

Document No. 335

KENNEDY, HAROLD W.
    County Viewpoints on Metropolitan Government - Is the Lakewood
    Plan the Answer? Los Angeles: (s.n.), 1958. 19p., (Presented
    to the Metropolitan Government Symposium, Held under the Auspices
    of the Los Angeles Chamber of Commerce, April 8, 1958, Hotel
    Statler-Hilton, Los Angeles).

    Descriptor: County Government

BIBLIOGRAPHY

Document No. 336

KENT, JR., T.J.
    City and County Planning for the Metropolitan San Francisco Bay Area. Berkeley, California: Institute of Governmental Studies, University of California, 1963. iii, 22p.

    Descriptors: Planning Commissions
                   Regional Agencies

Document No. 337

KENT, JR., T.J.
    Open Space for the San Francisco Bay Area: Organizing to Guide Metropolitan Growth. Berkeley, California: Institute of Governmental Studies, University of California, 1970. viii, 85p.

    Descriptors: Councils of Government
                   Planning Commissions
                   Regional Agencies

Document No. 338

KENT, JR., T.J.
    Regional Planning and Metropolitan Government Proposals for the San Francisco Bay Area. (s.l.): (s.n.), 1959. 11p., (Statement presented at the National Convention of the American Institute of Planners in Seattle; July, 1959).

    Descriptors: Planning Commissions
                   Regional Agencies

Document No. 339

KENTUCKY. LEGISLATIVE RESEARCH COMMISSION.
    Metropolitan Government. Prepared by the Staff of the Legislative Research Commission. Frankfort, Kentucky: The Commission, 1959. xi, 95p., (Research Publication No. 64).

    Descriptors: Annexation and Boundary Changes
                   Federation
                   Governmental Consolidation
                   Governmental Separation
                   Special Districts and Authorities

REFORM OF LOCAL GOVERNMENT STRUCTURES IN THE UNITED STATES: 1945-1971.

Document No. 340

KENTUCKY. LEGISLATIVE RESEARCH COMMISSION.
Municipal Government: Home Rule; State Assistance. Prepared by the Research Staff, Legislative Research Commission, Frankfort, Kentucky: The Commission, 1957. iv, 27p., (Research Publication No. 53).

Descriptors: Charters
Home Rule

Document No. 341

KENTUCKY. LEGISLATIVE RESEARCH COMMISSION.
First Report of the Advisory Committee on Metropolitan Government. Prepared by the Staff of the Legislative Research Commission. Frankfort, Kentucky: The Commission, 1959. iv, 17p., (Informational Bulletin No. 25).

Descriptors: Annexation and Boundary Changes
Incorporation
Municipal Government
Special Districts and Authorities

Document No. 342

KENTUCKY. LEGISLATIVE RESEARCH COMMISSION.
Second Report of the Advisory Committee on Metropolitan Government. Frankfort, Kentucky: The Commission, 1959. vii, 20p., (Informational Bulletin No. 27).

Descriptors: Annexation and Boundary Changes
Home Rule
Municipal Government
Special Districts and Authorities

Document No. 343

KENTUCKY. LEGISLATIVE RESEARCH COMMISSION.
State-Local Fiscal Relations: A Report to the Committee on Functions and Resources of State Government. Frankfort, Kentucky: The Commission, 1952. iii, 63p., (Research Publication No. 31).

Descriptor: County Government

Document No. 344

KERSTETTER, JOHN R.
Joint City-County Occupancy of Public Office Buildings. Washington, D.C.: American Municipal Association, 1952. 3p., (18).

Descriptor: Intergovernmental Cooperation

BIBLIOGRAPHY

Document No. 345

KLOSS, HENRY.
    California's Local Agency Formation Commissions - Planning Local Governmental Structure. Sacramento: (s.n.), 1970. 10p., (Paper submitted to National Association of Counties Convention, Atlanta, Georgia, July 28, 1970).

    Descriptors: Planning Commissions
                        Regional Agencies

Document No. 346

KOSAKI, RICHARD H.
    Home Rule in Hawaii. Honolulu: Legislative Reference Bureau, University of Hawaii, 1954. 46p., (Report No. 2).

    Descriptors: Charters
                        Home Rule

Document No. 347

KRAMER, LEONARD J.
    Some Political Aspects of Metropolitanism in Indiana. (s.l.): (s.n.), 1959. 54p. vi., (A research project of the Indiana Citizenship Clearing House Done in Connection with the Department of Government at Indiana University.).

    Descriptor: Municipal Government

Document No. 348

KWEDER, B. JAMES.
    The Roles of the Manager, Mayor, and Councilmen in Policy Making: A Study of Twenty-one North Carolina Cities. Chapel Hill, North Carolina: Institute of Government, University of North Carolina at Chapel Hill, 1965. vi, 138p.

    Descriptors: Council - Manager Government
                        Policy Planning
                        Political Leadership

Document No. 349

LAKE TAHOE JOINT STUDY COMMITTEE.
    Report of the Lake Tahoe Joint Study Committee. (s.l.): Lake Tahoe Joint Study Committee, 1967. 56p.

    Descriptors: Planning Commissions
                        Regional Agencies

REFORM OF LOCAL GOVERNMENT STRUCTURES IN THE UNITED STATES: 1945-1971.

Document No. 350

LAMB, JOHN S.
    Handbook for Washington Third Class City Officials. John S. Lamb; revision of Report No. 134 originally prepared by Robert Yee. Seattle: Bureau of Governmental Research and Services, University of Washington; in cooperation with Association of Washington Cities, 1962. viii, 205p., (Report No. 148).

    Descriptors: Annexation and Boundary Changes
                  Commission Government
                  Council - Manager Government
                  Governmental Consolidation
                  Incorporation
                  Mayor - Council Government

Document No. 351

LAMBERT, WALTER N.
    Governments in Knox County. Knoxville, Tennessee: Bureau of Public Administration, University of Tennessee, 1965. xi, 145p.

    Descriptors: County Government
                  Intergovernmental Cooperation

Document No. 352

LARSEN, CHRISTIAN L.
    Columbia City Government. Christian L. Larsen and Robert H. Stoudemire. Columbia, South Carolina: Bureau of Public Administration, University of South Carolina, 1948. 97p.

    Descriptors: Administrative Reorganization
                  Commission Government
                  Mayor - Council Government
                  Planning Commissions

Document No. 353

LARSEN, CHRISTIAN L.
    The Government of Rockville. Christian L. Larsen and Richard D. Andrews. College Park, Maryland: Bureau of Public Administration, College of Business and Public Administration, University of Maryland, 1950. iv, 76p.

    Descriptors: Administrative Reorganization
                  Charters
                Mayor - Council Government

BIBLIOGRAPHY

Document No. 354

LARSEN, CHRISTIAN L.
    Metropolitan Charleston. Christian L. Larsen and Robert H. Stoudemire. Columbia, South Carolina: Bureau of Public Administration, University of South Carolina, 1949. 48p.

    Descriptors: Annexation and Boundary Changes
                    Special Districts and Authorities

Document No. 355

LEADLEY, SAMUEL M.
    Establishing Multi-County Organizations for Planning and Development. Ithaca, New York: New York State College of Agriculture and Life Sciences, 1968. 8p., (Cornell Community and Resource Development Series; Bulletin 5).

    Descriptors: Planning Commissions
                    Policy Planning
                    Regional Agencies

Document No. 356

LEAGUE OF ARIZONA CITIES AND TOWNS.
    Annexation Manual for Arizona. Phoenix, Arizona: The League, 1963. 12p.

    Descriptor: Annexation and Boundary Changes

Document No. 357

LEAGUE OF ARIZONA CITIES AND TOWNS.
    Municipal Incorporation in Arizona: Special Report. Phoenix, Arizona: League of Arizona Cities and Towns, 1965. 17p.

    Descriptor: Incorporation

Document No. 358

LEAGUE OF ARIZONA CITIES AND TOWNS.
    1967 Municipal Policy Statement of the League of Arizona Cities and Towns. Phoenix, Arizona: League of Arizona Cities and Towns, 1967. 8p.

Document No. 359

LEAGUE OF CALIFORNIA CITIES.
    City - County Relations Report. Berkeley, California; Los Angeles, California: League of California Cities, 1960. 32p.

    Descriptor: Intergovernmental Cooperation

REFORM OF LOCAL GOVERNMENT STRUCTURES IN THE UNITED STATES: 1945-1971.

Document No. 360

LEAGUE OF CALIFORNIA CITIES.
    Inter-Municipal Cooperation Through Contractual Agreements. Berkeley, California; Los Angeles, California: League of California Cities, 1963. ii, 48p.

    Descriptor: Intergovernmental Cooperation

Document No. 361

LEAGUE OF VIRGINIA MUNICIPALITES. COMMITTEE ON CONSOLIDATION OF LOCAL GOVERNMENT.
    Statement of Committee on Consolidation of Local Governments of the League of Virginia Municipalities to the Virginia Advisory Legislative Council. Richmond, Virginia: Committee on Consolidation of Local Governments, League of Virginia Municipalities, 1959. 12p.

    Descriptor: Governmental Consolidation

Document No. 362

LEAGUE OF WOMEN VOTERS OF BEAVERTON, MILWAUKIE, OSWEGO AND PORTLAND (OREGON).
    A Tale of Three Counties: One Metropolitan Community. (s.l.): The League, 1960. 32p.

    Descriptors: Annexation and Boundary Changes
                   Governmental Consolidation
                   Governmental Separation
                   Special Districts and Authorities

Document No. 363

LEAGUE OF WOMEN VOTERS OF COLORADO. COMMITTEE FOR THE STUDY OF GOVERNMENTAL RELATIONSHIPS.
    Cooperation of Confusion?: Local Government in Colorado. Denver: League of Women Voters of Colorado, 1960. 46p., (1) leaf of plates.

    Descriptors: Annexation and Boundary Changes
                   County Government
                   Governmental Consolidation
                   Municipal Government
                   Planning Commissions
                   Special Districts and Authorities

BIBLIOGRAPHY

Document No. 364

LEAGUE OF WOMEN VOTERS OF COLORADO. COMMITTEE FOR THE STUDY OF
GOVERNMENTAL RELATIONSHIPS.
    Cooperation of Confusion?: Part II. The Urban and Metropolitan
    Problem in Colorado. Denver: League of Women Voters of Colorado,
    1961. 61p.

    Descriptors: Annexation and Boundary Changes
                    Governmental Consolidation
                    Governmental Separation
                    Intergovernmental Cooperation
                    Special Districts and Authorities

Document No. 365

LEAGUE OF WOMEN VOTERS OF GRAND RAPIDS, MICHIGAN.
    Our Metropolitan County: A Study of Local Government in Kent
    County. 2d ed. Grand Rapids, Michigan: League of Women Voters
    of Grand Rapids, 1957. 61p.

    Descriptors: County Government
                    Home Rule
                    Municipal Government

Document No. 366

LEAGUE OF WOMEN VOTERS OF INDIANAPOLIS.
    Who's in Charge Here?: A Look at Local Government. Indianapolis:
    League of Women Voters of Indianapolis, 1959. 47p.

    Descriptors: Annexation and Boundary Changes
                    Federation
                    Governmental Consolidation
                    Governmental Separation
                    Planning Commissions
                    Special Districts and Authorities

Document No. 367

LEAGUE OF WOMEN VOTERS OF KING COUNTY (SEATTLE).
    The Municipality of Metropolitan Seattle. 3d. ed. Seattle:
    League of Women Voters of King County, 1965. 12p.

    Descriptors: Council Government
                    Municipal Corporations

REFORM OF LOCAL GOVERNMENT STRUCTURES IN THE UNITED STATES: 1945-1971.

Document No. 368

LEAGUE OF WOMEN VOTERS OF MONTGOMERY COUNTY, MARYLAND. LOCAL GOVERNMENT COMMITTEE.
   Montgomery County's Charter: The Challenge of Change. Silver Springs, Maryland: League of Women Voters of Montgomery County, Maryland, 1965. 17p., (Publication No. 65-06).

   Descriptors: Citizen Participation
                Council - Manager Government

Document No. 369

LEAGUE OF WOMEN VOTERS OF PORTLAND AND EAST MULTNOMAH COUNTY (OREGON).
   City County Consolidation. Portland, Oregon: (League of Women Voters of Portland), 1970. 12p.

   Descriptors: Councils of Government
                Governmental Consolidation
                Special Districts and Authorities

Document No. 370

LEAGUE OF WOMEN VOTERS OF SEATTLE-BELLEVUE-RENTON-HIGHLINE.
   Municipality of Metropolitan Seattle. Seattle: League of Women Voters, 1961. 14p.

   Descriptors: Council Government
                Municipal Corporation

Document No. 371

LEAGUE OF WOMEN VOTERS OF TERRE HAUTE, INDIANA.
   Who's in Charge Here?: A Look at Local Government in Terre Haute and Vigo County. Terre Haute, Indiana: The League, 1967. 61p.

   Descriptors: County Government
                Mayor - Council Government

Document No. 372

LEAGUE OF WOMEN VOTERS OF WEST VIRGINIA.
   A Study of the Condition of West Virginia: County Organization. Charleston, West Virginia: League of Voters of West Virginia, 1962. 16p.

   Descriptor: County Government

BIBLIOGRAPHY

Document No. 373

LEASK, JR., SAMUEL.
    Metropolitan Government for Los Angeles: A Workable Solution. Samuel Leask, Jr. and George A. Terhune. Los Angeles: Office of City Administrative Officer, 1961. 15, 9p., (5) leaves of plates (1 fold.).

    Descriptors: Advisory Councils
                    Federation
                    Planning Commissions
                    Regional Agencies
                    Special Districts and Authorities

Document No. 374

LEASK, JR., SAMUEL.
    A Metropolitan Municipal Bill of Rights. Los Angeles: City Managers Department, League of California Cities, 1958. 13p.

    Descriptor: Municipal Government

Document No. 375

LEE, JR., ROBERT D.
    A Study of Government in the Greater Hazelton Area. Robert D. Lee, Jr., and Jeffery C. Rinehart; with the assistance of Edgar C. Leduc. University Park, Pennsylvania: Institute of Public Administration, Pennsylvania State University, 1970. xii, 180p.

    Descriptors: Commission Government
                    Governmental Consolidation
                    Intergovernmental Cooperation
                    Special Districts and Authorities

Document No. 376

LEEMANS, A.F.
    Changing Patterns of Local Government. The Hague: International Union of Local Authorities, 1970. 224p.

    Descriptors: Citizen Participation
                    Community Control
                    Decentralization
                    Intergovernmental Cooperation

REFORM OF LOCAL GOVERNMENT STRUCTURES IN THE UNITED STATES: 1945-1971.

Document No. 377

LeGATES, RICHARD T.
California Local Agency Formation Commissions. Berkeley, California: Institute of Governmental Affairs, University of California, Berkeley, 1970. x, 128p.

Descriptors: Annexation and Boundary Changes
Incorporation
Planning Commissions
Regional Agencies
Special Districts and Authorities

Document No. 378

LEHMAN, MAXWELL.
"Home Rule" vs. Super-Government: A Political Science Paper. Maxwell Lehman, Frank Smallwood, Arthur Prager. New York: Metropolitan Regional Council, 1961. 27p.

Descriptors: Home Rule
Regional Agencies
Special Districts and Commissions

Document No. 379

LEIFFER, DON B.
Homelands Zoning District No. 22: Incorporation Feasibility Study. Don B. Leiffer, Richard Bigger, James Harmon. San Diego: Public Affairs Research Institute, San Diego State College, 1959. 20p.

Descriptor: Incorporation

Document No. 380

LEIFFER, DON B.
Solana Beach, 1959. Don B. Leiffer, Richard Bigger, James Harmon. San Diego: Public Affairs Research Institute, San Diego State College, 1959. 60p.

Descriptor: Incorporation

Document No. 381

LEIFFER, DON B.
Spring Valley Today and Tomorrow. Don B. Leiffer, Richard Bigger, Orin K. Cope. San Diego: Public Affairs Research Institute, San Diego State College, 1958. 54p.

Descriptors: Annexation and Boundary Changes
Incorporation

BIBLIOGRAPHY

Document No. 382

LEVENSON, ROSALINE.
    County Government in Connecticut - Its History and Demise.
    Storrs, Connecticut: Institute of Public Service, University
    of Connecticut, 1966. xi, 237p.

    Descriptor: County Government

Document No. 383

LEVENSON, ROSALINE.
    Intergovernmental Cooperation Through Municipal Associations:
    An Examination of the Municipal League Movement in the United
    States and its Significance for Connecticut Municipalities.
    Storrs, Connecticut: Institute of Public Service, University
    of Connecticut, 1961. 25p., (Informational Bulletin No. 17).

    Descriptor: Intergovernmental Cooperation

Document No. 384

LITTLE, RICHARD.
    The Politics of Overlapping Government in Los Angeles.
    Los Angeles: Department of Political Science, University
    of California, 1961. 30p.

    Descriptors: Governmental Consolidation
                 Incorporation

Document No. 385

LITTLEFIELD, NEIL O.
    The Legal Framework for Intermunicipal and Regional Action in
    Connecticut: Catalog and Critique. Storrs, Connecticut:
    Institute of Urban Research, University of Connecticut, 1960.
    58p., (Connecticut Urban Research Reports No. 10).

    Descriptors: Intergovernmental Cooperation
                 Regional Agencies

Document No. 386

LITTLEFIELD, NEIL.
    Metropolitan Area Problems and Municipal Home Rule. Ann Arbor,
    Michigan: University of Michigan Law School, 1962. vi, 83p.

    Descriptors: District Government
                 Home Rule

REFORM OF LOCAL GOVERNMENT STRUCTURES IN THE UNITED STATES: 1945-1971.

Document No. 387

LOCAL GOVERNMENT IMPROVEMENT COMMITTEE, JEFFERSON COUNTY, KENTUCKY.
    The Plan for Improvement of the Local Government Improvement Committee, Jefferson County, Kentucky. Louisville, Kentucky: Local Government Improvement Committee, 1956. 24p.

    Descriptors: Annexation and Boundary Changes
                     County Government

Document No. 388

LOCAL GOVERNMENT PROBLEMS IN URBANIZING RURAL AREAS.
    Baton Rouge, Louisiana: Department of Agricultural Economics and Agribusiness, Louisiana State University, 1965. 53p., (Southern Land Economics Research Publication No. 4, Papers presented at Local Economics and Local Government Seminar, Louisiana State University).

    Descriptors: Municipal Government
                     Regional Planning

Document No. 389

LOCAL GOVERNMENT WORKSHOP, STATE UNIVERSITY COLLEGE OF EDUCATION AT ALBANY, 1960.
    Proceedings...Albany, New York: New York Executive Department, Office for Local Government, 1960. 94p.

    Descriptors: Intergovernmental Cooperation
                     Policy Planning

Document No. 390

LOCAL GOVERNMENT WORKSHOP, STATE UNIVERSITY COLLEGE OF EDUCATION AT ALBANY, 1961.
    Proceedings...Albany, New York: New York Executive Department, Office for Local Government, 1961. vi, 161p.

    Descriptors: Citizen Participation
                     Intergovernmental Cooperation

BIBLIOGRAPHY

Document No. 391

LOS ANGELES. CITY CHARTER COMMISSION.
    City Government For the Future: Report of the Los Angeles City Charter Commission. Los Angeles: City Hall, 1969. xi, 224p.

    Descriptors: Advisory Councils
                     Charters
                     Citizen Participation
                     Community Control
                     Little City Halls
                     Mayor - Council Government
                     Neighborhood Control
                     Ombudsman

Document No. 392

LOS ANGELES COUNTY. CHARTER STUDY COMMISSION.
    Recommendations of the Charter Study Committee presented to the Board of Supervisors. Los Angeles: Los Angeles County Charter Commission, 1958. vii, 34, 53p.

    Descriptors: Administrative Reorganization
                     Charters
                     Citizen Participation

Document No. 393

LOS ANGELES COUNTY. CHIEF ADMINISTRATIVE OFFICE.
    Annexation of Territory to an Incorporated City: Inhabited and Uninhabited. Los Angeles: The Office, 1965. 10p.

    Descriptors: Annexation and Boundary Changes
                     Regional Agencies
                     Planning Commissions

Document No. 394

LOS ANGELES COUNTY. CHIEF ADMINISTRATIVE OFFICE. COUNTY-CITY SERVICES SECTION.
    Effect of Incorporation and Annexation on Special Districts. Los Angeles: Chief Administrative Office, Special Services Division, County-City Services Section, 1964. 11p.

    Descriptors: Annexation and Boundary Changes
                     Incorporation
                     Special Districts and Authorities

REFORM OF LOCAL GOVERNMENT STRUCTURES IN THE UNITED STATES: 1945-1971.

Document No. 395

LOUISIANA. LEGISLATIVE COUNCIL.
    Municipal Government in Louisiana and in Other States. Baton Rouge, Louisiana: Louisiana Legislative Council, 1961. 28p., (Report to the Council No. 33).

    Descriptors: Charters
                    Municipal Government

Document No. 396

MacCORKLE, STUART A.
    Municipal Annexation in Texas. Austin, Texas: Institute of Public Affairs, University of Texas, 1965. 41p., (Public Affairs Series No. 63).

    Descriptors: Annexation and Boundary Changes
                    Governmental Consolidation
                    Governmental Separation
                    Home Rule

Document No. 397

McGREW, JAMES WILSON.
    A Study of the Fringe Areas of Modesto, California: An Analysis and Recommendations Pertaining to the Problems of the Unincorporated Areas Surrounding the City of Modesto, California. James Wilson McGrew and Arthur Bruce Winter. Denver: Department of Government Management, University of Denver, 1948. xii, 219, (33)p.

    Descriptors: Annexation and Boundary Changes
                    Incorporation
                    Municipal Corporations
                    Special Districts and Authorities

Document No. 398

McKENNA, JOSEPH M.
    The Growth and Problems of Metropolitan Wyandotte County. Lawrence, Kansas: Governmental Research Center, University of Kansas, 1963. 49p., (Citizen's Pamphlet Series No. 32).

    Descriptors: Commission Government
                    County Government
                    Special Districts and Authorities

BIBLIOGRAPHY

Document No. 399

McKENNA, JOSEPH M.
    The Topeka Metropolitan Area: Its Political Units and Characteristics. Lawrence, Kansas: Governmental Research Center, University of Kansas, 1962. 59p., (Citizen's Pamphlet Series No. 30).

    Descriptors: Commission Government
                Municipal Government
                Special Districts and Authorities

Document No. 400

MADDOX, RUSSELL WEBBER.
    Extraterritorial Powers of Municipalities in the United States. Corvallis, Oregon: Oregon State University, 1955. v, 114p., (Oregon State Monographs: Studies in Political Science No. 2).

    Descriptors: Annexation and Boundary Changes
                Special Districts and Authorities

Document No. 401

MAINE. INTERGOVERNMENTAL RELATIONS COMMISSION.
    Report by the Maine Intergovernmental Relations Commission to Governor John H. Reed, Members of 102nd Legislature, General Public. Augusta, Maine: The Commission, 1965. ii, 12p.

    Descriptors: Governmental Consolidation
                Intergovernmental Cooperation

Document No. 402

MAINE. INTERGOVERNMENTAL RELATIONS COMMISSION.
    Report by the Maine Intergovernmental Relations Commission on County Government to Governor, Members of the 103rd Legislature, General Public. Augusta, Maine: The Commission, 1966. 29p.

    Descriptor: County Government

REFORM OF LOCAL GOVERNMENT STRUCTURES IN THE UNITED STATES: 1945-1971.

Document No. 403

MAKIELSKI, JR., S.J.
    Special District Government in Virginia. S.J. Makielski, Jr. and David G. Temple. Charlottesville, Virginia: Institute of Government, University of Virginia, 1967. vii, 131p.

    Descriptors: District Government
                    Governmental Separation
                    Municipal Corporations
                    Regional Agencies
                    Special Districts and Authorities

Document No. 404

MANN, MAVIS ANDREE.
    The Structure of City Government in West Virginia. Morgantown, West Virginia: Bureau of Government Research, West Virginia University, 1953. v, 16p., (16) leaves of plates, (Publication No. 12).

    Descriptors: Charters
                    Commission Government
                    Council - Manager Government
                    Home Rule
                    Incorporation
                    Mayor - Council Government
                    Municipal Government

Document No. 405

MANN, SEYMOUR Z.
    Government in Granite City: A Reorganization and Operations Study. Seymour Z. Mann, Arthur S. Johnson, Gary R. Roberts. Edwardsville, Illinois: Metropolitan Affairs Program, Southern Illinois University, 1961. iv, 218p.

    Descriptors: Administrative Reorganization
                    Council - Manager Government

Document No. 406

MANVEL, ALLEN D.
    Urban America and the Federal System: Commission Findings and Proposals. Washington: Advisory Commission on Intergovernmental Relations, 1969. xiv, 140p.

    Descriptors: Federation
                    Intergovernmental Cooperation
                  Neighborhood Control
                  Planning Commissions
                  Policy Planning
                  Regional Agencies

BIBLIOGRAPHY

Document No. 407

MARION COUNTY GOVERNMENT STUDY COMMITTEE (INDIANA).
Tentative Proposals of the Marion County Government Study Committee. Indianapolis: Marion County Government Study Committee, 1966. 7p.

Descriptor: Governmental Consolidation

Document No. 408

MARS, DAVID.
The Urban County. Milwaukee: Metropolitan Study Commission, Research Coordinating Committee, 1960. 37p., (Third in a series of seminars presenting alternative solutions to metropolitan area problems sponsored by Metropolitan Study Commission).

Descriptor: County Government

Document No. 409

MARTENS, SHARON WILSON.
Reorganization of County Government in North Dakota. Sharon Wilson Martens; editorial assistance by Lloyd Omdahl. Grand Forks, North Dakota: Bureau of Governmental Affairs, University of North Dakota, 1970. 48p., (Special Report No. 10).

Descriptors: County Government
Governmental Consolidation

Document No. 410

MARTIN, ROSCOE C.
Metropolis in Transition: Local Government Adaptation to Changing Urban Needs. Washington, D.C.: Housing and Home Finance Agency, 1963. viii, 159p., (Prepared for the Housing and Home Finance Agency under the Urban Studies and Housing Research Program.).

Descriptors: Councils of Government
Municipal Corporations
Planning Commissions
Regional Agencies
Special Districts and Authorities

REFORM OF LOCAL GOVERNMENT STRUCTURES IN THE UNITED STATES: 1945-1971.

Document No. 411

MARYLAND. STATE PLANNING DEPARTMENT.
    The Counties of Maryland and Baltimore City: Their Origin, Growth, and Development, 1634-1963. Baltimore: State Planning Department, 1963. 106p., (Publication No. 126).

    Descriptors: County Government
                   Municipal Government

Document No. 412

MASSACHUSETTS. EXECUTIVE OFFICE FOR ADMINISTRATION AND FINANCE. OFFICE OF PLANNING AND PROGRAM COORDINATION.
    A Progress Report on Substate Regionalization in Massachusetts. Boston: Executive Office for Administration and Finance. Office of Planning and Program Coordination, 1968. 73p., (12) leaves of plates, (Publication No. 1059).

    Descriptors: Planning Commissions
                   Regional Agencies

Document No. 413

MASSACHUSETTS. LEGISLATIVE RESEARCH COUNCIL.
    Report Relative to Voluntary Municipal Merger Procedures. Boston: Wright and Potter, Legislative Printers, 1970. 238p., (No. 5453 - House).

    Descriptors: Governmental Consolidation
                   Home Rule

Document No. 414

MASSACHUSETTS. LEGISLATIVE RESEARCH COUNCIL.
    Report Submitted by the Legislative Research Council Relative to Municipal Home Rule. Boston: Legislative Research Council, 1961. 160p., (Senate - No. 580).

    Descriptor: Home Rule

Document No. 415

MASSACHUSETTS. SPECIAL COMMISSION TO STUDY THE ORGANIZATION AND OPERATION OF THE METROPOLITAN DISTRICT COMMISSION.
    Report of the Special Commission to Study the Organization and Operation of the Metropolitan District Commission. Boston: Wright and Potter, Legislative Printers, 1960. 16p., (15) fold. leaves of plates, (House - No. 3370).

    Descriptors: Advisory Councils
                 Special Districts and Authorities

BIBLIOGRAPHY

Document No. 416

MASSACHUSETTS. UNIVERSITY. BUREAU OF GOVERNMENT RESEARCH.
State-Local Relations in Massachusetts: Part 1 Home Rule, Part 2 State Reporting. Amherst, Massachusetts: Bureau of Government Research, University of Massachusetts, 1957. 16p.

Descriptor: Home Rule

Document No. 417

MATHEWSON, KENT.
A New Approach to the Metropolitan Problem. Salem, Oregon: City of Salem, 1961. 16p., (Address, League of Minnesota Municipalities, June 1961, Hotel Lowry, Minneapolis, Minnesota).

Descriptors: Intergovernmental Cooperation
Regional Agencies

Document No. 418

MATHEWSON, KENT.
Regional Goals Setting: An Overview for Southeast Michigan. Kent Mathewson and Donn Shelton; in consultation with Bertram M. Gross. Detroit: Metropolitan Fund, 1970. 26p.

Descriptors: Citizen Participation
Councils of Government
Planning Commissions
Regional Agencies

Document No. 419

MAY, SAMUEL C.
The States Interest in Metropolitan Problems. Samuel C. May and James M. Fales, Jr. Berkeley, California: Bureau of Public Administration, University of California, 1955. 31p.

Descriptors: Annexation and Boundary Changes
Home Rule
Special Districts and Authorities

REFORM OF LOCAL GOVERNMENT STRUCTURES IN THE UNITED STATES: 1945-1971.

Document No. 420

MEISENHELDER, III, EDWARD W.
    Laws for City-County Cooperation in Tennessee. Edward W. Meisenhelder, III and Robert A. Lovelace. Knoxville, Tennessee: Bureau of Public Administration, University of Tennessee, 1960. ii, 56p.

    Descriptors: Governmental Consolidation
                    Intergovernmental Cooperation

Document No. 421

MEMPHIS AND SHELBY COUNTY PLANNING COMMISSION (TENNESSEE).
    Annexation: A Must for a Growing Memphis. Memphis, Tennessee: Memphis and Shelby County Planning Commission, 1967, ii, 37p., (31).

    Descriptor: Annexation and Boundary Changes

Document No. 422

MEMPHIS AND SHELBY COUNTY CHARTER COMMISSION (TENNESSEE).
    Charter of the Consolidated Government of Memphis and Shelby County. Memphis, Tennessee: The Commission, 1962. xii, 176p.

    Descriptors: Advisory Councils
                    Charters
                    Governmental Consolidation
                    Planning Commissions

Document No. 423

MEMPHIS AND SHELBY COUNTY CHARTER COMMISSION (TENNESSEE).
    Shelby Unity Plan: A Recommended Charter for the City of Memphis and the County of Shelby. Memphis, Tennessee: Memphis and Shelby County Charter Commission, 1962. 78p.

    Descriptors: Charters
                    Governmental Consolidation

Document No. 424

MERELMAN, JACK M.
    Association of Bay Area Governments - An Exciting New High in California City-County Cooperation: Summary of Organization. (s.l.): (s.n.), 1960. 7p., (Before the Silver Anniversary Conference of the National Association of County Officials, Program on Multi-County Approach to Area Wide Problems).

    Descriptors: Councils of Government
                    Regional Agencies

BIBLIOGRAPHY

Document No. 425

MERRIAM, ROBERT E.
    The Charters of Chicago. A Summary by Robert E. Merriam and Norman N. Elkin. (s.l.): (s.n.), 1952. 32p., (2).

    Descriptors: Charters
                     Governmental Consolidation

Document No. 426

METROPOLITAN AREA PLANNING CONFERENCE, 1st, CHICAGO, 1958.
    Proceedings...Chicago: Northeastern Illinois Metropolitan Area Planning Commission, 1958. 34p.

    Descriptors: Planning Commissions
                     Regional Agencies

Document No. 427

METROPOLITAN AREA PLANNING CONFERENCE, 2d, CHICAGO, 1959.
    Proceedings...Chicago: Northeastern Illinois Metropolitan Area Planning Commission, 1959. iv, 56p.

    Descriptors: Planning Commissions
                     Regional Agencies

Document No. 428

METROPOLITAN AREA PLANNING CONFERENCE, 3d, CHICAGO, 1960.
    Proceedings...Chicago: Northeastern Illinois Metropolitan Area Planning Commission, 1960. 82p.

    Descriptors: Planning Commissions
                     Regional Agencies

Document No. 429

METROPOLITAN AREA PLANNING CONFERENCE, 4th, CHICAGO, 1961.
    Partnerships for Metropolitan Progress: Proceedings...Chicago: Northeastern Illinois Metropolitan Area Planning Commission, 1961. 67p.

    Descriptors: Planning Commissions
                     Regional Agencies

REFORM OF LOCAL GOVERNMENT STRUCTURES IN THE UNITED STATES: 1945-1971.

Document No. 430

METROPOLITAN ATLANTA COUNCIL OF LOCAL GOVERNMENTS.
    MACLOG Self-Analysis. Atlanta, Georgia: The Council, 1968. iii, 27p.

    Descriptors: Councils of Government
                  Planning Commissions
                  Regional Agencies

Document No. 431

METROPOLITAN FUND.
    Regional Organization. Detroit: Metropolitan Fund, 1965. 2v.

    Descriptors: Advisory Councils
                  Annexation and Boundary Changes
                  Home Rule
                  Planning Commissions
                  Regional Agencies

Document No. 432

METROPOLITAN GOVERNMENT SYMPOSIUM, LOS ANGELES, 1958.
    Proceedings, Metropolitan Government Symposium. Los Angeles: Los Angeles Chamber of Commerce, State and Local Government Committee, 1958. 113p., (1) fold. leaf of plates.

    Descriptors: County Government
                  Municipal Government

Document No. 433

METROPOLITAN PROBLEMS ADVISORY COMMITTEE (SEATTLE, WASHINGTON).
    Report of the Metropolitan Problems Advisory Committee. Seattle: Metropolitan Problems Advisory Committee, 1956. 11p.

    Descriptors: Council Government
                  Policy Planning

Document No. 434

METROPOLITAN PROBLEMS ADVISORY COMMITTEE (SEATTLE, WASHINGTON).
    Report of Metropolitan Problems Advisory Committee. Seattle: Metropolitan Problems Advisory Committee, 1957. 6p., (3) leaves of plates.

    Descriptors: Municipal Corporations
                  Policy Planning

BIBLIOGRAPHY

Document No. 435

METROPOLITAN ST. LOUIS SURVEY.
    Backgroung for Action. University City, Missouri: Metropolitan St. Louis Survey, 1957. 85p., (First Report of the St. Louis Metropolitan Survey).

    Descriptors: Citizen Participation
                    Commission Government
                    Mayor - Council Government

Document No. 436

METROPOLITAN ST. LOUIS SURVEY (MISSOURI).
    Path of Progress for Metropolitan St. Louis. University City, Missouri: Metropolitan St. Louis Survey, 1957. 121p.

    Descriptors: Annexation and Boundary Changes
                    District Governement
                    Governmental Consolidation

Document No. 437

METROPOLITAN WASHINGTON COUNCIL OF GOVERNMENTS.
    Governments of the Washington Metropolitan Area. Washington, D.C.: Metropolitan Washington Council of Governments, 1965. viii, 164p.

    Descriptors: Councils of Government
                    Intergovernmental Relations
                    Municipal Government
                    Regional Agencies
                    Special Districts and Authorities

Document No. 438

MIAMI, FLORIDA. CITY PLANNING BOARD.
    Miami City Planning 1946. Miami, Florida: City Planning Board, 1946. 33p.

    Descriptors: Planning Commissions
                    Policy Planning

REFORM OF LOCAL GOVERNMENT STRUCTURES IN THE UNITED STATES: 1945-1971.

Document No. 439

MICHIGAN. CONSTITUTIONAL CONVENTION. CITIZEN'S ADVISORY COMMITTEE ON LOCAL GOVERNMENT.
    Citizens' Advisory Committee Report: Local Government. Lansing, Michigan: Citizens Advisory Committee on Local Government, 1961. 6, 4p.

    Descriptor: Home Rule

Document No. 440

MICHIGAN. GOVERNOR'S SPECIAL COMMISSION ON URBAN PROBLEMS.
    Urban Growth and Problems: Report to Governor George Romney. Special Commission on Urban Problems, State of Michigan. Lansing, Michigan: The Commission, 1968. 82p.

    Descriptors: Councils of Government
                Home Rule
                Planning Commissions

Document No. 441

MICHIGAN. GOVERNOR'S STUDY COMMISSION ON COUNTY HOME RULE.
    County Home Rule: Report to the Honorable George Romney, Governor of Michigan. Lansing, Michigan: The Committee, 1964. 10p.

    Descriptor: Home Rule

Document No. 442

MICHIGAN. GOVERNOR'S STUDY COMMISSION ON METROPOLITAN AREA PROBLEMS.
    Final Report Governor's Study Commission on Metropolitan Area Problems. Lansing, Michigan: The Committee, 1960. 28p.

    Descriptors: Citizen Participation
                Intergovernmental Cooperation
                Policy Planning

Document No. 443

MICHIGAN. SUPERVISORS INTER-COUNTY COMMITTEE.
    Supervisors Inter-County Committee: What it is, How it Works, its Accomplishments. Detroit: Supervisors Inter-County Committee, 1963. 30p.

    Descriptor: Regional Agencies

BIBLIOGRAPHY

Document No. 444

MINNESOTA. COMMISSION ON MUNICIPAL ANNEXATION AND CONSOLIDATION.
Report of the Commission on Municipal Annexation and Consolidation: submitted to the 1959 Legislature of the State of Minnesota. St. Paul, Minneosta: Commission on Municipal Annexation and Consolidation, 1959. 48p.

Descriptors: Annexation and Boundary Changes
Governmental Consolidation

Document No. 445

MINNESOTA. LEGISLATIVE RESEARCH COMMITTEE.
Metropolitan Government. St. Paul, Minnesota: Legislative Research Committee, 1968. 18p., (Publication No. 112).

Descriptors: Advisory Councils
Federation
Governmental Consolidation
Governmental Separation
Special Districts and Authorities

Document No. 446

MINNESOTA. LEGISLATIVE RESEARCH COMMITTEE.
A Study of Legislation for Local Units of Government. St. Paul, Minnesota: Legislative Research Committee, 1964. 52p., (Publication No. 99).

Descriptors: Administrative Reorganization
Home Rule

Document No. 447

MINNESOTA. LEGISLATURE. INTERIM COMMISSION ON LOCAL GOVERNMENTAL FISCAL PROBLEMS.
Report of the Minnesota Legislative Interim Commission on Local Governmental Fiscal Problems: submitted to the Governor and the Minnesota Legislature. St. Paul, Minnesota: Interim Commission on Local Governmental Fiscal Problems, 1959. 54p.

Descriptors: County Government
Municipal Government

REFORM OF LOCAL GOVERNMENT STRUCTURES IN THE UNITED STATES: 1945-1971.

Document No. 448

MINNESOTA. LEGISLATURE. INTERIM COMMISSION TO STUDY COUNTY AND TOWNSHIP GOVERNMENTS.
    Report of the Legislative Interim Commission to Study County and Township Governments to the Legislature of the State of Minnesota. St. Paul, Minnesota: Interim Commission to Study County and Township Governments, 1961. 40p.

    Descriptors: Administrative Reorganization
                  County Government

Document No. 449

MISSISSIPPI - ARKANSAS - TENNESSEE COUNCIL OF GOVERNMENTS.
    1969 Annual Report: Mississippi-Arkansas-Tennessee Council of Governments. Memphis, Tennessee: Mississippi-Arkansas-Tennessee Council of Governments, 1970. 17p.

    Descriptor: Councils of Government

Document No. 450

MISSOURI. GENERAL ASSEMBLY. JOINT COMMITTEE ON LOCAL GOVERNMENT.
    Interim Report of the Committee on Local Government. Jefferson County, Missouri: State of Missouri, 1959. 21p.

    Descriptors: Administrative Reorganization
                  Policy Planning

Document No. 451

MISSOURI. GENERAL ASSEMBLY. JOINT INTERIM COMMITTEE ON GOVERNMENTAL PROBLEMS IN ST. LOUIS AND ST. LOUIS COUNTY.
    Final Report of the Joint Interim Committee on Governmental Problems in St. Louis and St. Louis County to the Seventy-second General Assembly of the State of Missouri. Jefferson County, Missouri: Joint Interim Committee on Governmental Problems in St. Louis and St. Louis County, 1962. 24p.

    Descriptors: Municipal Corporations
                  Regional Agencies

BIBLIOGRAPHY

Document No. 452

MISSOURI. GOVERNOR'S ADVISORY COUNCIL ON LOCAL GOVERNMENT LAW.
Missouri Local Government at the Crossroads: Report of the Governor's Advisory Council on Local Government Law. Jefferson County, Missouri: Governor's Advisory Council on Local Government Law, 1968. ix, 69p.

    Descriptors: Annexation and Boundary Changes
                 County Government
                 Incorporation
                 Planning Commissions
                 Special Districts and Authorities

Document No. 453

MISSOURI. UNIVERSITY. KANSAS CITY. SCHOOL OF LAW.
Cooperative Localism: (Preparation and Implementation of Unified Comprehensive Plans for Suburban Municipalities in Western Missouri Through Intergovernmental Cooperation): Final Report. Kansas City, Missouri: The School, 1970. 4p., (92).

    Descriptor: Intergovernmental Cooperation

Document No. 454

MISSOURI PUBLIC EXPENDITURE SURVEY.
Possible Areas of Cooperation Between City of St. Joseph, Buchanan County, St. Joseph School District. Jefferson City, Missouri: Missouri Public Expenditure Survey, 1959. 8p.

    Descriptor: Intergovernmental Cooperation

Document No. 455

MOAK, LENNOX L.
The Philadelphia Experiment. (s.l.): (s.n.), 1960. 10p.

    Descriptors: Home Rule
                 Mayor - Council Government

Document No. 456

MOGULOF, MELVIN B.
Citizen Participation: The Local Perspective. Washington, D.C.: The Urban Institute, 1970. iv, 182p., (Urban Institute Paper 138-5).

    Descriptors: Advisory Councils
                 Citizen Participation
                 Community Control

REFORM OF LOCAL GOVERNMENT STRUCTURES IN THE UNITED STATES: 1945-1971.

Document No. 457

MOGULOF, MELVIN B.
    Citizen Participation: A Review and Commentary on Federal Policies and Practices. Washington, D.C.: The Urban Institute, 1970. iii, 113p., (Urban Institute Paper 102-1).

    Descriptors: Citizen Participation
                Model Cities
                Neighborhood Control

Document No. 458

MOGULOF, MELVIN B.
    Federal Regional Councils: Their Current Experience and Recommendations for Further Development. Washington, D.C.: The Urban Institute, 1970. iii, ix, 164p., (Urban Institute Paper 138-7).

    Descriptors: Advisory Councils
                Regional Agencies

Document No. 459

MONROE COUNTY, NEW YORK. CHARTER COMMISSION.
    Proposed Monroe County Charter. Rochester, New York: The Commission, 1964. 77p.

    Descriptors: Charters
                Council - Manager Governments

Document No. 460

MONTANA. LEGISLATIVE COUNCIL.
    Local Government: A Report to the Forty-second Legislative Assembly by the Montana Legislative Council. Helena, Montana: Montana Legislative Council, 1970. vii, 39p., (Report No. 34).

    Descriptor: Planning Policy

Document No. 461

MONYPENNY, PHILLIP.
    A Case Study of a Municipal Merger Movement in Illinois. Phillip Monypenny, Gilbert Y. Steiner. Urbana, Illinois: (Institute of Government and Public Affairs, University of Illinois), 1949. 22p.

    Descriptor: Governmental Consolidation

BIBLIOGRAPHY

Document No. 462

MOTT, RODNEY L.
    Home Rule for America's Cities. Chicago: American Municipal Association, 1949. 23p.

    Descriptors: Charters
                     Home Rule

Document No. 463

MUSKEGON, MICHIGAN. GREATER MUSKEGON'S PUBLIC STUDY COMMITTEE ON CONSOLIDATION. SUBCOMMITTEE ON ADMINISTRATIVE ASPECTS.
    Government in Greater Muskegon. Muskegon, Michigan: Greater Muskegon's Public Study Committee on Administrative Aspects, 1956. 37p.

    Descriptors: Administrative Reorganization
                     Municipal Government

Document No. 464

MYLLENBECK, WESLEY L.
    Approaches to Local Government Reorganization, Tri-Cities, Washington. Wesley L. Myllenbeck, Ronald C. Cease, Michael F. Rosenberger. Portland, Oregon: Columbian Research Institute, 1970. v, 123p., (Prepared for Benton Franklin Governmental Conference).

    Descriptors: Councils of Government
                     Federation
                     Governmental Consolidation
                     Governmental Separation
                     Special Districts and Authorities

Document No. 465

NASHVILLE, TENNESSEE. METROPOLITAN GOVERNMENT CHARTER COMMISSION.
    Proposed Charter of the Metropolitan Government of Nashville and Davidson County. Nashville, Tennessee: The Commission, 1962. xiv, 94p., (61).

    Descriptors: Charters
                     Governmental Consolidation
                     Municipal Corporations

REFORM OF LOCAL GOVERNMENT STRUCTURES IN THE UNITED STATES: 1945-1971.

Document No. 466

NASHVILLE AND DAVIDSON COUNTY PLANNING COMMISSIONS (TENNESSEE).
    Plan of Metropolitan Government for Nashville and Davidson
    County. Nashville: Nashville and Davidson County Planning
    Commission, 1956. v, 69p., (4) fold. leaves of plates.

    Descriptors: Governmental Consolidation
                    Municipal Government

Document No. 467

NATIONAL ASSOCIATION OF COUNTIES.
    City-County Consolidation: Separations and Federations.
    Washington, D.C.: National Associations of Counties, 1970.
    88p.

    Descriptors: Federation
                    Governmental Consolidation
                    Governmental Separation

Document No. 468

NATIONAL ASSOCIATION OF COUNTIES.
    Guide to County Organization and Management. Washington, D.C.:
    National Association of Counties, 1968. 453p.

    Descriptors: Advisory Councils
                    County Government
                    Councils of Government
                    Special Districts and Authorities

Document No. 469

NATIONAL CONFERENCE OF COUNCIL OF GOVERNMENTS, 1st, WASHINGTON, D.C., 1967.
    A Summary of Proceedings. Washington, D.C.: Metropolitan
    Washington Council of Governments, 1967. 24p.

    Descriptors: Councils of Government
                    Planning Commissions
                    Regional Agencies

BIBLIOGRAPHY

Document No. 470

NATIONAL CONFERENCE ON METROPOLITAN PROBLEMS, MICHIGAN STATE UNIVERSITY, 1956.
    Proceedings...New York: Government Affairs Foundation, 1957. 99p., (Held at Kellogg Center, Michigan State University, East Lansing, Michigan, April 29 to May 2, 1956).

    Descriptor: Municipal Government

Document No. 471

NATIONAL LEAGUE OF CITIES.
    New Concepts in Municipal Government. Washington, D.C.: National League of Cities, 1967. 42p.

    Descriptors: Citizen Participation
                 Neighborhood Control
                 Planning Commissions

Document No. 472

NATIONAL LEAGUE OF CITIES. DEPARTMENT OF URBAN STUDIES.
    Adjusting Municipal Boundaries: Law and Practice. Washington, D.C.: Department of Urban Studies, National League of Cities, 1966. iii, 354p.

    Descriptor: Annexation and Boundary Changes

Document No. 473

NATIONAL LEAGUE OF CITIES. DEPARTMENT OF URBAN STUDIES.
    Reorganizing Local Government for the Future. Washington, D.C.: Department of Urban Studies, National League of Cities, 1967. 23p., (Staff Report No. 67-3).

    Descriptors: Advisory Councils
                 Annexation and Boundary Changes
                 Citizen Participation
                 Federation
                 Governmental Consolidation
                 Special Districts and Authorities

Document No. 474

NATIONAL MUNICIPAL LEAGUE.
    Model City Charter. 6th ed. New York: National Municipal League, 1964. xx, 76p.

    Descriptor: Charters

REFORM OF LOCAL GOVERNMENT STRUCTURES IN THE UNITED STATES: 1945-1971.

Document No. 475

NATIONAL MUNICIPAL LEAGUE.
    Model Council-Manager Plan Enabling Act. New York: National Municipal League, 1965. vii, 47p.

    Descriptor: Council - Manager Government

Document No. 476

NATIONAL MUNICIPAL LEAGUE.
    Model County Charter. Introduction by John E. Bebout. New York: National Municipal League, 1956. xxxviii, 71p.

    Descriptor: Charters

Document No. 477

NATIONAL MUNICIPAL LEAGUE. COMMITTEE ON A GUIDE FOR CHARTER COMMISSIONS.
    A Guide for Charter Commissions. 3d ed. New York: National Municipal League, 1957. iv, 44p.

    Descriptor: Charters

Document No. 478

NATIONAL SERVICE TO REGIONAL COUNCILS.
    Regional Opportunities 1968: Proceedings of Second Annual Conference of Regional Councils. Washington, D.C.: National Service to Regional Councils, 1968. 24p.

    Descriptors: Citizen Participation
                Councils of Government
                Regional Agencies

Document No. 479

NATIONAL SERVICE TO REGIONAL COUNCILS.
    Regional Councils and the Urban Cities: Proceeding of Third Annual Conference of Regional Councils. Washington, D.C.: National Service to Regional Councils, 1969. 20p.

    Descriptors: Councils of Government
                Regional Agencies

BIBLIOGRAPHY

Document No. 480

NATIONAL SERVICE TO REGIONAL COUNCILS.
    Regional Review: An Experiment in Intergovernmental Coordination. Washington, D.C.: National Service to Regional Councils, 1969. 8p.

    Descriptors: Councils of Government
                    Intergovernmental Cooperation
                    Regional Agencies

Document No. 481

NATIONAL SERVICE TO REGIONAL COUNCILS.
    Special Report: Program Implementation. Washington, D.C.: National Service to Regional Councils, 1968. 12p., (Special Report No. 6).

    Descriptors: Policy Planning
                    Regional Agencies

Document No. 482

NATIONAL SERVICE TO REGIONAL COUNCILS.
    Special Report: Regional Alternatives. Washington, D.C.: National Service to Regional Councils, 1968. 8p., (Special Report No. 2).

    Descriptors: Councils of Government
                    Regional Agencies

Document No. 483

NATIONAL SERVICE TO REGIONAL COUNCILS.
    Special Report: Regional Councils and States. Washington, D.C.: National Service to Regional Councils, 1968. 16p., (Special Report No. 8).

    Descriptors: Administrative Reorganization
                    Councils of Government
                    Planning Commissions
                    Regional Agencies
                    Special Districts and Authorities

REFORM OF LOCAL GOVERNMENT STRUCTURES IN THE UNITED STATES: 1945-1971.

Document No. 484

NEBRASKA. LEGISLATIVE COUNCIL. COMMITTEE ON COUNTY GOVERNMENT.
    Report of the Nebraska Legislative Council Committee on County Government. Lincoln, Nebraska: Nebraska Legislative Council, 1956. 29p., (Committee Report No. 74).

    Descriptor: County Government

Document No. 485

NEBRASKA. LEGISLATIVE COUNCIL. COMMITTEE ON COUNTY GOVERNMENT REORGANIZATION.
    Report of the Nebraska Legislative Council Committee on County Government Reorganization. Lincoln, Nebraska: Nebraska Legislative Council, 1966. 34p., (Committee Report No. 149).

    Descriptors: County Government
                 Governmental Consolidation

Document No. 486

NEBRASKA. LEGISLATIVE COUNCIL. COMMITTEE ON MUNICIPAL ANNEXATION.
    Report of the Nebraska Legislative Council Committee on Municipal Annexation. Lincoln, Nebraska: Nebraska Legislative Council, 1966. 23p., (Committee Report No. 148).

    Descriptor: Annexation and Boundary Changes

Document No. 487

NEBRASKA. LEGISLATIVE COUNCIL. COMMITTEE ON REORGANIZATION OF COUNTY GOVERNMENT.
    Report of the Legislative Committee on Reorganization of County Government. Lincoln, Nebraska: Nebraska Legislative Council, 1950. 49p., (Committee Report No. 32).

    Descriptors: County Government
                 Governmental Consolidation

Document No. 488

NEW JERSEY. COMMISSION OF MUNICIPAL GOVERNMENT.
    Local Self-Government in New Jersey: A Proposed Optional Charter Plan: Report of the Commission on Municipal Government. Trenton, New Jersey: Commission on Municipal Government, 1949, xii, 120p.

    Descriptors: Charters
                 Commission Government
                 Council - Manager Government
                 Incorporation
                 Mayor - Council Government

BIBLIOGRAPHY

Document No. 489

NEW JERSEY. COUNTY AND MUNICIPAL GOVERNMENT STUDY COMMISSION.
County Government: Challenge and Change: Second Report.
County and Municipal Study Commission. Trenton, New Jersey:
The Commission, 1969. xxiv, 128p., (1) fold. leaf of plates.

Descriptors: Administrative Reorganization
County Government

Document No. 490

NEW JERSEY. COUNTY AND MUNICIPAL GOVERNMENT STUDY COMMISSION.
County Government: Supplementary Readings and Research
Materials. compiled and edited by Bartley R. Carhart.
Trenton, New Jersey: County and Municipal Government
Study Commission, 1970. 239p., (1) leaf of plates.

Descriptors: Administrative Reorganization
Charters
County Government

Document No. 491

NEW JERSEY. COUNTY AND MUNICIPAL GOVERNMENT STUDY COMMISSION.
Creative Localism: A Prospectus: An Interim Report of the
County and Municipal Government Study Commission. Trenton,
New Jersey: County and Municipal Study Commission, 1968.
xxvi, 104p.

Descriptors: County Government
Intergovernmental Cooperation
Municipal Government

Document No. 492

NEW JERSEY. COUNTY AND MUNICIPAL GOVERNMENT STUDY COMMISSION.
Joint Services - A Local Response to Area Wide Problems:
Third Report. State of New Jersey, County and Municipal
Government Study Commission. Trenton, New Jersey: The
Commission, 1970. xv, 50p.

Descriptors: Intergovernmental Cooperation
Municipal Government

REFORM OF LOCAL GOVERNMENT STRUCTURES IN THE UNITED STATES: 1945-1971.

Document No. 493

NEW JERSEY. COUNTY AND MUNICIPAL LAW REVISION COMMISSION.
    Public Hearing on Tentative Draft of Municipal Powers Law
    (Title 40) before County and Municipal Law Revision
    Commission. Trenton, New Jersey: County and Municipal
    Law Revision Commission, 1961. 73p.

    Descriptor: Municipal Government

Document No. 494

NEW YORK (CITY). CHARTER REVISION FOR THE CITY OF NEW YORK.
    Proposed Charter for the City of New York: Filed with the
    City Clerk on August 4, 1961. Charter Commission of the City
    of New York. New York: The Commission, 1961. ii, 155p.

    Descriptor: Charters

Document No. 495

NEW YORK (CITY). MAYOR'S TASK FORCE ON THE CONSTITUTIONAL CONVENTION.
    Report and Proposed Constitutional Amendments. New York:
    The Task Force, 1967. iii, 72p.

    Descriptor: Home Rule

Document No. 496

NEW YORK (CITY). MAYOR'S TASK FORCE ON REORGANIZATION OF THE CITY
OF NEW YORK GOVERNMENT.
    Report and Proposed Local Law. New York: Institute of
    Public Administration, 1966. 42, 79p.

    Descriptor: Administrative Reorganization

Document No. 497

NEW YORK (STATE). COMMISSION ON GOVERNMENTAL OPERATIONS OF THE CITY
OF NEW YORK.
    A New Charter for the City of New York. New York: New York
    State Commission on Governmental Operations of the City of
    New York, 1961. 32p.

    Descriptor: Charters

BIBLIOGRAPHY

Document No. 498

NEW YORK (STATE). DEPARTMENT OF AUDIT AND CONTROL.
Interlocal Cooperation in New York State: Extent of Cooperation and Statutory Authorization for Cooperative Activity: prepared for the Governor's Committee on Home Rule. Comptroller. Albany, New York: Department of Audit and Control, 1958. 60p.

Descriptor: Intergovernmental Cooperation

Document No. 499

NEW YORK (STATE). EXECUTIVE DEPARTMENT. OFFICE OF LOCAL GOVERNMENT.
Annual Report, 1959-1960. Albany, New York: State of New York, Executive Department, 1961. 20p.

Descriptors: Advisory Councils
Home Rule

Document No. 500

NEW YORK (STATE). EXECUTIVE DEPARTMENT. OFFICE FOR LOCAL GOVERNMENT.
Annual Report, 1961-1962. Albany, New York: State of New York, Executive Department, 1963. 44p.

Descriptor: Advisory Councils

Document No. 501

NEW YORK (STATE). EXECUTIVE DEPARTMENT. OFFICE FOR LOCAL GOVERNMENT.
Annual Report, 1963-1964. Albany, New York: State of New York, Executive Department, 1965. 43p.

Descriptors: Charters
Home Rule
Municipal Government

Document No. 502

NEW YORK (STATE). EXECUTIVE DEPARTMENT. OFFICE FOR LOCAL GOVERNMENT.
Annual Report, 1965-1966. Albany, New York: State of New York, Executive Department, 1967. 40p.

Descriptors: Administrative Reorganization
Charters

Document No. 503

NEW YORK (STATE). EXECUTIVE DEPARTMENT. OFFICE FOR LOCAL GOVERNMENT.
Annual Report, 1967-1968. Albany, New York: State of New York, Executive Department, 1969. 44p.

Descriptor: Administrative Reorganization

REFORM OF LOCAL GOVERNMENT STRUCTURES IN THE UNITED STATES: 1945-1971.

Document No. 504

NEW YORK (STATE). EXECUTIVE DEPARTMENT. OFFICE FOR LOCAL GOVERNMENT. Annual Report, 1969-1970. Albany, New York: State of New York, Executive Department, 1971. 43p.

   Descriptor: Administrative Reorganization

Document No. 505

NEW YORK (STATE). EXECUTIVE DEPARTMENT. OFFICE FOR LOCAL GOVERNMENT. County Charters in New York State: A Comparative Guide to Leading Charter Provisions. Albany, New York: State of New York, Office for Local Government, 1963. v, 69p.

   Descriptors: Charters
                County Government

Document No. 506

NEW YORK (STATE). EXECUTIVE DEPARTMENT. OFFICE FOR LOCAL GOVERNMENT. Local Government: A Brief Summary of Local Government Structures, Organizations, and Functions in New York State. Albany, New York: State of New York, Executive Department, Office for Local Government, 1966. 13p.

   Descriptors: Charters
                Home Rule
                Special Districts and Authorities

Document No. 507

NEW YORK (STATE). EXECUTIVE DEPARTMENT. OFFICE FOR LOCAL GOVERNMENT. Local Government Cooperation: Uses--Procedures--Case Studies: A Guide for Municipal Officials. Albany, New York: State of New York, Office for Local Government, 1963. vi, 33p.

   Descriptors: Intergovernmental Cooperation
                Special Districts and Authorities

Document No. 508

NEW YORK (STATE). EXECUTIVE DEPARTMENT. OFFICE FOR LOCAL GOVERNMENT. Local Government Seminar for State Officials, October 14, 1964, Albany, New York. Albany, New York: State of New York, Executive Department, Office for Local Government, 1964. 81p., (2) leaves of plates.

   Descriptor: Municipal Government

BIBLIOGRAPHY

Document No. 509

NEW YORK (STATE). LEGISLATURE. JOINT LEGISLATIVE COMMITTEE ON METROPOLITAN AREAS STUDY.
    Metropolitan Action: A Six County Inventory of Practical Programs. Albany, New York: State of New York, Joint Legislative Committee on Metropolitan Areas Study, 1960. viii, 141p., (1) leaf of plates.

    Descriptor: County Government

Document No. 510

NEW YORK (STATE). LEGISLATURE. JOINT LEGISLATIVE COMMITTEE ON METROPOLITAN AREAS STUDY.
    Municipal Cooperation: A Digest of the Law of New York Permitting Intergovernmental Service Agreements Among Municipalities of the State. rev. ed. Albany, New York: State of New York, Joint Legislative Committee on Metropolitan Areas Study, 1959. viii, 171p.

    Descriptors: Annexation and Boundary Changes
                  Governmental Consolidation
                  Intergovernmental Cooperation

Document No. 511

NEW YORK (STATE). LEGISLATURE. JOINT LEGISLATIVE COMMITTEE ON METROPOLITAN AREAS STUDY.
    Municipal Cooperation: A Digest of the Law of New York Permitting Intergovernmental Service Arrangements Among Municipalities of the State: 1960 Supplement. Albany, New York: State of New York, Joint Legislative Committee on Metropolitan Areas Study, 1960. vi, 27p.

    Descriptors: Intergovernmental Cooperation
                  Special Districts and Authorities

Document No. 512

NEW YORK (STATE). LEGISLATURE. JOINT LEGISLATIVE COMMITTEE ON METROPOLITAN AREAS STUDY.
    One Hundred New Answers to Problems of Urban Growth: Recent Legislative Action...Albany, New York: Joint Legislative Committee on Metropolitan Areas Study, 1960. 16p.

    Descriptor: Municipal Government

REFORM OF LOCAL GOVERNMENT STRUCTURES IN THE UNITED STATES: 1945-1971.

Document No. 513

NEW YORK (STATE). LEGISLATURE. JOINT COMMITTEE ON METROPOLITAN AREAS STUDY.
    1958 Report of the Joint Legislative Committee on Metropolitan Areas Study to the Legislature of the State of New York, March 20, 1958. Albany, New York: Joint Legislative Committee on Metropolitan Areas Study, 1958. 84p., (Legislative Document (1958) No. 30).

    Descriptors: Intergovernmental Cooperation
                  Municipal Government

Document No. 514

NEW YORK (STATE). LEGISLATURE. JOINT COMMITTEE ON METROPOLITAN AREAS STUDY.
    1959 Report of the Joint Legislative Committee on Metropolitan Areas Study to the Legislature of the State of New York, March 20, 1959. Albany, New York: Joint Legislative Committee on Metropolitan Areas Study, 1959. 109p., (Legislative Document (1959) No. 19).

    Descriptors: Home Rule
                  Intergovernmental Cooperation
                  Municipal Government

Document No. 515

NEW YORK (STATE). LEGISLATURE. JOINT COMMITTEE ON METROPOLITAN AREAS STUDY.
    1960 Report of the Joint Legislative Committee on Metropolitan Areas Study to the Legislature of the State of New York, March 21, 1960. Albany, New York: Joint Legislative Committee on Metropolitan Areas Study, 1960. 107p., (Legislative Document (1960) No. 17).

    Descriptors: Intergovernmental Cooperation
                  Municipal Government

Document No. 516

NEW YORK (STATE). LEGISLATURE. JOINT COMMITTEE ON METROPOLITAN AREAS STUDY.
    1961 Report of the Joint Legislative Committee on Metropolitan Areas Study to the Legislature of the State of New York, March 15, 1961. Albany, New York: Joint Legislative Committee on Metropolitan Areas Study, 1961. 149p., (Legislative Document (1961) No. 18).

    Descriptors: Intergovernmental Cooperation
                  Municipal Government

BIBLIOGRAPHY

Document No. 517

NEW YORK (STATE). LEGISLATURE. JOINT COMMITTEE ON METROPOLITAN AREAS STUDY.
    1962 Report of the Joint Legislative Committee on Metropolitan Areas Study to the Legislature of the State of New York, March 15, 1962. Albany, New York: Joint Legislative Committee on Metropolitan Areas Study, 1962. 96p.

    Descriptors: Intergovernmental Cooperation
                     Municipal Government

Document No. 518

NEW YORK (STATE). LEGISLATURE. JOINT COMMITTEE ON METROPOLITAN AREAS STUDY.
    1963 Report of the Joint Legislative Committee on Metropolitan Areas Study to the Legislature of the State of New York, March 31, 1963. Albany, New York: Joint Legislative Committee on Metropolitan Areas Study, 1963. 70p., (Legislative Document (1963) No. 23).

    Descriptors: Intergovernmental Cooperation
                     Municipal Government

Document No. 519

NEW YORK (STATE). LEGISLATURE. JOINT COMMITTEE ON METROPOLITAN AREAS STUDY.
    1964 Report of the Joint Legislative Committee on Metropolitan Areas Study to the Legislature of the State of New York, March 15, 1964. Albany, New York: Joint Legislative Committee on Metropolitan Areas Study, 1964. 57p., (Legislative Document (1964) No. 18).

    Descriptor: Municipal Government

Document No. 520

NEW YORK (STATE). LEGISLATURE. JOINT COMMITTEE ON METROPOLITAN AREAS STUDY.
    1965 Report of the Joint Legislative Committee on Metropolitan Areas Study to the Legislature of the State of New York, March 15, 1965. Albany, New York: Joint Legislative Committee on Metropolitan Areas Study, 1965. 57p., (Legislative Document (1965) No. 13).

    Descriptor: Municipal Government

REFORM OF LOCAL GOVERNMENT STRUCTURES IN THE UNITED STATES: 1945-1971.

Document No. 521

NEW YORK (STATE). LEGISLATURE. JOINT COMMITTEE ON METROPOLITAN AND REGIONAL AREA STUDIES.
    1966 Report of the Joint Legislative Committee on Metropolitan and Regional Area Studies to the Legislature of the State of New York, March 31, 1966. Albany, New York: Joint Legislative Committee on Metropolitan and Regional Area Studies, 1966. 96p., (Legislative Document (1966) No. 24).

    Descriptors: Planning Commissions
                  Policy Planning
                  Regional Agencies

Document No. 522

NEW YORK (STATE). LEGISLATURE. JOINT COMMITTEE ON METROPOLITAN AND REGIONAL AREAS STUDY.
    Governing Urban Areas: Realism and Reform: The 1967 Report of the Joint Legislative Committee on Metropolitan and Regional Areas Study to the Governor and the Legislature of the State of New York. Albany, New York: Joint Legislative Committee on Metropolitan and Regional Areas Study, 1967. 122p., (Legislative Document (1967) No. 42).

    Descriptors: Planning Commissions
                  Regional Agencies

Document No. 523

NEW YORK (STATE). LEGISLATURE. JOINT COMMITTEE ON METROPOLITAN AND REGIONAL AREAS STUDY.
    Governing Urban Areas: Realism and Reform: Appendix XI of the 1967 Report of the Joint Legislative Committee on Metropolitan and Regional Areas Study to the Governor and the Legislature of the State of New York. Albany, New York: Joint Legislative Committee on Metropolitan and Regional Areas Study, 1967. 83p., (Legislative Document (1967) No. 42A).

    Descriptor: Municipal Government

BIBLIOGRAPHY

Document No. 524

NEW YORK (STATE). LEGISLATURE. JOINT COMMITTEE ON METROPOLITAN AND REGIONAL AREAS STUDY.
>Governing Urban Areas: Strengthening Local Government Through Regionalism: The 1968 Report of the Joint Legislative Committee on Metropolitan and Regional Areas Study to the Governor and the Legislature of the State of New York. Albany, New York: Joint Legislative Committee on Metropolitan and Regional Areas Study, 1968. 251p., (Legislative Document (1968) No. 33).

>Descriptors: Charters
>Planning Commissions
>Policy Planning
>Regional Agencies

Document No. 525

NEW YORK (STATE). LEGISLATURE. JOINT LEGISLATIVE COMMITTEE ON METROPOLITAN AND REGIONAL AREAS STUDY.
>Public Hearing... New York: New York Reporting Services, 1966. ii, 303p.

>Descriptor: Municipal Government

Document No. 526

NEW YORK (STATE). TEMPORARY STATE COMMISSION ON THE CONSTITUTIONAL CONVENTION.
>Local Government. New York: The Commission, 1967. 150p.

>Descriptors: Home Rule
>Municipal Government

Document No. 527

NEW YORK (STATE). TEMPORARY STATE COMMISSION TO STUDY THE ORGANIZATIONAL STRUCTURE OF THE GOVERNMENT OF THE CITY OF NEW YORK.
>Four Steps to Better Government of New York City: A Plan for Action. New York: Temporary State Commission to Study the Organizational Structure of the City of New York, 1953-1954. 2v.

>Descriptors: Administrative Reorganization
>Municipal Government

Document No. 528

NEW YORK CHAMBER OF COMMERCE.
>A New Charter for the City of New York. New York: New York Chamber of Commerce, 1961. 9p.

>Descriptor: Charters

REFORM OF LOCAL GOVERNMENT STRUCTURES IN THE UNITED STATES: 1945-1971.

Document No. 529

NEW YORK CHAMBER OF COMMERCE.
    Proposition I: Proposed Charter for the City of New York: Proposition II: Minority Representation. New York: New York Chamber of Commerce, 1961. 6p.

    Descriptor: Charters

Document No. 530

NICHOLS, GLENN W.
    Interlocal Cooperation in Idaho. Moscow, Idaho: Bureau of Public Affairs Research, University of Idaho, 1968. 75p.

    Descriptor: Intergovernmental Cooperation

Document No. 531

NICKS, ROY S.
    Kingsport and Annexation. prepared by Roy S. Nicks, Edward S. Overman, Simon Perry. Knoxville, Tennessee: Bureau of Public Administration and the Municipal Advisory Service, Division of University Extension, University of Tennessee; in cooperation with the Tennessee Municipal League, 1956. iv, 153p., (3) leaves of plates.

    Descriptor: Annexation and Boundary Changes

Document No. 532

NORRGARD, DAVID L.
    Regional Law Enforcement: A Study of Intergovernmental Cooperation and Coordination. Chicago: Public Administration Service, 1969. viii, 58p.

    Descriptors: Councils of Government
               Governmental Consolidation
               Home Rule
               Intergovernmental Cooperation
               Municipal Government
               Regional Agencies

Document No. 533

NORTH CAROLINA. LOCAL GOVERNMENT STUDY COMMISSION.
    Report of the Local Government Study Commission to the Governor of North Carolina and the General Assembly of 1969. Raleigh, North Carolina: Local Government Study Commission, 1969. viii, 188p.

    Descriptors: Advisory Councils
               County Government
               Planning Commissions
               Regional Agencies

BIBLIOGRAPHY

Document No. 534

NORTH CAROLINA. MUNICIPAL GOVERNMENT STUDY COMMISSION.
    Report of the Municipal Government Study Commission. Raleigh, North Carolina: Municipal Government Study Commission, 1958. 37p.

    Descriptors: Annexation and Boundary Changes
                   Municipal Government
                   Policy Planning

Document No. 535

NORTH CAROLINA. MUNICIPAL GOVERNMENT STUDY COMMISSION.
    Report of the Municipal Government Study Commission: North Carolina General Assembly Supplementary Report. Raleigh, North Carolina: Municipal Government Study Commission, 1959. 15p.

    Descriptor: Annexation and Boundary Changes

Document No. 536

NORTH CAROLINA. UNIVERSITY. INSTITUTE OF GOVERNMENT.
    Materials on Municipal Government in North Carolina. edited by Warren J. Wicker, Chapel Hill, North Carolina: Institute of Government, University of North Carolina at Chapel Hill, 1969. x, 458p.

    Descriptors: Council - Manager Government
                   Mayor - Council Government
                   Municipal Government
                   Policy Planning

Document No. 537

NORTH CAROLINA. UNIVERSITY. INSTITUTE OF GOVERNMENT.
    Revenues and Service Costs for General Fund Activities: A Special Report on Annexation for the City of Durham. Institute of Government and Planning Department, City of Durham. Durham, North Carolina: Institute of Government, University of North Carolina, 1957. 28p.

    Descriptor: Annexation and Boundary Changes

REFORM OF LOCAL GOVERNMENT STRUCTURES IN THE UNITED STATES: 1945-1971.

Document No. 538

NORTHEASTERN ILLINOIS METROPOLITAN AREA LOCAL GOVERNMENTAL SERVICES COMMISSION.
    1963 Findings and Recommendations: Report of the Northeastern Illinois Metropolitan Area Local Governmental Services Commission to the 73rd General Assembly. Chicago: Northeastern Illinois Metropolitan Area Local Governmental Services Commission, 1963. iv, 52p.

    Descriptors: Annexation and Boundary Changes
                       County Government
                       Governmental Consolidation
                       Governmental Separation
                       Incorporation
                       Planning Commissions

Document No. 539

NORTHEASTERN ILLINOIS METROPOLITAN AREA LOCAL GOVERNMENTAL SERVICES COMMISSION.
    Governmental Problems in the Chicago Metropolitan Area: A Report of the Northeastern Illinois Metropolitan Area Local Governmental Services Commission. Edited by Leverett S. Lyon. Chicago: University of Chicago Press, 1957. xii, 283p., (6) fold. leaves of plates.

    Descriptors: Municipal Government
                       Policy Planning

Document No. 540

NORTHEASTERN ILLINOIS METROPOLITAN AREA LOCAL GOVERNMENTAL SERVICES COMMISSION.
    Metropolitan Area Services: Second Report of the Northeastern Illinois Metropolitan Area Local Governmental Services Commission. Edited by Gilbert Y. Steiner, Lois Me. Pelekoudas. Urbana, Illinois: Institute of Government and Public Affairs, University of Illinois, 1959. v, 59p.

    Descriptors: Municipal Government
                       Policy Planning

Document No. 541

NORTHEASTERN ILLINOIS METROPOLITAN AREA LOCAL GOVERNMENTAL SERVICES COMMISSION.
    Recommendations of the Northeastern Illinois Metropolitan Area Local Governmental Services Commission to the Seventieth Session of the General Assembly of the State of Illinois. Chicago: The Commission, 1957. ii, 25p.

    Descriptor: Planning Commissions

BIBLIOGRAPHY

Document No. 542

NORTHEASTERN ILLINOIS METROPOLITAN AREA LOCAL SERVICES COMMISSION.
Summary of Hearing by and Report to the Northeastern Illinois Metropolitan Area Local Government Services Commission: A Report to the Seventieth Session of the General Assembly of the State of Illinois. Chicago: The Commission, 1957. 20, 7, 13p.

Descriptors: Intergovernmental Cooperation
Policy Planning

Document No. 543

NORTHEASTERN ILLINOIS PLANNING COMMISSION.
Handbook on Annexation and Incorporation Procedures. Chicago: Northeastern Illinois Planning Commission, 1964. 31p., xxvi. (Local Planning Aid No. 7).

Descriptors: Annexation and Boundary Changes
Governmental Consolidation
Governmental Separation
Incorporation
Neighborhood Control

Document No. 544

NORTHEASTERN ILLINOIS PLANNING COMMISSION.
Manual for Intercommunity Councils. Chicago: Northeastern Illinois Planning Commission, 1964. 44p., (Local Planning Aid No. 8).

Descriptors: Advisory Councils
Intergovernmental Cooperation

Document No. 545

NORTON, JAMES A.
The Metro Experience. Cleveland: Press of Western Reserve University, 1963. iii, 80p.

Descriptor: Municipal Government

REFORM OF LOCAL GOVERNMENT STRUCTURES IN THE UNITED STATES: 1945-1971.

Document No. 546

NUQUIST, ANDREW E.
    Town Government in Vermont: or Making Democracy "Democ".
    Burlington, Vermont: Government Research Center, University
    of Vermont, 1964. xiv, 276p., (State Series No. 2).

    Descriptors: Citizen Participation
                 County Government
                 Special Districts and Authorities

Document No. 547

O'HARE, ROBERT J.M.
    A Guide for Charter Commissions. Boston: Bureau of Public
    Affairs, Boston College; Bureau of Government Research,
    University of Massachusetts, 1969. 60p., (Part III in a
    Series on Modernizing Local Government in Massachusetts).

    Descriptors: Charters
                 Home Rule

Document No. 548

OHIO. DEPARTMENT OF URBAN AFFAIRS.
    Councils of Government in Ohio. (Prepared by Gretchen McBeath).
    Columbus, Ohio: Ohio Department of Urban Affairs, Division of
    Intergovernmental Services, 1969. iii, 70p.

    Descriptors: Councils of Government
                 Federation
                 Governmental Consolidation
                 Regional Agencies
                 Special Districts and Authorities

Document No. 549

OHIO. LEGISLATIVE SERVICE COMMISSION.
    Municipal Incorporation and Annexation in Ohio. Research
    Staff. Columbus, Ohio: Ohio Legislative Service Commission,
    1965. 70p., (Staff Research Report No. 69).

    Descriptors: Annexation and Boundary Changes
                 Incorporation

BIBLIOGRAPHY

Document No. 550

OHIO. LEGISLATIVE SERVICE COMMISSION.
Selected Metropolitan Area Problems: Section 1. The Municipal Income Tax, Section 2. Mass Transportation in Ohio, Section 3. Alternative Forms of County Government. Columbus, Ohio: Ohio Legislative Service Commission, 1959. 70p., (Staff Research Report No. 34).

Descriptors: Charters
County Government
Municipal Government

Document No. 551

OMDAHL, LLOYD B.
Investigating Home Rule in North Dakota. Grand Forks, North Dakota: Bureau of Governmental Affairs, University of North Dakota, 1971. iii, 26p., (Special Report No. 23).

Descriptors: Charters
Home Rule

Document No. 552

OPPERMANN, PAUL.
Midwest Metropolis - Six Counties Plan for a Century of Promise. Chicago: (s.n.), 1958. 16p., (Remarks before Joint Meeting of Metropolitan Housing and Planning Council and South Side Planning Board, Palmer House, May 7, 1958).

Descriptors: Municipal Government
Planning Commissions

Document No. 553

ORANGE COUNTY, FLORIDA. LOCAL GOVERNMENT STUDY COMMISSION.
Final Report: Findings and Recommendations of the Local Government Study Commission of Orange County. Orlando, Florida: Local Government Commission of Orange County, 1967. ix, 188p.

Descriptors: County Government
Mayor - Council Government

REFORM OF LOCAL GOVERNMENT STRUCTURES IN THE UNITED STATES: 1945-1971.

Document No. 554

OREGON. LEGISLATIVE ASSEMBLY. INTERIM COMMITTEE ON CITY-COUNTY CONSOLIDATION IN MULTNOMAH COUNTY.
    Report of the Interim Committee on City-County Consolidation in Multnomah County: submitted to the Governor of Oregon and the Forty-sixth Legislative Assembly, January 10, 1951. Salem, Oregon: Interim Committee on City-County Consolidation in Multnomah County, 1951. 12p.

    Descriptor: Governmental Consolidation

Document No. 555

OREGON. LEGISLATIVE ASSEMBLY. INTERIM COMMITTEE ON LOCAL GOVERNMENT.
    Findings and Recommendations: Report of the Joint Legislative Interim Committee on Local Government. Salem, Oregon: Interim Committee on Local Government, 1956. 204p., (14) leaves of plates (10 fold.).

    Descriptors: County Government
                 Municipal Government

Document No. 556

OREGON. LEGISLATIVE ASSEMBLY. INTERIM COMMITTEE ON LOCAL GOVERNMENT.
    Metropolitan and Urban Area Problems in Oregon: Report of the Legislative Interim Committee on Local Government: submitted to His Excellency the Governor of Oregon and Members of the Fifty-second Legislative Assembly. Salem, Oregon: Interim Committee on Local Government, 1963. 57p.

    Descriptors: Advisory Councils
                 Annexation and Boundary Changes
                 Special Districts and Authorities

Document No. 557

OREGON. LEGISLATIVE ASSEMBLY. INTERIM COMMITTEE ON LOCAL GOVERNMENT.
    Report of the Legislative Interim Committee on Local Government: Submitted to Members of the Fifty-fifth Legislative Assembly. Salem, Oregon: Interim Committee on Local Government, 1968. vii, 43p.

    Descriptors: Annexation and Boundary Changes
                 Governmental Consolidation
                 Special Districts and Authorities

BIBLIOGRAPHY

Document No. 558

OREGON. LEGISLATIVE ASSEMBLY. INTERIM COMMITTEE ON LOCAL GOVERNMENT.
Summary of Tentative Findings and Recommendations of the
Joint Legislative Interim Committee on Local Government.
Salem, Oregon: Legislative Committee on Local Government,
1956. 9p.

Descriptors: Annexation and Boundary Changes
Special Districts and Authorities

Document No. 559

OREGON. UNIVERSITY. BUREAU OF GOVERNMENTAL RESEARCH AND SERVICE.
Central Lane Metropolitan Study: Structure Brief No. 2: The
Role of the County in Metropolitan Areas. prepared by Bureau
of Research and Service, University of Oregon, Eugene, Oregon,
1969. 23p.

Descriptors: County Government
Governmental Consolidation

Document No. 560

OREGON. UNIVERSITY. BUREAU OF GOVERNMENTAL RESEARCH.
Municipal Annexation in Oregon: Legal Requirements, Effects
on Special Districts, Illustrative Documents. rev. Eugene,
Oregon: Bureau of Municipal Research and Service, University
of Oregon, 1967. 71p., (Legal Bulletin No. 11).

Descriptors: Annexation and Boundary Changes
Special Districts and Authorities

Document No. 561

OREGON. UNIVERSITY. BUREAU OF MUNICIPAL RESEARCH AND SERVICE.
Background Information on Local Government in Oregon. Eugene,
Oregon: Bureau of Municipal Research and Service, University
of Oregon, 1967. 149p. in various pagings.

Descriptors: Intergovernmental Cooperation
Policy Planning

Document No. 562

OREGON. UNIVERSITY. BUREAU OF MUNICIPAL RESEARCH AND SERVICE.
Local Intergovernmental Cooperation in the Tri-county Area.
Eugene, Oregon: Bureau of Governmental Research and Service,
University of Oregon, 1966. 55p., (Information Bulletin No. 150).

Descriptor: Intergovernmental Cooperation

REFORM OF LOCAL GOVERNMENT STRUCTURES IN THE UNITED STATES: 1945-1971.

Document No. 563

OREGON. UNIVERSITY. BUREAU OF MUNICIPAL RESEARCH AND SERVICE.
Model Charter for Oregon Cities: Council-Manager Form of Government. 3d rev. Eugene, Oregon: Bureau of Municipal Research and Service, University of Oregon, 1967. vi, 37p., (Legal Bulletin No. 7).

Descriptors: Charters
Council - Manager Government

Document No. 564

OREGON. UNIVERSITY. BUREAU OF MUNICIPAL RESEARCH AND SERVICE.
Model Charter for Oregon Cities: Mayor-Council Form of Government. 3d rev. Eugene, Oregon: Bureau of Governmental Research and Service, University of Oregon, 1967. vi, 34p., (Legal Bulletin No. 7).

Descriptors: Charters
Mayor - Council Government

Document No. 565

OREGON. UNIVERSITY. BUREAU OF MUNICIPAL RESEARCH AND SERVICE.
The Organization of Municipal Services in the North Lincoln Beach Area. Prepared by the Bureau of Municipal Research and Service. Eugene, Oregon: The Bureau, University of Oregon, 1964. iii, 55p., (2).

Descriptors: Annexation and Boundary Changes
Governmental Consolidation

Document No. 566

OREGON. UNIVERSITY. BUREAU OF MUNICIPAL RESEARCH AND SERVICE.
Problems of Urban Fringe. Eugene, Oregon: Bureau of Municipal Research and Service, University of Oregon, 1957. 2 v. (Prepared for the Legislative Interim Committee on Local Government).

Descriptors: Annexation and Boundary Changes
Special Districts and Authorities

Document No. 567

OREGON. UNIVERSITY. BUREAU OF MUNICIPAL RESEARCH AND SERVICE.
A Proposed Constitutional Amendment for County Home Rule Charter: Background Information. Eugene, Oregon: Bureau of Governmental Research and Service, University of Oregon, 1958. 24p.

Descriptors: Charters
Home Rule

BIBLIOGRAPHY

Document No. 568

OREGON. UNIVERSITY. BUREAU OF MUNICIPAL RESEARCH AND SERVICE.
The Units of Local Government in Oregon. Eugene, Oregon:
Bureau of Municipal Research and Service, University of
Oregon, 1962. 17p., (Information Bulletin No. 129).

Descriptors: County Government
Special Districts and Authorities

Document No. 569

OREGON TAX RESEARCH.
Special Taxing Districts in Oregon. Portland, Oregon:
Oregon Tax Research, 1956. 36p.

Descriptor: Special Districts and Authorities

Document No. 570

OVERBECK, JR., JOHN H.
Constitutional Municipal Home Rule for Illinois: A Redefinition
of State-Local Relations: A report to the Illinois Cities and
Villages Municipal Problems Commission and the Illinois Con-
stitutional Study Commission. John H. Overbeck, Jr. and
Charles B. Hetrick. Park Ridge, Illinois: (s.n.), 1966. 7p.

Descriptor: Home Rule

Document No. 571

PACIFIC COAST CONFERENCE ON METROPOLITAN PROBLEMS, BERKELEY,
CALIFORNIA, 1958.
Metropolitan Area Problems. edited by Stanley Scott. Berkeley,
California: Bureau of Public Administration and University
Extension, University of California, 1960. viii, 249p.

Descriptors: County Government
Municipal Government

Document No. 572

PAGLIN, MORTON.
The Economics of Metropolitan Consolidation. Portland, Oregon:
Portland State College, 1967. 24, 2p., (Prepared for the
Urban Studies Center for Presentation to the Metropolitan
Study Commission.).

Descriptor: Governmental Consolidation

REFORM OF LOCAL GOVERNMENT STRUCTURES IN THE UNITED STATES: 1945-1971.

Document No. 573

PALMER, PHILIP F.
    The Allouez Study: Governmental Organization for the Town of Allouez (Brown County, Wisconsin): Summary of Findings and Courses of Action. Madison, Wisconsin: Bureau of Government, University of Wisconsin, 1961. xiv, 132p., (Report NS 10; A Report to the Special Committee of the Town of Allouez (Brown County), Wisconsin).

    Descriptors: Annexation and Boundary Changes
                  Community Control

Document No. 574

PARK COLLEGE, MISSOURI. GOVERNMENTAL RESEARCH BUREAU.
    The Special Districts of Platte County, Missouri. Parkville, Missouri: The Bureau, 1958. 2v., (Government Research Bureau Series C - Nos. 1 and 2).

    Descriptor: Special Districts and Authorities

Document No. 575

PEACHEY, PAUL.
    New Town, Old Habits: Citizen Participation At Fort Lincoln. Washington, D.C.: Washington Center for Metropolitan Studies, 1970. vii, 52p., (Community Governance No. 1).

    Descriptors: Advisory Councils
                  Citizen Participation
                  Community Control

Document No. 576

PENJERDEL.
    Organizing a Metropolitan Research and Information Program: Annual Report, 1959-1960. Philadelphia: Pennsylvania-New Jersey-Delaware Metropolitan Project, 1960. 11p.

    Descriptor: Regional Agencies

Document No. 577

PENJERDEL.
    Annual Report 1960-1961: A Year of Progress. Philadelphia: Pennsylvania-New Jersey-Delaware Metropolitan Project, 1961. 19p.

    Descriptor: Regional Agencies

BIBLIOGRAPHY

Document No. 578

PENJERDEL.
    Annual Report, 1962. Philadelphia: Pennsylvania-New Jersey-Delaware Metropolitan Project, 1963. 23p.

    Descriptor: Regional Agencies

Document No. 579

PENJERDEL.
    Annual Report, 1963. Philadelphia: Pennsylvania-New Jersey-Delaware Metropolitan Project, 1964. 28p.

    Descriptor: Regional Agencies

Document No. 580

PENJERDEL.
    What is Penjerdel? Philadelphia: Pennsylvania-New Jersey-Delaware Metropolitan Project, 1958. 31p.

    Descriptor: Regional Agencies

Document No. 581

PENNSYLVANIA. CONSTITUTIONAL CONVENTION, 1967-1968.
    Local Government. Prepared for the Delagates by the Preparatory Committee. Harrisburg: Commonwealth of Pennsylvania, 1967. xii, 288p., (Reference Manual No. 9).

    Descriptors: Annexation and Boundary Changes
                    County Government
                    Home Rule
                    Municipal Government
                    Regional Agencies
                    Special Districts and Authorities

Document No. 582

PENNSYLVANIA. DEPARTMENT OF COMMERCE. BUREAU OF COMMUNITY DEVELOPMENT.
    County and Regional Planning. Department of Commerce. Harrisburg: Commonwealth of Pennsylvania, Department of Commerce, Bureau of Community Development, 1963. 77p., (Publication No. 11).

    Descriptors: Planning Commissions
                    Regional Agencies

Document No. 583

PENNSYLVANIA. METROPOLITAN STUDY COMMISSION.
    Report of the Metropolitan Study Commission: A Summary of this Commission's 296-Page Report. Pittsburgh: Pittsburgh Chamber of Commerce, 1955. 24p., (1).

    Descriptor: County Government

REFORM OF LOCAL GOVERNMENT STRUCTURES IN THE UNITED STATES: 1945-1971.

Document No. 584

PENNSYLVANIA. METROPOLITAN STUDY COMMISSION OF ALLEGHENY COUNTY.
An Urban Home Rule Charter for Allegheny County: A Report of the Metropolitan Study Commission of Allegheny County. Pittsburgh: Metropolitan Study Commission of Allegheny County, 1955. 296p.

Descriptors: Charters
Home Rule

Document No. 585

PENNSYLVANIA. STATE UNIVERSITY. INSTITUTE OF PUBLIC ADMINISTRATION.
A Study of Local Government in the Greater Hazleton Area. University Park, Pennsylvania: Institute to Public Administration, Pennsylvania State University, 1967. ix, 180p.

Descriptors: Annexation and Boundary Changes
Governmental Consolidation

Document No. 586

PENNSYLVANIA ECONOMY LEAGUE. EASTERN DIVISION.
Challenges and Choices In Improving the Performance of Local Government in the Penjerdel Region. Philadelphia: Pennsylvania Economy League, 1964. v, 14p.

Descriptor: Regional Agencies

Document No. 587

PERFECTING MUNICIPAL HOME RULE: A SYMPOSIUM.
Edited by Charles B. Hetrick. Park Ridge, Illinois: City of Park Ridge, 1965. 16p., (Sponsored by the Northwest Municipal Conference of Northwest Suburban Cook County).

Descriptor: Home Rule

Document No. 588

PHILADELPHIA. CHARTER COMMISSION.
Philadelphia Home Rule Charter: Annotated. Philadelphia: Philadelphia Charter Commission, 1951. xxi, 213p.

Descriptors: Charters
Home Rule

BIBLIOGRAPHY

Document No. 589

PHILADELPHIA. STUDY COMMISSION OF THE PHILADELPHIA AREA.
    A Metropolis Expands: A Look at the Growth of the Metropolitan Territory Bordering the Middle Delaware 1920-1957. Philadelphia: Study Commission of the Philadelphia Metropolitan Area, 1958. 22p., (5) fold. leaves of plates.

    Descriptor: Annexation and Boundary Changes

Document No. 590

PHILLIPS, WALTER M.
    A Future for Penjerdel: A Report on Penjerdel, the Organization and the Region, With Recommendations for New Directions. Philadelphia: Pennsylvania-New Jersey-Delaware Metropolitan Project, 1965. x, 94p.

    Descriptors: Planning Commissions
                Regional Agencies

Document No. 591

PICKARD, JEROME P.
    Metropolitanization of the United States. Washington, D.C.: Urban Land Institute, 1959. 95p., (Research Monograph 2).

    Descriptor: Regional Agencies

Document No. 592

PIERCE, DORIS S.
    Forms of City Government in Kansas. Lawrence, Kansas: Government Research Center, University of Kansas, 1957. 33p., (Citizen's Pamphlet Series No. 21).

    Descriptors: Commission Government
                Council - Manager Government
                Mayor - Council Government

Document No. 593

PINELLAS COUNTY, FLORIDA. GOVERNMENTAL STUDY COMMISSION.
    Report and Recommendations of the Pinellas County Governmental Study Commission to the Board of County Commissioners, the Legislative Delegation and the Citizens of Pinellas County. Clearwater, Florida: Pinellas County Governmental Study Commission, 1966. iii, 106p.

    Descriptors: Administrative Reorganization
                Commission Government
                Home Rule

REFORM OF LOCAL GOVERNMENT STRUCTURES IN THE UNITED STATES: 1945-1971.

Document No. 594

PITTSBURGH. UNIVERSITY. INSTITUTE OF LOCAL GOVERNMENT.
    The Council-Manager Form of Government in Pennsylvania: A Citizen's Handbook. Pittsburgh: Institute of Local Government, Graduate School of Public and International Affairs, University of Pittsburgh, 1962. 50p.

    Descriptor: Council - Manager Government

Document No. 595

PITTSBURGH. UNIVERSITY. INSTITUTE OF LOCAL GOVERNMENT.
    Patterns of Pennsylvania Local Government. Pittsburgh: Institute of Local Government, Graduate School of Public and International Affairs, University of Pittsburgh, 1967. 59p.

    Descriptors: County Government
                  Intergovernmental Cooperation
                  Special Districts and Authorities

Document No. 596

POCK, MAX A.
    Independent Special Districts: A Solution to the Metropolitan Area Problems. Ann Arbor, Michigan: University of Michigan Law School, 1962. vii, 193p.

    Descriptors: Annexation and Boundary Changes
                  District Government
                  Special Districts and Authorities

Document No. 597

PORTLAND, OREGON METROPOLITAN STUDY COMMISSION.
    Interim Report. Portland, Oregon: Portland Metropolitan Study Commission, 1966. 25p., (2).

    Descriptors: Annexation and Boundary Changes
                  Charters
                  Councils of Government
                  Governmental Consolidation
                  Special Districts and Authorities

BIBLIOGRAPHY

Document No. 598

PORTLAND, OREGON METROPOLITAN STUDY COMMISSION. STATE AND LOCAL AFFAIRS COMMITTEE.
    State Aid to Local Government: A Report to the State and Local Affairs Committee, Portland Metropolitan Study Commission. Staff Report by Dwight K. Hunter and Michael McElligott. Portland, Oregon: Portland Metropolitan Study Commission, 1968. v, 84p.

    Descriptors: Advisory Councils
                    Intergovernmental Cooperation
                    Regional Agencies

Document No. 599

PORTLAND STATE COLLEGE. URBAN STUDIES CENTER.
    Annexation, Incorporation, and Consolidation in the Portland Metropolitan Area: A Study Prepared for the Portland Metropolitan Study Commission. Portland, Oregon: Urban Studies Center, Portland State College, 1968. iii, 131p.

    Descriptors: Annexation and Boundary Changes
                    Governmental Consolidation
                    Incorporation

Document No. 600

PORTLAND STATE RESEARCH BUREAU.
    Voter Participation in Special Districts: A Report prepared for the Portland Metropolitan Study Commission. Portland, Oregon: The Bureau, 1965. 47p.

    Descritpors: Citizen Participation
                    Special Districts and Authorities

Document No. 601

POWERS OF IDAHO CITIES REGARDING URBAN FRINGE AREAS: A STUDY OF ANNEXATION AND EXTRATERRITORIAL POWERS IN IDAHO AND OTHER STATES.
    Herbert Sydney Duncombe, John Robertson Porter, Robert Harwood, Michael T. Nelson, Glenn W. Nichols. Moscow, Idaho: Bureau of Public Affairs Research, University of Idaho, 1968, 42p.

    Descriptors: Annexation and Boundary Changes
                    Decentralization

REFORM OF LOCAL GOVERNMENT STRUCTURES IN THE UNITED STATES: 1945-1971.

Document No. 602

PRESS, O. CHARLES.
　　Alternative Arrangements for the Provision of Urban Services. East Lansing, Michigan: Institute for Community Development, Michigan State University, 1960. 10p., (Technical Bulletin B-11).

　　Descriptors: Annexation and Boundary Changes
　　　　　　　　　Incorporation
　　　　　　　　　Special Districts and Authorities

Document No. 603

PRESS, CHARLES.
　　Farmers and Urban Expansion: A Study of Michigan Township. Charles Press and Clarence J. Hein. Washington, D.C.: U.S. Department of Agriculture, Farm Economics Division, Economic Research Service; in cooperation with Institute of Community Development and Services, Michigan State University, 1962. 28p., (ERS-92).

　　Descriptors: Annexation and Boundary Changes
　　　　　　　　　Community Control

Document No. 604

PRESS, CHARLES.
　　When One-Third of a City Moves to the Suburbs: A Report on the Grand Rapids Metropolitan Area. East Lansing, Michigan: Institute for Community Development and Services, Michigan State University, 1959. vii, 79p., (Research Report No. 1).

　　Descriptors: Intergovernmental Cooperation
　　　　　　　　　Municipal Government

Document No. 605

PUBLIC ADMINISTRATION SERVICE.
　　The Government of Metropolitan Miami. Chicago: Public Service Administration, 1954. xii, 194p.

　　Descriptors: Administrative Reorganization
　　　　　　　　　County Government
　　　　　　　　　Municipal Government

Document No. 606

PUBLIC ADMINISTRATION SERVICE.
　　The Government of Metropolitan Sacramento. Chicago: Public Administration Service, 1957. 261p.

　　Descriptors: Governmental Consolidation
　　　　　　　　　Municipal Government

BIBLIOGRAPHY

Document No. 607

PUBLIC ADMINISTRATION SERVICE.
    Local Government in Battle Creek City and Battle Creek Township. Chicago: Public Service Administration, 1957. x, 186p.

    Descriptors: Annexation and Boundary Changes
                        District Government
                        Federation
                        Governmental Consolidation
                        Governmental Separation
                        Special Districts and Authorities

Document No. 608

PUBLIC ADMINISTRATION SERVICE.
    Local Government in the Twin Cities Area. Chicago: Public Administration Services, 1957. 99p.

    Descriptors: Annexation and Boundary Changes
                        Federation
                        Governmental Consolidation
                        Special Districts and Authorities

Document No. 609

PUBLIC ADMINISTRATION SERVICE.
    Local Government Under the Alaska Constitution: A Survey Report. Chicago: Public Administration Service, 1959. xi, 82p.

    Descriptors: Annexation and Boundary Changes
                        Home Rule
                        Incorporation

Document No. 610

PUBLIC ADMINISTRATION SERVICE.
    The Organization and Activities of the Mid Willamette Valley Council of Governments. Chicago: Public Service Administration, 1970. vi, 53p.

    Descriptors: Councils of Government
                        Planning Commissions

REFORM OF LOCAL GOVERNMENT STRUCTURES IN THE UNITED STATES: 1945-1971.

Document No. 611

PUBLIC ADMINISTRATION SERVICE.
A Plan for the Future: The Government of Fairfax County. Chicago: Public Administration Service, 1958. vii, 124p., (3), (11) leaves of plates.

Descriptors: Citizen Participation
County Government
Political Leadership

Document No. 612

PUBLIC ADMINISTRATION SERVICE.
Regional Government Agencies and Programs in the San Francisco Bay Area: An Inventory and Analysis. Chicago: Public Service Administration, 1968. 43, 55p., (Prepared for the Association of Bay Area Governments).

Descriptors: Planning Commissions
Regional Agencies
Special Districts and Authorities

Document No. 613

PUBLIC ADMINISTRATION SERVICE.
State and Local Government Relationships in the State of Hawaii. Chicago: Public Administration Service, 1962. x, 234p.

Descriptors: County Government
Intergovernmental Relations

Document No. 614

PUBLIC ADMINISTRATION SERVICE.
Summary Report on Administrative Survey: City of Minneapolis. Chicago: Public Administration Service, 1947. iv, 43p., (13) leaves (5 fold.).

Descriptors: Administrative Reorganization
Council - Manager Government
Mayor - Council Government

BIBLIOGRAPHY

Document No. 615

PUBLIC AFFAIRS RESEARCH (OAKLAND, CALIFORNIA).
Pleasant Hill Government Study. Oakland, California: Public Affairs Research, 1958. 45p., (1) leaf of plates.

Descriptors: Annexation and Boundary Changes
Incorporation

Document No. 616

PUBLIC AFFAIRS RESEARCH (OAKLAND, CALIFORNIA).
Should We Annex?: Financial, Economic and Political Effects of Annexing Alvarado - Decoto Area to City of Fremont. Oakland, California: Public Affairs Research, 1957. 47p.

Descriptor: Annexation and Boundary Changes

Document No. 617

PUBLIC POLICY FORUM ON NEW JERSEY LOCAL GOVERNMENT, RUTGERS UNIVERSITY, 1967.
Proceedings...New Brunswick, New Jersey: Bureau of Government Research and University Extension Division, Rutgers University, 1967. 51p.

Descriptors: County Government
Municipal Government

Document No. 618

PUBLIC POLICY FORUM ON THE FUTURE STRUCTURES OF LOCAL GOVERNMENT, RUTGERS UNIVERSITY.
Proceedings...New Brunswick, New Jersey: Bureau of Government Research and University Extension Division, Rutgers University, 1969. 66p.

Descriptors: County Government
Municipal Government

Document No. 619

PUBLIC RESEARCH AND MANAGEMENT (ATLANTA, GEORGIA).
South Carolina Local Government Study. Prepared by Public Research and Management for the Office of the Governor, State Planning and Grants Division, State of South Carolina. Columbia, South Carolina: Municipal Association of South Carolina, 1969. 232p.

Descriptors: Administrative Reorganization
Advisory Councils
Planning Commissions

REFORM OF LOCAL GOVERNMENT STRUCTURES IN THE UNITED STATES: 1945-1971.

Document No. 620

QUINN, KENT.
    Brookfield, Missouri Abandons the Council Manager Plan.
    Parkville, Missouri: Government Research Bureau, Park College,
    1960. 28p., (Government Research Bureau Series D - No. 2).

    Descriptor: Council - Manager Government

Document No. 621

RAY, JOSEPH M.
    Improving Government in Silver Spring. College Park, Maryland:
    Bureau of Public Administration, College of Business and Public
    Administration, University of Maryland, 1949. 44p.

    Descriptors: Annexation and Boundary Changes
                  Charters
                  Planning Commissions

Document No. 622

RAY, JOSEPH M.
    Improving the Government of Cumberland: A Report to the Mayor
    and Council of Cumberland, Maryland. College Park, Maryland:
    Department of Government and Politics, College of Business and
    Public Administration, University of Maryland, 1947. 32p.

    Descriptors: Commission Government
                  Home Rule

Document No. 623

RAY, JOSEPH M.
    Improving the Government of Hagerstown: A Report to the Mayor
    and Council of Hagerstown, Maryland. College Park, Maryland:
    Department of Government and Politics, College of Business and
    Public Administration, University of Maryland, 1946. 21p.

    Descriptors: Charters
                  Council - Manager Government
                  Planning Commissions

Document No. 624

RAY, JOSEPH M.
    Improving the Government of Pocomoke. College Park, Maryland:
    Bureau of Public Administration, College of Business and Public
    Administration, University of Maryland, 1948. 30p., (3) leaves
    of plates.

    Descriptors: Council - Manager Government
                  Home Rule
                  Planning Commissions

BIBLIOGRAPHY

Document No. 625

RAY, JOSEPH M.
    Improving the Government of Salisbury. College, Park, Maryland: Bureau of Public Administration, College of Business and Public Administration, University of Maryland, 1949. iv, 42p., (1) leaf of plates.

    Descriptors: Citizen Participation
                  Home Rule
                  Mayor - Council Government

Document No. 626

REED, DORIS D.
    The Cincinnati Area Must Solve Its Own Metropolitan Problems: A Report to the Stephen H. Wilder Foundation. Doris D. Reed and Thomas H. Reed. Cincinnati: Stephen H. Wilder Foundation, 1953. 44p., (1) fold. leaf of plates.

    Descriptors: Annexation and Boundary Changes
                  Federation
                  Incorporation

Document No. 627

REED, THOMAS H.
    Preliminary Observation on the Charleston Metropolitan Problem. Thomas H. and Doris D. Reed. Charleston, South Carolina: (s.n.), 1956. 5p., (for the Greater Charleston Chamber of Commerce).

    Descriptors: Administrative Reorganization
                  Annexation and Boundary Changes

Document No. 628

RESEARCH AND PLANNING COUNCIL (SAN ANTONIO, TEXAS).
    The Miami Story. San Antonio, Texas: Research and Planning Council, 1962. 16p., (Preliminary Metro Study No. 5).

    Descriptors: Charters
                  Municipal Government

Document No. 629

THE RESEARCH GROUP (ATLANTA, GEORGIA).
    A Program of Work for the Chattanooga Area Regional Council of Governments. The Research Group; assisted by Eric Hill Associates. Atlanta, Georgia: The Research Group, 1969. iii, 60p.

    Descriptors: Councils of Government
                  Planning Commissions

REFORM OF LOCAL GOVERNMENT STRUCTURES IN THE UNITED STATES: 1945-1971.

Document No. 630

THE RESEARCH GROUP (ATLANTA, GEORGIA).
    Regional Coordination Recommendations and Revised Work Program for the Chattanooga Area Regional Council of Governments. Atlanta, Georgia: The Research Group, 1970. ii, 60p.

    Descriptors: Councils of Government
                 Planning Commissions
                 Regional Agencies

Document No. 631

RICHARDSON, RICHARD J.
    Orleans Parish Offices: Notes on a City Parish Consolidation. New Orleans: Bureau of Governmental Research, 1961. iv, 68p., (The Edgar B. Stern Memorial Honors Fellowship Series, Volume 1).

    Descriptor: County Government

Document No. 632

RICHMOND, VIRGINIA CITY COUNCIL AND HENRICO COUNTY. BOARD OF SUPERVISORS. ADVISORY COMMITTEES FOR THE CONSOLIDATION OF RICHMOND AND HENRICO COUNTY.
    Report....Richmond, Virginia: Advisory Committees for the Consolidation of Richmond and Henrico County, 1961. 211p.

    Descriptors: Charters
                 Governmental Consolidation

Document No. 633

RIDER, DONALD G.
    Municipal Development in New Mexico. Albuquerque, New Mexico: Division of Government Research, University of New Mexico, 1964. 55p.

    Descriptors: Annexation and Boundary Changes
                 Municipal Government

Document No. 634

RIEGELMAN, HAROLD.
    Key Issues in the Revision of the New York City Charter. New York: Citizens Budget Commission, 1961. 11p., (Statement to the Charter Commission at the City Bar Association, May 11, 1961).

    Descriptor: Charters

BIBLIOGRAPHY

Document No. 635

RIGGS, FRED W.
    Convergences in the Study of Comparative Public Administration and Local Government. Gainsville, Florida: Public Administration Clearing Service of the University of Florida, 1962. 23p., (Studies in Public Administration No. 23).

    Descriptor: Administrative Reorganization

Document No. 636

RINGGENBERG, CLAYTON L.
    Council-Manager Government in Iowa. Iowa City: Institute of Public Affairs, State University of Iowa; in cooperation with the League of Iowa Municipalities, 1953. 96p.

    Descriptor: Council - Manager Government

Document No. 637

ROBERTS AND RYDER.
    Brief of the Town of Speedway on Tentative Proposals of the Marion County Government Study Commission. Indianapolis: Roberts and Ryder, 1963. 13p., (9) leaves of plates.

    Descriptors: County Government
                  Planning Commissions

Document No. 638

ROLLINS COLLEGE, WINTER PARK, FLORIDA. CENTER FOR PRACTICAL POLITICS.
    Metropolitan Regionalism in Florida. Edited by Paul Douglass, Alice McMahon, Franklin Albert, Carl Feiss, Frederick Eberle. 2d rev. and enl. ed. Winter Park, Florida: Center for Practical Politics, Rollins College, 1959. iii, 99, 8p., (15) leaves of plates.

    Descriptors: Municipal Government
                  Neighborhood Control
                  Planning Commissions
                  Regional Agencies

REFORM OF LOCAL GOVERNMENT STRUCTURES IN THE UNITED STATES: 1945-1971.

Document No. 639

ROLLINS COLLEGE, WINTER PARK, FLORIDA. CENTER FOR PRACTICAL POLITICS.
    Patterns of Urban Government. Winter Park, Florida: Center for Practical Politics, Rollins College, 1968. 47p., (12) leaves of plates.

    Descriptors: Council - Manager Government
                  Municipal Government
                  Regional Agencies

Document No. 640

ROSS, MYRON H.
    Probable Economic Impact of a Consolidated Urban Area. rev. Kalamazoo, Michigan: Kalamazoo County Citizens Study Committee on Community Services, 1967. 25p., (Staff Paper No.11).

    Descriptor: Governmental Consolidation

Document No. 641

ROSS, MYRON H.
    Ranking of Urban Government Services in Terms of Local Versus Areawide Operation. Kalamazoo, Michigan: Kalamazoo County Citizens Study Committee on Community Services, 1967. 3p., (Staff Report No. 12).

    Descriptor: Policy Planning

Document No. 642

RUSCO, ELMER R.
    Municipal Home Rule: Guidelines for Idaho, A Compendium of Legislative and Judicial Interpretation in the United States. Moscow, Idaho: Bureau of Public Affairs Research, University of Idaho, 1966. 101p., (Research Memorandum No. 1).

    Descriptor: Home Rule

Document No. 643

RUTHERFORD, GEDDES W.
    Administrative Problems in a Metropolitan Area: The National Capital Region. Chicago: Public Administration Service, 1952. xiv, 63p.

    Descriptors: Administrative Reorganization
                  Planning Commissions
                  Policy Planning

BIBLIOGRAPHY

Document No. 644

ST. LOUIS, MISSOURI. BOARD OF FREEHOLDERS.
    Proposed Charter of the City of St. Louis. Prepared by the 1956-57 Board of Freeholders. St. Louis: The Board, 1957. ii, 91p., (For Submission to the Voters of the City of St. Louis. Volume XL No. 3).

    Descriptor: Charters

Document No. 645

ST. LOUIS - ST. LOUIS COUNTY, MISSOURI. METROPOLITAN BOARD OF FREEHOLDERS.
    Proposed Plan of the Greater St. Louis City-County District. Prepared by Metropolitan Board of Freeholders. St. Louis: The Board, 1959. v, 55p.

    Descriptor: District Government

Document No. 646

SACRAMENTO CITY-COUNTY CHAMBER OF COMMERCE. METROPOLITAN DEVELOPMENT COMMITTEE.
    New City Incorporations? Sacramento: Sacramento City-County Chamber of Commerce, Metropolitan Development Committee, 1961. 13p.

    Descriptor: Incorporation

Document No. 647

SACRAMENTO COUNTY, CALIFORNIA. PLANNING DEPARTMENT.
    A Suburban Administrative Center for Sacramento County. Sacramento: The Department, 1957. 25p., (2).

    Descriptors: Administrative Reorganization
                  Decentralization

Document No. 648

SACRAMENTO METROPOLITAN AREA ADVISORY COMMITTEE.
    Final Report by the Sacramento Metropolitan Area Advisory Committee on the Metropolitan Area Study. Sacramento: Sacramento Metropolitan Area Advisory Committee, 1957. 13p.

    Descriptors: Council - Manager Government
                  Federation

REFORM OF LOCAL GOVERNMENT STRUCTURES IN THE UNITED STATES: 1945-1971.

Document No. 649

SACRAMENTO METROPOLITAN AREA ADVISORY COMMITTEE.
Government Reorganization for Metropolitan Sacramento: Final Report of the Metropolitan Government Committee. Sacramento: Sacramento Metropolitan Area Advisory Committee, 1959. 31p.

Descriptors: Annexation and Boundary Changes
Governmental Consolidation

Document No. 650

SAN DIEGO. CITIZENS CHARTER REVISION COMMITTEE.
Report of the Citizens Charter Committee. San Diego, California: Citizens Charter Review Committee, 1962. 36p.

Descriptors: Administrative Reorganization
Charters
Policy Planning

Document No. 651

SAN FRANCISCO. CITIZENS CHARTER REVISION COMMITTEE.
Report of the San Francisco Citizens Charter Revision Committee to the Mayor and Board of Supervisors: First Annual Report, June 1969. San Francisco: San Francisco Citizens Charter Revision Committee, 1969. 138p.

Descriptor: Charters

Document No. 652

SAN FRANCISCO. CITIZENS CHARTER REVISION COMMITTEE.
Staff Report to the San Francisco Citizens Charter Revision Committee: Part 1, Staff Recommendations for Discussion Only. San Francisco: San Francisco Citizens Charter Revision Committee, 1969. 45p.

Descriptors: Administrative Reorganization
Charters
Citizen Participation

BIBLIOGRAPHY

Document No. 653

SAN FRANCISCO. CITIZENS CHARTER REVISION COMMITTEE.
　　Staff Report to the San Francisco Citizens Charter Revision
　　Committee: Part 2, Text and Commentary for Discussion Only.
　　San Francisco: San Francisco Citizens Charter Revision
　　Committee, 1969. vii, 91p.

　　Descriptors:　Administrative Reorganization
　　　　　　　　　Advisory Councils
　　　　　　　　　Charters
　　　　　　　　　Citizen Participation
　　　　　　　　　Community Control
　　　　　　　　　Neighborhood Control

Document No. 654

SAN FRANCISCO. CITIZENS CHARTER REVISION COMMITTEE.
　　Staff Report to the San Francisco Citizens Charter Revision
　　Committee: Part 3, Disposition of Existing Sections for
　　Discussion Only. San Francisco: San Francisco Citizens
　　Charter Revision Committee, 1969. 94p.

　　Descriptor:　Charters

Document No. 655

SAN FRANCISCO. CITIZENS CHARTER REVISION COMMITTEE.
　　Appendix A to the Report of the San Francisco Citizens
　　Charter Revision Committee to the Mayor and the Board of
　　Supervisors, June 1969. San Francisco: San Francisco
　　Citizens Charter Revision Committee, 1969. 93p.

　　Descriptor:　Charters

Document No. 656

SAN FRANCISCO BAY CONSERVATION AND DEVELOPMENT COMMISSION.
　　Government: Part of a Detailed Study of San Francisco Bay.
　　San Francisco: San Francisco Bay Conservation and Develop-
　　ment Commission, 1967. 23p.

　　Descriptors:　Planning Commissions
　　　　　　　　　Regional Agencies

REFORM OF LOCAL GOVERNMENT STRUCTURES IN THE UNITED STATES: 1945-1971.

Document No. 657

SAN LUIS OBISPO COUNTY, CALIFORNIA. OFFICE OF THE DISTRICT ATTORNEY.
　　Summary of Special Districts. San Luis Obispo, California:
　　Office of the District Attorney, 1968. iii, 41p.

　　Descriptor: Special Districts and Authorities

Document No. 658

SANTA CLARA COUNTY COUNCIL ON INTERGOVERNMENTAL RELATIONS (CALIFORNIA).
　　A Practical Basis for Developing Better Intergovernmental
　　Relations: An Experiment Conducted in Santa Clara County.
　　San Jose, California: The Council, 1947. x, 50p.

　　Descriptors: Advisory Councils
　　　　　　　　　Intergovernmental Cooperation
　　　　　　　　　Planning Commissions

Document No. 659

SAUSE, GEORGE G.
　　Municipal Authorities: The Pennsylvania Experience.
　　Harrisburg: Commonwealth of Pennsylvania, Department
　　of Internal Affairs, 1962. vi, 52p.

　　Descriptor: Special Districts and Authorities

Document No. 660

SCHEIBER, WALTER A.
　　Regional Council Administration: An Emerging Art.
　　Washington, D.C.: National Service to Regional
　　Councils, 1970. 6p.

　　Descriptors: Councils of Government
　　　　　　　　　Regional Agencies

Document No. 661

SCHMANDT, HENRY J.
　　The Metropolitan Federation and Special District. Milwaukee:
　　Research Coordinating Committee, Metropolitan Study Commission,
　　1960, 20p., (Second in a series of seminars presenting alter-
　　native solutions to metropolitan area problems, sponsored by
　　Metropolitan Study Commission; Transcript of a Seminar on the
　　Metropolitan Federation and Special District as a possible
　　solution to metropolitan area problems).

　　Descriptors: Federation
　　　　　　　　　Special Districts and Authorities

BIBLIOGRAPHY

Document No. 662

SCHMANDT, HENRY J.
    Metropolitan Reform in St. Louis: A Case Study. Henry J. Schmandt, Paul G. Steinbicker, George D. Wendel. New York: Holt, Rinehart and Winston, 1961. xi, 73p.

    Descriptors: Citizen Participation
                      Municipal Government
                      Political Leadership

Document No. 663

SCHMANDT, HENRY J.
    The Milwaukee Metropolitan Study Commission. Henry J. Schmandt; with William H. Standing. Bloomington, Indiana: Indiana University Press, 1965. xiii, 331p., (Metropolitan Action Studies No. 3).

    Descriptors: Advisory Councils
                      Citizen Participation
                      Political Leadership

Document No. 664

SCHMANDT, HENRY J.
    The Municipal Incorporation Trend, 1950-1960. Madison, Wisconsin: Bureau of Government, University of Wisconsin, 1961. iii, 23p., (Report NS 11).

    Descriptor: Incorporation

Document No. 665

SCOTT, STANLEY.
    Annexation? Incorporation?: A Guide for Community Action. Stanley Scott and Lewis Keller. 3d. ed., rev., Berkeley, California: Bureau of Public Administration, University of California, 1959. 228p.

    Descriptors: Annexation and Boundary Changes
                      Incorporation

Document No. 666

SCOTT, STANLEY.
    California Legislation Governing Municipal Incorporation: A Criticism and Suggested New Policies. Berkeley, California: Bureau of Public Administration, University of California, 1960. 14p., (Prepared for a meeting of the California Governor's Commission on Metropolitan area Problems, March 4-6, 1960, Sacramento, California).

    Descriptor: Incorporation

REFORM OF LOCAL GOVERNMENT STRUCTURES IN THE UNITED STATES: 1945-1971.

Document No. 667

SCOTT, STANLEY.
    Governing a Metropolitan Region: The San Francisco Bay Area.
    Stanley Scott, John C. Bollens. Berkeley, California:
    Institute of Governmental Studies, University of California,
    1968. xiii, 162p.

    Descriptors: Councils of Government
                      Federation
                      Governmental Consolidation
                      Political Leadership
                      Regional Agencies

Document No. 668

SCOTT, STANLEY.
    Home Rule for California's General Law Counties. (s.l.):
    (s.n.), 1960. 7p., (Prepared at the request of the Assembly
    Interim Committee on Municipal and County Government, for a
    hearing to be held in Sacramento on June 15, 1960. Based on
    a statement prepared for a similar hearing of the committee
    held on June 6, 1958.).

    Descriptor: Home Rule

Document No. 669

SCOTT, STANLEY.
    Local Governmental Boundaries and Areas: New Policies for
    California. Stanley Scott, Lewis Keller, John C. Bollens.
    Los Angeles: (s.n.), 1960. 29p., (38), (Prepared for
    Governor's Commission on Metropolitan Area Problems, June
    3-4, 1960, Los Angeles, California).

    Descriptor: Annexation and Boundary Changes

Document No. 670

SCOTT, STANLEY.
    Local Government in a Changing World: A Seminar for City and
    County Managers 1965-1966. Stanley Scott, editor. Berkeley,
    California: Institute of Governmental Studies, University of
    California, 1967. xiii, 200p.

    Descriptors: Citizen Participation
                      Community Control
                      Home Rule
                      Intergovernmental Cooperation
                      Regional Agencies

BIBLIOGRAPHY

Document No. 671

SCOTT, STANLEY.
Metropolitan Agencies and Concurrent Office-Holding: A Survey of Selected Districts and Authorities. Stanley Scott and Willis Culver. Berkeley, California: Bureau of Public Administration, University of California, 1961. 31p., (1961 Legislative Problems: No. 7).

Descriptor: Administrative Reorganization

Document No. 672

SCOTT, STANLEY.
Metropolitan District Legislation: Some Problems and Issues. Berkeley, California: Bureau of Public Administration, University of California, 1958. 28p., (Revised February 20, 1959).

Descriptor: Special Districts and Authorities

Document No. 673

SCOTT, STANLEY.
Metropolitan Problems and Programs for State Action. San Francisco: Americans for Democratic Action, 1962. 20p., (For ADA's State Policy Committee).

Descriptors: Regional Agencies
Special Districts and Authorities

Document No. 674

SCOTT, STANLEY.
Special Districts in the San Francisco Bay Area: Some Problems and Issues. Stanley Scott and John Corzine. Berkeley, California: Institute of Government Studies, University of California, 1963. 39p., (Prepared at the request of the Association of Bay Area Governments).

Descriptor: Special Districts and Authorities

Document No. 675

SEATTLE. METROPOLITAN COUNCIL.
Metro -- The First Ten Years, 1958-1968. Seattle: Metropolitan Council, 1965. 38p.

Descriptors: Citizen Participation
Municipal Government

REFORM OF LOCAL GOVERNMENT STRUCTURES IN THE UNITED STATES: 1945-1971.

Document No. 676

SEATTLE. OFFICE OF EXECUTIVE DIRECTOR.
Municipality of Metropolitan Seattle. Interim Report (Period of September 9, 1958 to July 15, 1959). Seattle: Office of Executive Director, 1959. 8p., (2), (1) Fold. Leaf of plates.

Descriptor: Municipal Government

Document No. 677

SENGSTOCK, FRANK S.
Annexation: A Solution to the Metropolitan Area Problem. Ann Arbor, Michigan: University of Michigan Law School, 1960. vi, 120p.

Descriptor: Annexation and Boundary Changes

Document No. 678

SENGSTOCK, FRANK S.
Consolidation: Building A Bridge Between City and Suburb. Frank S. Sengstock, Phillip A. Fellin, Lawrence E. Nicholson, Charles I. Mundale. St. Louis: School of Law, Saint Louis University, 1964. vii, 136p., (4) Fold. leaves of plates.

Descriptors: Citizen Participation
Federation
Governmental Consolidation

Document No. 679

SENGSTOCK, FRANK S.
Extraterritorial Powers in the Metropolitan Area. Ann Arbor, Michigan: University of Michigan Law School, 1962. v, 72p.

Descriptor: Annexation and Boundary Changes

Document No. 680

SERINO, GUSTAVE.
Miami's Metropolitan Experiment. Gainsville, Florida: Public Administration Clearing Service of the University of Florida, 1958. 24p., (Civic Information Series No. 28).

Descriptor: Municipal Government

BIBLIOGRAPHY

Document No. 681

SHARP, VEE J.
    Report on Local Government: Reorganization and Consolidation: A Staff Report for the Planning and Organization Committee of the Utah Legislative Council. Salt Lake City: Utah Legislative Council, 1970. v, 138p.

    Descriptors: Commission Government
                     Council - Manager Government
                     Councils of Government
                     Federation
                     Governmental Consolidation
                     Governmental Separation
                     Mayor - Council Government

Document No. 682

SIFFIN, CATHERINE FOX.
    Shadow over the City: Special Legislature for Tennessee Municipalities. Knoxville, Tennessee: Bureau of Public Administration and the Municipal Technical Advisory Service, 1951. xiii, 80p., (University of Tennessee Record Extension Series, Volume XXVII, No. 3).

    Descriptors: Citizen Participation
                     Home Rule
                     Municipal Government

Document No. 683

SMALL, JOSEPH F.
    Governmental Alternatives Facing the Chicago Metropolitan Area. Chicago: Center for Research in Urban Government, Loyola University, 1966. 39p., (No. 6).

    Descriptors: Advisory Councils
                     Governmental Separation
                     Planning Commissions

Document No. 684

THE SMALL CITY IN THE METROPOLITAN SEA: ITS PROBLEMS, LEGITIMACY AND FUTURE.
    Donald G. Hagman, William G. Coleman, James C. Johnson, Royal Sorensen and John R. Ficklin. Los Angeles: Institute of Government and Public Affairs, University of California, 1968. 38p., (MR-114).

    Descriptor: Municipal Government

REFORM OF LOCAL GOVERNMENT STRUCTURES IN THE UNITED STATES: 1945-1971.

Document No. 685

SMITH, CRAIG M.
    Considerations for Dealing with the Problems of Local Government in a Metropolitan Area: Presented to the New York Joint Legislative Committee on Metropolitan and Regional Areas Study. Rochester, New York: Rochester Bureau of Municipal Research, 1966, 9p.

    Descriptors: Municipal Government
                       Policy Planning

Document No. 686

SMITH, HARRY R.
    Home Rule for Iowa? Iowa City: Institute for Public Affairs, University of Iowa, 1962. vii, 49p.

    Descriptors: Home Rule

Document No. 687

SMITH, HARRY R.
    A Survey of Municipal Organization and Administration - Des Moines, Iowa. Iowa City: Institute of Public Affairs, University of Iowa, 1965. viii, 107p.

    Descriptors: Administrative Reorganization
                       Council Government
                       Municipal Government

Document No. 688

SMITH, HARRY R.
    Units of Government in Siouxland. Harry R. Smith and H. Paul Friesema. Iowa City: Institute of Public Affairs, University of Iowa, 1963. xiii, 62p., (Siouxland Studies No. 1).

    Descriptors: County Government
                       Special Districts and Authorities

Document No. 689

SMITH, ROBERT G.
    Public Authorities, Special Distircts and Local Government. Washington, D.C.: National Association of Counties, 1964. xxv, 225p.

    Descriptors: Special Districts and Authorities

BIBLIOGRAPHY

Document No. 690

SMITH, STEPHEN C.
    Economic Conflicts in the Rural-Urban Fringe: A Problem of Metropolitan Organization. (s.l.): (s.n.), 1958. 19p., (Talk prepared for the Joint Meeting of the Western Economic Association and the Western Farm Economic Association, Pullman, Washington, August 14, 1958).

    Descriptor: Annexation and Boundary Changes

Document No. 691

SNADEN, JOHN W.
    Annexation Study: Charleston, West Virginia. Charleston, West Virginia: Municipal Planning Commission, 1956, 47p., (17) leaves of plates (13 fold.).

    Descriptor: Annexation and Boundary Changes

Document No. 692

SNOWISS, SYLVIA.
    Urban Problems and Governmental Organization. Los Angeles: Institute of Government and Public Affairs, University of California, Los Angeles, 1967. 19p., (MR-88).

    Descriptors: Annexation and Boundary Changes
                 Governmental Consolidation
                 Regional Agencies

Document No. 693

SO, FRANK S.
    Metropolitan Planning Policy Implementation. Chicago: American Society of Planning Officials, 1970. 40p., (Report No. 262).

    Descriptor: Policy Planning

Document No. 694

SOFEN, EDWARD.
    The Miami Metropolitan Experiment. Bloomington, Indiana: Indiana University Press, 1963. XIV, 313p., (Metropolitan Action Studies No. 2).

    Descriptors: Charters
                 Governmental Consolidation

REFORM OF LOCAL GOVERNMENT STRUCTURES IN THE UNITED STATES: 1945-1971.

Document No. 695

SOKOLOW, ALVIN D.
Local Government in Michigan's Upper Peninsula: Some Problems and Opportunities. East Lansing, Michigan: Institute for Community Development, Michigan State University, 1963. 17p., (Speech Series No. 1; Speech presented to Annual Meeting of the Upper Peninsula Committee on Area Problems (UPCAP) Newberry, Michigan, June 15, 1963).

Descriptor: Governmental Consolidation

Document No. 696

SOURS, JAMES K.
Some Observations on the Management of Large Cities. Wichita, Kansas: University of Wichita, 1967. 15p., (University of Wichita Bulletin, University Studies No. 37, Volume XXII No. 3).

Descriptor: Municipal Government

Document No. 697

SOUTH CAROLINA. UNIVERSITY. BUREAU OF PUBLIC ADMINISTRATION.
A Report to the Mayor and the Council Committee to Study Merger in the Charleston Area. Charleston, South Carolina: Bureau of Public Administration, University of South Carolina, 1955. 19p.

Descriptors: Annexation and Boundary Changes
Governmental Consolidation

Document No. 698

SOUTH DAKOTA. LEGISLATIVE RESEARCH COUNCIL.
County and Township Government in South Dakota, Including Alternatives for Organizational Reform. Pierre, South Dakota: State Legislative Research Council, 1967. 55p., (Staff Background Memorandum No. 14).

Descriptors: Councils of Government
County Government
Governmental Consolidation
Home Rule

BIBLIOGRAPHY

Document No. 699

SOUTH DAKOTA. GOVERNMENT STUDY COMMISSION.
    Functional Cooperation Among and Between South Dakota Political Subdivisions. Pierre, South Dakota: State Legislative Research Council, 1968. i, 124p.

    Descriptors: County Government
                    Intergovernmental Cooperation

Document No. 700

SOUTH DAKOTA. LOCAL GOVERNMENT STUDY COMMISSION.
    Report of the 1966 Local Government Study Commission of the State of South Dakota: submitted to the members of the Forty-second Legislature. Compiled and edited by the Staff of the State Legislative Council. Pierre, South Dakota: The Council, 1967. iv, 81p., (1) leaf of plates.

    Descriptors: Administrative Reorganization
                    Special Districts and Authorities

Document No. 701

SOUTH DAKOTA. LOCAL GOVERNMENT STUDY COMMISSION.
    First Annual Report. Pierre, South Dakota: State Legislative Research Council, 1968. iii, 12p.

    Descriptors: Administrative Reorganization
                    County Government

Document No. 702

SOUTH DAKOTA. LOCAL GOVERNMENT STUDY COMMISSION.
    Second Annual Report. Pierre, South Dakota: State Legislative Research Council, 1969. iii, 14p.

    Descriptors: Administrative Reorganization
                    County Government

Document No. 703

SOUTH DAKOTA. LOCAL GOVERNMENT STUDY COMMISSION.
    Third Annual Report. Pierre, South Dakota: State Legislative Research Council, 1970. iii, 12p.

    Descriptors: Administrative Reorganization
                    County Government

REFORM OF LOCAL GOVERNMENT STRUCTURES IN THE UNITED STATES: 1945-1971.

Document No. 704

SOUTHERN, DODD A.
    Michigan Mayor - Council Charters. Dodd A. Southern and Charles T. Canterbury. Ann Arbor, Michigan: Institute of Public Administration, University of Michigan, 1964. 129p., (Papers in Public Administration No. 45).

    Descriptors: Charters
                    Mayor - Council Government

Document No. 705

SOUTHERN ILLINOIS UNIVERSITY, CARBONDALE. LOCAL GOVERNMENT CENTER.
    Organization and Management of the Government of East St. Louis. Carbondale, Illinois: Local Government Center, Southern Illinois University, 1961. 85p., (1).

    Descriptors: Commission Government
                    Intergovernmental Cooperation

Document No. 706

SOUTHERN ILLINOIS UNIVERSITY, EDWARDSVILLE. REGIONAL AND URBAN DEVELOPMENT STUDIES AND SERVICES.
    East St. Louis - Studied and Re-Studied. Robert Mendelson, William Tudor, Sally Ferguson, Sophie Junz. Edwardsville, Illinois: Regional and Urban Development Studies and Services, Southern Illinois University, 1969. vii, 96p., (RUD Report No. 2).

    Descriptor: Municipal Government

Document No. 707

SPANGLE (WILLIAM) AND ASSOCIATES.
    Municipal, State and Federal Programs Affecting San Francisco Bay: Part of a Detailed Study of the Bay. William Spangle and Associates; jointly with Paul Sedway and Associates. Menlo Park, California: William Spangle and Associates, Paul Sedway Associates, 1966. iii, 96p., (6) leaves of plates (3 fold.)., (prepared for the San Francisco Bay Conservation and Development Commission).

    Descriptors: Intergovernmental Cooperation
                    Regional Agencies

BIBLIOGRAPHY

Document No. 708

SPENCER, JEAN E.
    Contemporary Local Government in Maryland. College Park, Maryland: Bureau of Governmental Research, College of Business and Public Administration, University of Maryland, 1965. x, 116p.

    Descriptors: Commission Government
                    Council - Manager Government
                    County Government
                    Home Rule
                    Mayor - Council Government

Document No. 709

STEINER, GILBERT Y.
    Metropolitan Government and the Real World: The Case of Chicago. Chicago: Center for Research in Urban Government, Loyola University, 1966. 36p., (Volume 1, No. 3).

    Descriptors: Advisory Councils
                    Citizen Participation
                    Neighborhood Control

Document No. 710

STENE, EDWIN O.
    Abandonments of the Manager Plan: A Study of Four Small Cities. Edwin O. Stene and George K. Floro. Lawrence, Kansas: Governmental Research Center, University of Kansas, 1953. 107p., (Governmental Research Series No. 9).

    Descriptors: Administrative Reorganization
                    Council - Manager Government

Document No. 711

STONER, JOHN E.
    Intergovernmental Organization for Planning: A Case Study of the Lower Fox River Valley Area, Wisconsin. Eugene, Oregon: Bureau of Governmental Research and Service, University of Oregon, 1969. 92p.

    Descriptors: Councils of Government
                  Intergovernmental Cooperation
                  Planning Commissions
                  Regional Agencies

REFORM OF LOCAL GOVERNMENT STRUCTURES IN THE UNITED STATES: 1945-1971.

Document No. 712

STONER, JOHN E.
    Interlocal Governmental Cooperation: A Study of Five States. Washington, D.C.: U.S. Department of Agriculture, Economic Research Service, 1964. vii, 123p., (Agricultural Economic Report No. 118).

    Descriptors: Citizen Participation
                  Intergovernmental Cooperation
                  Planning Commissions
                  Regional Agencies

Document No. 713

STOYLES, JR., ROBERT L.
    A Guide to Annexation and Subdivision Control. Iowa City: Institute of Public Affairs, State University of Iowa; in cooperation with the League of Iowa Municipalities, 1959. 52p.

    Descriptor: Annexation and Boundary Changes

Document No. 714

STUART, PATRICIA.
    Forms of Town and City Government in Connecticut. Storrs, Connecticut: Institute of Public Service, University of Connecticut, 1964. 24p.

    Descriptors: Council - Manager Government
                  Mayor - Council Government

Document No. 715

STUART, PATRICIA.
    Forms of Town and City Government in Connecticut. Storrs, Connecticut: Institute of Public Service, University of Connecticut, 1970. v, 25p., (2).

    Descriptors: Council - Manager Government
                  Mayor - Council Government

BIBLIOGRAPHY

Document No. 716

STUART, PATRICIA.
    Summary of Charter Provisions in Connecticut Local Government: An Outline of Provisions Pertaining to Form of Government in Forty-one Council-Manager and Mayor-Council Communities. Storrs, Connecticut: Institute of Public Service, University of Connecticut, 1964. 46p.

    Descriptors: Charters
                       Council - Manager Government
                       Mayor - Council Government

Document No. 717

STUART, PATRICIA.
    Units of Local Government in Connecticut. Storrs, Connecticut: Institute of Public Service, University of Connecticut, 1965. 19p.

    Descriptors: Regional Agencies
                       Special Districts and Authorities

Document No. 718

SUNDERMANN, FREDERICK.
    A Survey of Municipal Organization and Administration, Sioux City, Iowa. Iowa City: Institute of Public Affairs, University of Iowa, 1963. xvi, 150p., (Siouxland Studies No.2).

    Descriptors: Council - Manager Government
                       Municipal Government

Document No. 719

SWANSON, K.T.W.
    Governmental Units in Spokane County: A Description of the Organization, Function, and Responsibility of the Units of Government. Spokane, Washington: County of Spokane, Planning Commission, 1955. 81p., (31) leaves of plates.

    Descriptors: County Government
                       Planning Commissions

REFORM OF LOCAL GOVERNMENT STRUCTURES IN THE UNITED STATES: 1945-1971.

Document No. 720

SYMPOSIUM AT TARRYTOWN, WESTCHESTER COUNTY NEW YORK, OCTOBER 16-17, 1970.
    Crisis in Local Government. Tarrytown, New York: Builders
    Institute of Westchester and Putnam Counties, 1970. 59p.

    Descriptors: County Government
                 Regional Agencies

Document No. 721

SYMPOSIUM ON METROPOLITAN REGIONALISM: DEVELOPING GOVERNMENTAL CONCEPTS.
    Philadelphia: Law School, University of Pennsylvania, 1957.
    vi, 616p., (University of Pennsylvania Law Review, Volume 105,
    No. 4).

    Descriptors: Municipal Government
                 Regional Agencies

Document No. 722

SYRACUSE, NEW YORK. CHARTER REVISION COMMITTEE.
    Considerations for Revising the City Charter. Syracuse, New
    York: Syracuse Charter Revision Committee, 1959, ii, 35p.,
    (3) fold. leaves of plates, (Second Interim Report).

    Descriptors: Charters
                 Mayor - Council Government

Document No. 723

SYRACUSE, NEW YORK. CHARTER REVISION COMMITTEE.
    A New Charter for Syracuse: Final Report and Proposed Charter.
    Syracuse, New York: Syracuse Charter Revision Committee, 1960.
    xix, 99p., (2) leaves of plates.

    Descriptors: Charters
                 Mayor - Council Government

Document No. 724

TAX RESEARCH ASSOCIATION OF HOUSTON AND HARRIS COUNTY (TEXAS).
    A Synopsis of the Report of the Harris County Home Rule
    Commission. Houston, Texas: Tax Research Association of
    Houston and Harris County, 1958. (5), (Special Newsletter).

    Descriptor: Home Rule

BIBLIOGRAPHY

Document No. 725

TENNESSEE. CHARTER 120.
    Charter 120, Public Acts of 1957. Assembly of the State of Tennessee. Nashville, Tennessee: The State, 1957. 13p.

    Descriptor: Municipal Government

Document No. 726

TENNESSEE. LEGISLATIVE COUNCIL COMMITTEE.
    Study on Structure of County Government 1966: Final Report of the Legislative Council Committee. Nashville, Tennessee: State of Tennessee, Legislative Council Committee, 1966. 347p. in various pagings.

    Descriptor: County Government

Document No. 727

TENNESSEE. UNIVERSITY. BUREAU OF PUBLIC ADMINISTRATION.
    Forms of Government Available to Tennessee Communities. Knoxville, Tennessee: Bureau of Public Administration, University of Tennessee, 1950. iv, 28p.

    Descriptors: Commission Government
                  Council - Manager Government
                  Incorporation
                  Mayor - Council Government

Document No. 728

TENNESSEE. UNIVERSITY. BUREAU OF PUBLIC ADMINISTRATION.
    Greeneville's Government: A Study of the Organization and Administration of the Government of Greeneville, Tennessee. Bureau of Public Administration, University of Tennessee; in cooperation with the Bureau of Research, College of Business Administration, University of Tennessee, Tennessee State Planning Commission, and Tennessee Valley Authority. Knoxville, Tennessee: The Bureau, 1950. ix, 160p.

    Descriptors: Administrative Reorganization
                  Mayor - Council Government

REFORM OF LOCAL GOVERNMENT STRUCTURES IN THE UNITED STATES: 1945-1971.

Document No. 729

TENNESSEE TAXPAYERS ASSOCIATION.
 Local Government in the Chattanooga-Hamilton County Metropolitan Area: Summary and Revision of Findings and Recommendations of the Original 1952 Report of the Tennessee Taxpayers Association for Hamilton County and the City of Chattanooga. Chattanooga, Tennessee: Tennessee Taxpayers Association, 1953. 38p.

 Descriptors: Annexation and Boundary Changes
        Governmental Consolidation

Document No. 730

TEXAS. LEGISLATIVE COUNCIL.
 Municipal Annexation. Prepared by the Staff of the Texas Legislative Council. Austin, Texas: The Council, 1954. 82p., xxv, (1) leaf of plates.

 Descriptors: Annexation and Boundary Changes
        Home Rule

Document No. 731

TEXAS. LEGISLATIVE COUNCIL. STUDY COMMITTEE ON COUNTY GOVERNMENT.
 County Government in Texas: A Report to the 60th Legislature. Austin, Texas: Texas Legislative Council, 1960. 12p. Report No. 59-5.

 Descriptor: County Government

Document No. 732

TEXAS. UNIVERSITY. INSTITUTE OF PUBLIC AFFAIRS.
 Texas Council-Manager Charters. Austin, Texas: Institute of Public Affairs, University of Texas, 1961. 71p., (Public Affairs Series No. 47).

 Descriptors: Charters
        Council - Manager Government

Document No. 733

TEXAS CONFERENCE ON METROPOLITAN PROBLEMS, 1958.
 Proceedings...Austin, Texas: Institute of Public Affairs, University of Texas, 1958. 102p.

 Descriptor: Municipal Government

BIBLIOGRAPHY

Document No. 734

TEXAS RESEARCH LEAGUE.
    Citizen Participation in the North Central Texas Council of Governments. Austin, Texas: Texas Research League, 1967. 32p.

    Descriptors: Citizen Participation
                  Councils of Government

Document No. 735

TEXAS RESEARCH LEAGUE.
    A Feasibility Study for the Proposed Consolidation of McAllen and Mission: An Analysis of the Possible Advantages and Disadvantages Which Could Result From the Consolidation of the Two Cities. Austin, Texas: The League, 1968. ix, 67p.

    Descriptor: Governmental Consolidation

Document No. 736

TEXAS RESEARCH LEAGUE.
    Metropolitan Texas: A Workable Approach to its Problems. Austin, Texas: Texas Research League, 1967. x, 79p., (A Report to Governor John Connally and the 60th Texas Legislature).

    Descriptors: County Government
                  Municipal Government
                  Policy Planning

Document No. 737

TEXAS RESEARCH LEAGUE.
    Regional Planning, Cooperation and Development in the Lower Rio Grande Valley. Austin, Texas: Texas Research League, 1967. 62p., (A Report to the Lower Rio Grande Valley Development Council).

    Descriptors: Planning Commissions
                  Regional Agencies

Document No. 738

THARP, CLAUDE R.
    A Manual of City Government in Michigan. rev. ed. Ann Arbor, Michigan: Bureau of Government, Institute of Public Administration, University of Michigan, 1957. 194p., (Michigan Governmental Studies No. 22).

    Descriptors: Charters
                  Commission Government
                  Council - Manager Government
                  Home Rule
                  Mayor - Council Government

REFORM OF LOCAL GOVERNMENT STRUCTURES IN THE UNITED STATES: 1945-1971.

Document No. 739

THARP, CLAUDE R.
    Michigan Cities and Villages: Organization and Administration. Ann Arbor, Michigan: University of Michigan Press, 1951. v, 40p., (Michigan Pamphlet No. 23).

    Descriptors: Charters
                Home Rule

Document No. 740

THROMBLEY, WOODWORTH G.
    Special Districts and Authorities in Texas. Austin, Texas: Institute of Public Administration, University of Texas, 1959. viii, 142p., (Public Affairs Series No. 39).

    Descriptor: Special Districts and Authorities

Document No. 741

TORGOVNIK, EFRAIM.
    Special Districts in Rhode Island. Kingston, Rhode Island: Bureau of Government, University of Rhode Island, 1968. 76p., (Metropolitan Study 2).

    Descriptor: Special Districts and Authorities

Document No. 742

TOSCANO, JAMES V.
    The Chief Elected Official in the Penjerdel Region: A Self Portrait. Philadelphia: Pennsylvania-New Jersey-Delaware Metropolitan Project, 1964. iii, 47p.

    Descriptors: Political Leadership
                Regional Agencies

Document No. 743

TOWARD A BAY AREA REGIONAL ORGANIZATION.
    Harriet Nathan and Stanley Scott, editors. Berkeley, California: Institute of Governmental Affairs, University of California, 1969. xii, 272p., (Report of the September 14, 1968 Conference presented by University Extension and the Institute of Governmental Studies of the University of California, Berkeley, on behalf of the Joint Committee on Bay Area Regional Organization).

    Descriptors: Citizen Participation
                Regional Agencies

BIBLIOGRAPHY

Document No. 744

TRENTON, NEW JERSEY. CHARTER COMMISSION.
    Report and Recommendations of the Trenton Charter Commission.
    Trenton, New Jersey: Charter Commission, 1961. v, 32p., (11).

    Descriptors: Charters
                      Commission Government
                      Mayor - Council Government

Document No. 745

TULSA METROPOLITAN AREA PLANNING COMMISSION.
    Indian Nations Council of Governments. Tulsa, Oklahoma:
    The Commission, 1967. 106p., (24).

    Descriptors: Councils of Government
                      Regional Agencies

Document No. 746

TWIN CITIES METROPOLITAN PLANNING COMMISSION (MINNESOTA).
    The Challenge of Metropolitan Growth. St. Paul, Minnesota:
    The Commission, 1958. 33p., (Report No. 1, December 1958).

    Descriptors: Planning Commission
                      Regional Agencies

Document No. 747

UNITED STATES. ADVISORY COMMISSION ON INTERGOVERNMENTAL RELATIONS.
    Alternative Approaches to Governmental Reorganization in
    Metropolitan Areas: A Commission Report. Washington:
    Advisory Commission on Intergovernmental Relations, 1962.
    88p., (A-11).

    Descriptors: Advisory Councils
                      Federation
                      Governmental Consolidation
                      Governmental Separation
                      Special Districts and Authorities

Document No. 748

UNITED STATES. ADVISORY COMMISSION ON INTERGOVERNMENTAL RELATIONS.
    Factors Affecting Voter Reactions to Governmental Reorganization
    in Metropolitan Areas: An Information Report. Washington:
    Advisory Commission on Intergovernmental Relations, 1962. v, 80p.,
    (1) leaf of plates., (M-15).

    Descriptor: Citizen Participation

REFORM OF LOCAL GOVERNMENT STRUCTURES IN THE UNITED STATES: 1945-1971.

Document No. 749

UNITED STATES. ADVISORY COMMISSION ON INTERGOVERNMENTAL RELATIONS.
Governmental Structure, Organization, and Planning in Metropolitan Areas: Suggested Action by Local, State and National Governments: A Report by the Advisory Commission on Intergovernmental Relations. Washington: U.S. Government Printing Office, 1961. ix, 121p.

Descriptors: Intergovernmental Cooperation
Planning Commissions

Document No. 750

UNITED STATES. ADVISORY COMMISSION ON INTERGOVERNMENTAL RELATIONS.
A Handbook for Interlocal Agreements and Contracts: An Information Report. Washington: Advisory Commission on Intergovernmental Relations, 1967. vi, 197p., (M-29).

Descriptor: Intergovernmental Cooperation

Document No. 751

UNITED STATES. ADVISORY COMMISSION ON INTERGOVERNMENTAL RELATIONS.
Intergovernmental Responsibilities for Mass Transportation Facilities and Services in Metropolitan Areas: A Commission Report. Washington: Advisory Commission on Intergovernmental Relations, 1961. v, 54p.

Descriptors: Intergovernmental Cooperation
Regional Agencies

Document No. 752

UNITED STATES. ADVISORY COMMISSION ON INTERGOVERNMENTAL RELATIONS.
Intergovernmental Responsibilities for Water Supply and Sewage Disposal in Metropolitan Areas: A Commission Report. Washington: Advisory Commission on Intergovernmental Relations, 1962. 135, 24p., (A-13).

Descriptor: Intergovernmental Cooperation

Document No. 753

UNITED STATES. ADVISORY COMMISSION ON INTERGOVERNMENTAL RELATIONS.
Metropolitan Social and Economic Disparities: Implications for Intergovernmental Relations in Central Cities and Suburbs. Washington: Advisory Commission on Intergovernmental Relations, 1965. viii, 253p., (A-25).

Descriptor: Intergovernmental Relations

BIBLIOGRAPHY

Document No. 754

UNITED STATES. ADVISORY COMMISSION ON INTERGOVERNMENTAL RELATIONS. Performance of Urban Functions: Local and Areawide: An Information Report. Washington: Advisory Commission on Intergovernmental Relations, 1963. viii, 281p., (M-21 revised).

Descriptor: Intergovernmental Relations

Document No. 755

UNITED STATES. ADVISORY COMMISSION ON INTERGOVERNMENTAL RELATIONS. The Problems of Special Districts in American Government: A Commission Report. Washington: Advisory Commission on Intergovernmental Relations, 1964. x, 112p., (A-22).

Descriptor: Special Districts and Authorities

Document No. 756

UNITED STATES. ADVISORY COMMISSION ON INTERGOVERNMENTAL RELATIONS. State Constitutional and Statutory Restrictions upon the Structural, Functional and Personnel Powers of Local Government. Washington: Advisory Commission on Intergovernmental Relations, 1962. ix, 80p., (A-12).

Descriptor: Administrative Reorganization

Document No. 757

UNITED STATES. ADVISORY COMMISSION ON INTERGOVERNMENTAL RELATIONS. Urban and Rural America: Policies for Future Growth: A Commission Report. Washington: Advisory Commission on Intergovernmental Relations, 1968. xvi, 186p.

Descriptors: Policy Planning
             Regional Agencies

Document No. 758

UNITED STATES. BUREAU OF THE CENSUS. Local Government Structure in the United States. (prepared under the supervision of Allen D. Manvel). Washington: U.S. Government Printing Office, 1954. 91p., (State and Local Government Special Studies No. 34).

Descriptors: County Government
             Municipal Government

REFORM OF LOCAL GOVERNMENT STRUCTURES IN THE UNITED STATES: 1945-1971.

Document No. 759

UNITED STATES. CONGRESS. HOUSE. COMMITTEE ON GOVERNMENT OPERATIONS. Federal-State-Local Relations: Dade County (Florida) Metropolitan Government: hearing before a Subcommittee of the Committee on Government Operations, House of Representatives, Eighty-fifth Congress, first session...Washington, D.C.: U.S. Government Printing Office, 1958. iii, 120p.

Descriptor: Intergovernmental Relations

Document No. 760

UNITED STATES. CONGRESS. HOUSE. COMMITTEE ON GOVERNMENT OPERATIONS. Government in Metropolitan Areas: Commentaries on a Report by the Advisory Commission on Intergovernmental Relations. Washington: U.S. Government Printing Office, 1962. vi, 123p., (87th Congress, 1st Session, Committee Print).

Descriptors: Intergovernmental Relations
Municipal Government

Document No. 761

UNITED STATES. CONGRESS. HOUSE. COMMITTEE ON GOVERNMENT OPERATIONS. Metropolitan Problems and Urban Development: hearing before a Subcommittee of the Committee on Government Operations, House of Representatives, Eighty-Sixth Congress, first session... Washington: U.S. Government Printing Office, 1959. iv, 151p.

Descriptor: Municipal Government

Document No. 762

UNITED STATES. CONGRESS. HOUSE. COMMITTEE ON GOVERNMENT OPERATIONS. Unshackling Local Government: A Survey of Proposals by the Advisory Commission on Intergovernmental Relations: Thirtieth Report by the Committee on Government Operations. Washington: U.S. Government Printing Office, 1966. viii, 47p., (89th Congress, 2d session, House Report No. 1643).

Descriptor: Intergovernmental Cooperation

BIBLIOGRAPHY

Document No. 763

UNITED STATES. CONGRESS. HOUSE. COMMITTEE ON GOVERNMENT OPERATIONS.
Unshackling Local Government: A Survey of Proposals by the Advisory Commission on Intergovernmental Relations: Twenty-Fourth Report by the Committee on Government Operations, rev. ed. Washington: U.S. Government Printing Office, 1968. viii, 72p., (90th Congress, 2d session, House Report No. 1270).

Descriptors: Intergovernmental Relations
Municipal Government

Document No. 764

UNITED STATES. CONGRESS. JOINT COMMITTEE ON WASHINGTON METROPOLITAN PROGRAMS.
The Governing of Metropolitan Washington: Staff Study for the Joint Committee on Washington Metropolitan Problems. Congress of the United States. Washington: U.S. Government Printing Office, 1958. v, 98p., (85th Congress, 2d session, Joint Committee Print).

Descriptor: Municipal Government

Document No. 765

UNITED STATES. CONGRESS. SENATE. COMMITTEE ON GOVERNMENT OPERATIONS. SUBCOMMITTEE ON REORGANIZATION AND INTERNATIONAL ORGANIZATIONS.
Create a Commission on Metropolitan Problems: hearing before the Subcommittee on Reorganization and International Organizations of the Committee on Government Operations, United States Senate, Eighty-Sixth Congress, first session on S. 1431, S. 2397...July 24, 1959. Washington: U.S. Government Printing Office, 1959. iii, 73p.

Descriptor: Advisory Councils

Document No. 766

UNITED STATES. CONGRESS. SENATE. COMMITTEE ON GOVERNMENT OPERATIONS. SUBCOMMITTEE ON INTERGOVERNMENTAL RELATIONS.
Problems of Federal-State-Local Relations: Hearing before the Subcommittee on Intergovernmental Relations of the Committee on Government Operations, United States Senate, Eighty-Seventh Congress, second session.... Washington: U.S. Government Printing Office, 1962. iii, 60p.

Descriptor: Intergovernmental Relations

REFORM OF LOCAL GOVERNMENT STRUCTURES IN THE UNITED STATES: 1945-1971.

Document No. 767

UNITED STATES. CONGRESS. SENATE. COMMITTEE ON GOVERNMENT OPERATIONS, SUBCOMMITTEE ON INTERGOVERNMENTAL RELATIONS.
> Role of the Federal Government in Metropolitan Areas: hearings before the Subcommittee on Intergovernmental Relations of the Committee on Government Operations, United States Senate, Eighty-Seventh Congress, second session....Washington: U.S. Government Printing Office, 1963. iii, 121p.

> Descriptors: Intergovernmental Relations
> Municipal Government

Document No. 768

UNITED STATES. CONGRESS. SENATE AND HOUSE COMMITTEES ON GOVERNMENT OPERATIONS. SUBCOMMITTEES ON INTERGOVERNMENTAL RELATIONS.
> Government in Metropolitan Areas (New York Metropolitan Region): Joint hearings before the Subcommittees on Intergovernmental Relations of the Senate and House Committees on Government Operations, Congress of the United States, Eighty-Eighth Congress, first session.... Washington: U.S. Government Printing Office, 1963. iv, 326p.

> Descriptor: Municipal Government

Document No. 769

UNITED STATES. DEPARTMENT OF HOUSING AND URBAN DEVELOPMENT.
> Citizen Participation in Model Cities, A HUD Guide. Washington, D.C.: U.S. Department of Housing and Urban Development, 1968. i, 27p., (Technical Assistance Bulletin No. 3).

> Descriptors: Citizen Participation
> Model Cities

Document No. 770

UNITED STATES. OFFICE OF ECONOMIC OPPORTUNITY.
> Participation of the Poor in the Community Decision-Making Process. Washington: Office of Economic Opportunity, Community Action Program, 1969. iii, 39p.

> Descriptors: Citizen Participation
> Community Control

BIBLIOGRAPHY

Document No. 771

UNITED STATES CONFERENCE OF MAYORS. COMMUNITY RELATIONS SERVICE.
City Hall and Neighborhood Residents: The Atlanta Approach.
Washington, D.C.: United States Conference of Mayors,
Community Relations Service, 1968. 16p., (Services Series:
Experience Report No. 110).

Descriptors: Citizen Participation
Little City Halls
Neighborhood Control

Document No. 772

THE URBAN DIMENSION IN MONTANA: PROCEEDINGS OF A CONFERENCE AT THE
UNIVERSITY OF MONTANA, MISSOULA, JULY 11, 1967.
Missoula, Montana: Bureau of Government Research,
University of Montana, 1968. 72p., (Publication No. 6).

Descriptors: Home Rule
Regional Agencies

Document No. 773

URBAN POLICY CONFERENCE, 5th, UNIVERSITY OF IOWA, 1968.
Proceedings.... Iowa City: Institute of Public Affairs,
University of Iowa, 1969. iii, 67p.

Descriptor: Community Control

Document No. 774

UTAH. LOCAL GOVERNMENT SURVEY COMMISSION.
A Report on Utah's Special Purpose Districts. Prepared by
J.D. Williams; with recommendations by the Local Government
Survey Commission, 1956. vii, 74p.

Descriptor: Special Districts and Authorities

Document No. 775

UTAH. UNIVERSITY. CENTER FOR ECONOMIC AND COMMUNITY DEVELOPMENT.
How to Increase the Efficiency and Cut the Costs of Local
Government. Provo, Utah: University of Utah, 1970. 104p.,
(80). (Local Government Modernization Study; Report No. 4).

Descriptor: Administrative Reorganization

REFORM OF LOCAL GOVERNMENT STRUCTURES IN THE UNITED STATES: 1945-1971.

Document No. 776

UTAH. UNIVERSITY. CENTER FOR ECONOMIC AND COMMUNITY DEVELOPMENT.
Modernizing Utah's Local Governments for the Years Ahead. Provo, Utah: University of Utah, 1970. 48, 19p., (2), (Local Government Modernization Study: Report No. 3).

Descriptor: Administrative Reorganization

Document No. 777

VANLANDINGHAM, KENNETH.
The Constitution and Local Government. Frankfort, Kentucky: Kentucky Legislative Research Commission, 1964, vii, 63p., (Information Bulletin No. 36).

Descriptors: Home Rule
Municipal Government

Document No. 778

VerBURG, KENNETH.
County Home Rule: What is it, Pro and Con Arguments. East Lansing, Michigan: Institute for Community Development and Services, Michigan State University, 1962. 9p., (Technical Bulletin B-34).

Descriptors: County Government
Home Rule

Document No. 779

VerBURG, KENNETH.
A Study of the Local Powers of Michigan Local Governments. rev. ed. East Lansing, Michigan: Institute for Community Development and Services, Michigan State University, 1967. viii, 37p.

Descriptors: Annexation and Boundary Changes
Governmental Consolidation
Incorporation

Document No. 780

VIRGINIA. ADVISORY LEGISLATIVE COUNCIL.
Annexation and Consolidation: Report of the Virginia Advisory Legislative Council to the Governor and the General Assembly of Virginia. Richmond, Virginia: Commonwealth of Virginia, Department of Purchases and Supply, 1964. 35p., (House Document No. 16).

Descriptors: Annexation and Boundary Changes
Governmental Consolidation

BIBLIOGRAPHY

Document No. 781

VIRGINIA. METROPOLITAN AREAS STUDY COMMISSION.
Metropolitan Virginia: A Program for Action. Richmond, Virginia: Virginia Metropolitan Areas Study Commission, 1967. 40p.

Descriptors: Councils of Government
Governmental Consolidation
Governmental Separation
Planning Commissions

Document No. 782

VIRGINIA. METROPOLITAN AREAS STUDY COMMISSION.
Metropolitan Virginia 1967: A Brief Assessment. Richmond, Virginia: Virginia Metropolitan Areas Study Commission, 1967. 40p.

Descriptor: Municipal Government

Document No. 783

VIRGINIA. METROPOLITAN AREAS STUDY COMMISSION. COMMITTEE ON GOVERNMENTAL STRUCTURE.
Governing the Virginia Metropolitan Areas: As Assessment. Richmond, Virginia: Virginia Metropolitan Areas Study Commission, 1967. 54p.

Descriptors: Annexation and Boundary Changes
County Government
Governmental Consolidation
Municipal Government

Document No. 784

VIRGINIA. UNIVERSITY. BUREAU OF PUBLIC ADMINISTRATION.
City Consolidation in the Lower Peninsula: A Report on the Advantages and Disadvantages of Consolidating the Cities of Hampton, Newport News and Warwick: With Supplementary Report Nos. 1,2,3,4,5. Prepared by the Bureau of Public Administration, University of Virginia. Charlottesville, Virginia: The Bureau, 1956. vii, 74p., (111).

Descriptor: Governmental Consolidation

REFORM OF LOCAL GOVERNMENT STRUCTURES IN THE UNITED STATES: 1945-1971.

Document No. 785

VIRGINIA. UNIVERSITY. BUREAU OF PUBLIC ADMINISTRATION.
    Report on an Administrative Survey of Fairfax County, Virginia.
    Charlottesville, Virginia: The Bureau, 1957. vii, 62p.

    Descriptors: Administrative Reorganization
                Commission Government
                County Government

Document No. 786

VIRGINIA. UNIVERSITY. INSTITUTE OF GOVERNMENT.
    The Financial Effects of the Incorporation of Fairfax County
    as a City. Charlottesville, Virginia: Institute of Government, University of Virginia, 1965. vii, 74p.

    Descriptor: Incorporation

Document No. 787

WARREN, ROBERT O.
    Government in Metropolitan Regions: A Reappraisal of
    Fractionated Political Organization. Davis, California:
    Institute of Governmental Affairs, University of
    California, 1966. 327p.

    Descriptors: Incorporation
                Municipal Government

Document No. 788

WASHINGTON (STATE). LEGISLATURE. JOINT COMMITTEE ON URBAN AREA
GOVERNMENT. CITIZENS ADVISORY COMMITTEE.
    City and Suburb - Community or Chaos: Report to the Joint
    Committee on Urban Area Government. Olympia, Washington:
    Legislature of the State of Washington, 1962. 35p.

    Descriptors: Governmental Consolidation
                Governmental Separation

Document No. 789

WASHINGTON (STATE). RESEARCH COUNCIL.
    City-County Consolidation: A Study of Its Possibilities for
    Walla Walla, Washington. Olympia: Washington State Research
    Council, 1967. ii, 67p.

    Descriptor: Governmental Consolidation

BIBLIOGRAPHY

Document No. 790

WASHINGTON. UNIVERSITY. BUREAU OF GOVERNMENTAL RESEARCH AND SERVICES.
Municipal Government in the State of Washington. Seattle: Bureau of Governmental Research and Services, University of Washington, 1962. xiii, 318p., (Report No. 149).

Descriptors: Commission Government
Council - Manager Government
Home Rule
Incorporation
Mayor - Council Government
Planning Commissions

Document No. 791

WAYNE STATE UNIVERSITY CITIZEN LEADER CONFERENCE, 1961.
Constitutional Revision and Local Government in Michigan. Edited by Louis L. Friedland. Detroit: Department of Political Science, Wayne State University, 1961. 63p., (Papers and panel summaries delivered to the Citizen Leader Conference conducted by the Department of Political Science, College of Liberal Arts, Wayne State University, June 10th, 1961).

Descriptor: Municipal Government

Document No. 792

WEEKS, J. DEVEREUX.
Drafting a Virginia Municipal Charter. J. Devereux Weeks and Walter Stoneham. Charlottesville, Virginia: Virginia Municipal League and Bureau of Public Administration, University of Virginia, 1963. iv, 69p., (Joint Report No. 18).

Descriptor: Charters

Document No. 793

WENTZ, JOHN B.
An Analysis of the Advisability of Annexing All or a Part of the Lakewood Area to the City of Long Beach. Long Beach, California: (s.n.), 1951. viii, 142p., (Sponsored by Long Beach City Manager).

Descriptors: Annexation and Boundary Changes
Incorporation

REFORM OF LOCAL GOVERNMENT STRUCTURES IN THE UNITED STATES: 1945-1971.

Document No. 794

WENUM, JOHN D.
    Annexation as a Technique for Metropolitan Growth: The Case of Phoenix, Arizona. Tempe, Arizona: Institute of Public Administration, Arizona State University, 1970. xi, 129p.

    Descriptor: Annexation and Boundary Changes

Document No. 795

WESTERN GOVERNMENTAL RESEARCH ASSOCIATION, 17th, LONG BEACH, CALIFORNIA, 1957.
    Workshop Discussion on Administrative Problems in Contractual Public Services: Transcript of Proceedings. Sacramento: Assembly Interim Committee on Municipal and County Government, 1957. 56p.

    Descriptors: County Government
                  Municipal Government

Document No. 796

WETMORE, RUTH Y.
    Council and Commission Manager Government. Lawrence, Kansas: Governmental Research Center, University of Kansas, 1960. 34p., (Citizen's Pamphlet Series No. 29).

    Descriptors: Commission Government
                  Council - Manager Government

Document No. 797

WHITE, MAX R.
    Forms of Town Government in Connecticut. Max R. White and Shirley Raissi. Storrs, Connecticut: Institute of Public Service, University of Connecticut, 1962. 21p.

    Descriptors: Council - Manager Government
                  Mayor - Council Government

Document No. 798

WICHITA REGIONAL CONFERENCE ON LOCAL GOVERNMENT PROBLEMS AND POLICIES.
    Wichita Tomorrow. Edited by Hugo Wall. Wichita, Kansas: Center for Urban Studies, Wichita State University, 1967. viii, 124p.

    Descriptors: Citizen Participation
                  Municipal Government

BIBLIOGRAPHY

Document No. 799

WILLIAMSBURG - JAMES CITY COUNTY JOINT CONSOLIDATION STUDY COMMISSION.
Report of the Williamsburg - James City County Joint Consolidation Study Commission: (and Attachments...). Williamsburg, Virginia: Williamsburg - James City County Joint Consolidation Study Commission, 1963. 2 v.

Descriptors: Council - Manager Government
              Governmental Consolidation

Document No. 800

WINTERS, JOHN M.
Interstate Metropolitan Areas. Ann Arbor, Michigan: University of Michigan Law School, 1962. vi, 110p.

Descriptors: Intergovernmental Relations
              Planning Commissions

Document No. 801

WINTERS, JOHN M.
State Constitutional Limitations on Solutions of Metropolitan Area Problems. Ann Arbor, Michigan: University of Michigan Law School, 1961. ix, 169p.

Descriptors: Intergovernmental Relations

Document No. 802

WISCONSIN. LEGISLATURE. INTERIM URBAN PROBLEMS COMMITTEE.
Report of the Interim Urban Problems Committee: submitted to the Governor and the 1959 Legislature. Madison, Wisconsin: Interim Urban Problems Committee, 1959. viii, 31p., (39).

Descriptors: Incorporation
              Intergovernmental Cooperation
              Planning Commissions

Document No. 803

WISCONSIN. LEGISLATIVE COUNCIL.
Preliminary Staff Report to the Urban Problems Committee. Madison, Wisconsin: Legislative Council, 1958. v, 57p., (Publication No. 59-8).

Descriptors: Intergovernmental Cooperation
              Municipal Government

REFORM OF LOCAL GOVERNMENT STRUCTURES IN THE UNITED STATES: 1945-1971.

Document No. 804

WISCONSIN. LEGISLATIVE REFERENCE BUREAU.
    Latest Thoughts on Local Government. (prepared by Patricia V. Robbins). Madison, Wisconsin: Legislative Reference Bureau, 1967. 19p., (Informational Bulletin 67-4).

    Descriptors: County Government
                   Intergovernmental Relations

Document No. 805

WISCONSIN. LEGISLATIVE REFERENCE BUREAU.
    A Summary Look at State Agencies of Local Affairs. (prepared by Patricia V. Robbins). Madison, Wisconsin: Legislative Reference Bureau, 1966. 12, 3p., (Informational Bulletin 66-12).

    Descriptors: Intergovernmental Cooperation
                   Regional Agencies

Document No. 806

WISCONSIN. LEGISLATIVE REFERENCE LIBRARY.
    One Hundred and One Proposed Constitutional Amendments to Change the Structure of County Government in Wisconsin 1901-1961. prepared by Wisconsin Legislative Reference Library; (prepared by Kathleen R. Kepner). Madison, Wisconsin: The Library, 1962. 16p., (Informational Bulletin 215).

    Descriptor: County Government

Document No. 807

WISCONSIN. METROPOLITAN STUDY COMMISSION.
    1958 Annual Report to the Governor of the State of Wisconsin. Milwaukee: Metropolitan Study Commission, 1958. iv, 53p.

    Descriptors: Municipal Government
                 Planning Commissions
                 Regional Agencies

BIBLIOGRAPHY

Document No. 808

WISCONSIN. METROPOLITAN STUDY COMMISSION.
    1959 Annual Report to the Governor of the State of Wisconsin.
    Milwaukee: Metropolitan Study Commission, 1959. 3, vii, 38p.

    Descriptors: Municipal Government
                   Planning Commissions
                   Regional Agencies

Document No. 809

WISCONSIN. METROPOLITAN STUDY COMMISSION.
    1960 Annual Report to the Governor of the State of Wisconsin.
    Milwaukee: Metropolitan Study Commission, 1960. ii, 67p.

    Descriptors: Municipal Government
                   Planning Commissions
                   Regional Agencies

Document No. 810

WISCONSIN. METROPOLITAN STUDY COMMISSION.
    Report to the 1961 Legislature of the State of Wisconsin.
    Milwaukee: Metropolitan Study Commission, 1961. 39p.

    Descriptors: Planning Commissions
                   Policy Planning
                 Regional Agencies

Document No. 811

WISCONSIN. METROPOLITAN STUDY COMMISSION.
    Final Report on Intergovernmental Cooperation in Milwaukee
    County. Milwaukee: Intergovernmental Cooperation
    Committee, Metropolitan Study Commission, 1961. iii, 77p.

    Descriptors: County Government
                   Intergovernmental Relations

Document No. 812

WISCONSIN. METROPOLITAN STUDY COMMISSION.
    Metropolitan Milwaukee: Problems - Solutions: Report of the
    Metropolitan Study Commission, State of Wisconsin. Milwaukee:
    Metropolitan Study Commission, 1961. 26p.

    Descriptors: Annexation and Boundary Changes
                   County Government

REFORM OF LOCAL GOVERNMENT STRUCTURES IN THE UNITED STATES: 1945-1971.

Document No. 813

WISCONSIN. METROPOLITAN STUDY COMMISSION. REVENUE SOURCES AND
DISTRIBUTION COMMITTEE.
    Final Report and Recommendations on Taxation and Revenue
Distribution in Milwaukee County. Milwaukee: Metropolitan
Study Commission, Revenue Sources and Distribution Committee,
1960. 35p., (8) leaves of plates.

    Descriptor: County Government

Document No. 814

WISCONSIN. TASK FORCE ON LOCAL GOVERNMENT FINANCE AND REORGANIZATION.
    County Administrative Organization. prepared by J. Devereux
Weeks, James R. Morgan. Madison, Wisconsin: Task Force on
Local Government Finance and Organization, 1968. 7p.,
(Government Organization Report No. 1).

    Descriptors: Administrative Reorganization
               County Government

Document No. 815

WISCONSIN. TASK FORCE ON LOCAL GOVERNMENT FINANCE AND ORGANIZATION.
    County Home Rule and Enrolled Resolution 49. prepared by
James R. Morgan, J. Devereux Weeks. Madison, Wisconsin:
Task Force on Local Government Finance and Organization,
1968, 6p., (Government Organization Report No. 3).

    Descriptors: County Government
               Home Rule

Document No. 816

WISCONSIN. TASK FORCE ON LOCAL GOVERNMENT FINANCE AND ORGANIZATION.
    Home Rule for Counties. prepared by J. Devereux Weeks and
James R. Morgan. Madison, Wisconsin: Task Force on Local
Government Finance and Organization, 1968. 5p., (1).
(Government Organization Report No. 2).

    Descriptors: County Government
               Home Rule

BIBLIOGRAPHY

Document No. 817

WISCONSIN. TASK FORCE ON LOCAL GOVERNMENT FINANCE AND ORGANIZATION.
    Merger of Local Units of Government. prepared by James R.
    Morgan, Richard Stauber. Madison, Wisconsin: Task Force
    on Local Government Finance and Organization, 1968. 3p.,
    (Government Organization Report No. 4).

   Descritpors: County Government
                Governmental Consolidation

Document No. 818

WISCONSIN. TASK FORCE ON LOCAL GOVERNMENT FINANCE AND ORGANIZATION.
    Metropolitan Government. prepared by C.K. Alexander,
    J. Devereux Weeks. Madison, Wisconsin: Task Force on
    Local Government Finance and Organization, 1968. 9p.,
    (Government Organization Report No. 10).

   Descriptor: Municipal Government

Document No. 819

WISCONSIN. TASK FORCE ON LOCAL GOVERNMENT FINANCE AND ORGANIZATION.
    Urban Growth Policy for Wisconsin: Draft Legislation for
    Municipal Boundary Controls. prepared by Douglas G. Weiford,
    Richard Lehmann, Richard Cutler, James R. Morgan. Madison,
    Wisconsin: Task Force on Local Government Finance and
    Organization, 1968. 33p., (Government Organization Report
    No. 14).

   Descriptor: Annexation and Boundary Changes

Document No. 820

WISCONSIN. TASK FORCE ON LOCAL GOVERNMENT FINANCE AND ORGANIZATION.
    Urban Growth Policy for Wisconsin: Legislative Proposals
    in the Area of Municipal Boundary Changes. prepared by
    Douglas G. Weiford, Richard Lehmann, Richard Cutler, James R.
    Morgan. Madison, Wisconsin: Task Force on Local Government
    Finance and Organization, 1968. 7p., (3). (Government
    Organization Report No. 8).

   Descriptor: Annexation and Boundary Changes

REFORM OF LOCAL GOVERNMENT STRUCTURES IN THE UNITED STATES: 1945-1971.

Document No. 821

WISCONSIN. UNIVERSITY. BUREAU OF GOVERNMENT.
    County Government Activities in Wisconsin. Bureau of Government, University Extension Division, University of Wisconsin, Madison, Wisconsin: The Bureau, 1961. xi, 72p., (Third in a Series of Reports on County Government in Wisconsin).

    Descriptor: County Government

Document No. 822

WISCONSIN. UNIVERSITY. BUREAU OF GOVERNMENT.
    Governmental Organization in Menomonee Falls. Madison, Wisconsin: Bureau of Government, University of Wisconsin, 1964. ii, 11, 31p., (Report NS 18).

    Descriptors: Commission Government
                  Council - Manager Government
                  Mayor - Council Government

Document No. 823

WISE, SIDNEY.
    Selected Areas of Intergovernmental Cooperation. Edited by Sidney Wise. Harrisburg: Commonwealth of Pennsylvania, Department of Internal Affairs, 1957. v, 46p.

    Descriptors: Intergovernmental Relations

Document No. 824

WISE, SIDNEY.
    Selected Areas of Intergovernmental Cooperation. rev. ed. Harrisburg: Commonwealth of Pennsylvania, Department of Internal Affairs, 1962. x, 39p.

    Descriptors: Intergovernmental Cooperation

Document No. 825

WOLFF, REINHOLD P.
    Miami Metro: The Road to Urban Unity. Coral Gables, Florida: Bureau of Business and Economic Research, University of Florida, 1960. x, 203p., (Area Development Series No. 9).

    Descriptors: Governmental Consolidation
                  Municipal Government

BIBLIOGRAPHY

Document No. 826

WOOD, ROBERT C.
    1400 Governments: The Political Economy of the New York Metropolitan Region. Robert C. Wood; with Vladimir V. Almendinger. Cambridge, Massachusetts: Harvard University Press, 1961. xviii, 267p.

    Descriptor: Municipal Government

Document No. 827

WORKSHOP ON METROPOLITAN AREA PROBLEMS, 1st, UNIVERSITY OF PENNSYLVANIA, 1956.
    The Formulation of Metropolitan Area Study Objectives. Philadelphia: Institute of Local and State Government, University of Pennsylvania, 1956. 18, 9p.

    Descriptor: Municipal Government

Document No. 828

WORKSHOP ON METROPOLITAN AREA PROBLEMS, 2d, UNIVERSITY OF PENNSYLVANIA, 1957.
    The Methodology for Achieving Metropolitan Study Objectives. Philadelphia: Institute of Local and State Government, University of Pennsylvania, 1957. 34pp. in various pagings.

    Descriptors: Municipal Government

Document No. 829

WORKSHOP ON VOLUNTARY MULTI-PURPOSE ORGANIZATIONS, SEATTLE, 1961.
    Summary of Discussion. Washington, D.C.: American Municipal Association, 1961. 17p., (1).

    Descriptors: Advisory Councils
                   Regional Agencies

Document No. 830

WORLD CONFERENCE OF LOCAL GOVERNMENTS, WASHINGTON, D.C., 1961.
    Local Government Structure and Organization: Problems of Metropolitan Areas. The Hague: Martinus Nijhoff, 1962. 119p.

    Descriptors: Council Government
                   Mayor - Council Government

Document No. 831

ZEIGLER, FRANK W.
    Consolidation of City and County Governments. (s.l.): (s.n.), 1957. 12p., (Presented at the Forty-Ninth Annual Convention of the Southern Association of Chamber of Commerce Executives at Charleston, South Carolina, March 12, 1957).

    Descriptors: County Government
                 Governmental Consolidation

REFORM OF LOCAL GOVERNMENT STRUCTURES IN THE UNITED STATES: 1945-1971.

Document No. 832

ZIMMER, KENNETH.
    A Study of the Effectiveness of a Citizens Association in Municipal Government: With Specific Reference to the Richmond (Virginia) Citizens Association. prepared by Kenneth Zimmer, Howard Davis, William Edwards. Richmond, Virginia: Richmond Professional Institute of the College of William and Mary, 1960. 41p., (Community Service Study No. 1).

    Descriptors: Advisory Councils
                   Citizen Participation

Document No. 833

ZIMMERMAN, JOSEPH F.
    Metropolitan Charters. Joseph F. Zimmerman, editor. Albany, New York: Graduate School of Public Affairs, University of New York at Albany, 1967. v, 195p.

    Descriptors: Charters
                   Municipal Government

Document No. 834

ZION, WILLIAM R.
    Coordination of Bay-Delta Governmental Studies with BCDC. prepared by William R. Zion; with the assistance of Robert Grunwald, Victor Jones, Stanley Scott, Paul H. Sedway. San Francisco: San Francisco Bay Conservation and Development Commission, 1967. 45p.

    Descriptors: Planning Commissions
                   Regional Agencies

Document No. 835

ZION, WILLIAM R.
    Final Report, Fresno Metropolitan Study, March 1960: prepared for the City of Fresno and the County of Fresno. William R. Zion and F. Patrick Henry. Fresno, California: Fresno Metropolitan Study Committee, 1960. 209p.

    Descriptors: Annexation and Boundary Changes
                   Special Districts and Commissions

Document No. 836

ZION, WILLIAM R.
    Report on Local Government Alternatives in the Calwa-Malaga Area. (s.l.): (s.n.), 1963. 37p., (Prepared for the Calwa-Malaga Development Association).

    Descriptors: Annexation and Boundary Changes
                   Incorporation

INDEX

ABERCROMBIE, CLAUDE. 468

ABERDEEN, S.D. 710

ABERS, JACOB H. 146

ACKERMAN, DUKE R. 001

ACKERMAN, WILLIAM C. 428

ADMINISTRATIVE REORGANIZATION. 003, 028, 085, 092, 095, 110, 116, 120, 126, 136, 160, 162, 166, 169, 175, 176, 177, 178, 185, 221, 267, 281, 283, 308, 333, 334, 352, 353, 392, 405, 446, 448, 450, 463, 483, 489, 490, 496, 502, 503, 504, 527, 593, 605, 614, 619, 627, 635, 643, 647, 650, 652, 653, 671, 687, 700, 701, 702, 703, 710, 728, 756, 775, 776, 785, 814

ADRIAN, CHARLES. 470

ADVISORY COUNCILS. 020, 026, 088, 114, 124, 134, 139, 147, 150, 160, 200, 216, 217, 220, 241, 248, 259, 263, 290, 331, 373, 391, 415, 422, 431, 445, 456, 458, 468, 473, 499, 500, 533, 544, 556, 575, 598, 619, 653, 658, 663, 683, 709, 747, 765, 829, 832

AKRON, OHIO. 085

ALABAMA. 004, 152, 170, 184, 218, 235, 268, 269, 472, 712, 758

ALABAMA. UNIVERSITY. BUREAU OF PUBLIC ADMINISTRATION. 152, 170, 218

ALABAMA LEAGUE OF MUNICIPALITIES. 170

ALAMEDA COUNTY, CALIFORNIA. 359

ALASKA. 005, 414, 468, 472, 609, 758

ALAUEDON TOWNSHIP, MICHIGAN. 603

ALBEMARLE COUNTY, VIRGINIA. 194

ALBEQUERQUE, NEW MEXICO. 107

ALBERT, FRANKLIN. 638

ALDERFER, HAROLD F. 002

ALDRICH, ELMER. 571

ALEXANDER, C.K. 818

ALEXANDRIA, VIRGINIA. 437

ALFORD, ROBERT. 670

REFORM OF LOCAL GOVERNMENT STRUCTURES IN THE UNITED STATES: 1945-1971.

ALIOTO, JOSEPH L. 743

ALLDRITT, DONALD. 798

ALLEGANY COUNTY, MARYLAND. 411, 622

ALLEGHENY COUNTY, PENNSYLVANIA. 470, 581, 583, 584

ALLEN, BOB. 238

ALLEN, WILLIAM R. 143

ALLOUEZ, WISCONSIN. 573

ALMENDINGER, VLADIMIR V. 826

ALPERT, MILTON. 508, 525

ALTWIES, ROBERT. 468

AMERICAN BAR ASSOCIATION. SECTION OF LOCAL GOVERNMENT LAW. 003

AMERICAN MUNICIPAL ASSOCIATION. 184, 214, 344, 462, 829

AMERICAN SOCIETY OF PLANNING OFFICIALS. 004, 693

AMERICANS FOR DEMOCRATIC ACTION. 673

ANCEL, LOUIS. 427, 587

ANCHORAGE, ALASKA. 005

ANDERSON, J.O. 058, 315, 767

ANDERSON, PAUL J. 059, 143

ANDERSON, ROBERT T. 006, 059, 064

ANDERSON, WAYNE F. 222

ANDREWS, ELTON R. 047, 204

ANN ARBOR, MICHIGAN. 608

ANN ARUNDEL COUNTY, MARYLAND. 411

INDEX

ANNEXATION AND BOUNDARY CHANGES. 001, 004, 008, 012, 021, 025, 033, 039, 043, 047, 051, 055, 057, 058, 059, 061, 064, 065, 078, 094, 097, 102, 103, 108, 112, 129, 130, 131, 133, 138, 154, 155, 170, 171, 181, 184, 198, 200, 203, 204, 205, 216, 219, 223, 227, 228, 232, 235, 241, 245, 253, 258, 262, 265, 270, 284, 285, 286, 294, 300, 308, 329, 332, 339, 341, 342, 350, 354, 356, 362, 363, 364, 366, 377, 381, 387, 393, 394, 396, 397, 400, 419, 421, 431, 436, 444, 452, 472, 473, 485, 510, 531, 534, 535, 537, 538, 543, 549, 556, 557, 558, 560, 565, 566, 573, 581, 585, 589, 596, 597, 599, 601, 602, 603, 607, 608, 609, 615, 616, 621, 626, 627, 633, 649, 665, 669, 677, 679, 690, 691, 692, 697, 713, 729, 730, 779, 780, 783, 793, 794, 812, 819, 820, 835, 836

ANTON, THOMAS J. 007, 117

ARAUZ, F. 830

ARCULEO, ANGELO. 523

ARIZONA. 024, 025, 040, 184, 266, 334, 356, 357, 358, 414, 472, 758, 794

ARIZONA. STATE UNIVERSITY. INSTITUTE OF PUBLIC ADMINISTRATION. 794

ARIZONA. UNIVERSITY. BUREAU OF BUSINESS AND PUBLIC RESEARCH. 024, 025

ARKANSAS. 008, 129, 184, 206, 209, 269, 449, 472, 758

ARKANSAS. LEGISLATIVE COUNCIL. RESEARCH DEPARTMENT. 008

ARLINGTON COUNTY, VIRGINIA. 437

ARMS, RICHARD. 427

ARNEBERGH, ROGER. 060, 432

ARONSON, STEPHEN. 009

ASCHER, C.S. 830

ASCHMAN, FREDERICK. 222, 426, 539

ASHTABULA COUNTY, OHIO. 548

ASKEW, J.T. 141

ASSOCIATION OF BAY AREA GOVERNMENTS. 011, 066, 667, 674, 707

ASSOCIATION OF WASHINGTON CITIES. 070, 350

ATKINS, RICHARD A. 508

ATKINSON, HAROLD E. 426

REFORM OF LOCAL GOVERNMENT STRUCTURES IN THE UNITED STATES: 1945-1971.

ATLANTA, GEORGIA. 220, 221, 227, 235, 329, 364, 410, 430, 771

AUGENBLICK, ALAN. 618

AUSTIN, TEXAS. 228

AYERS, EUNICE. 468

BABCOCK, RICHARD F. 426, 427

BACH, IRA J. 222, 428

BAILEY, SCOTT. 238

BAIN, CHESTER W. 012, 013

BAIN, HENRY. 014

BAIR, FRED. 212

BAKER, BENJAMIN. 015

BALDWIN, HERBERT. 768

BALDWIN, ROSALIND. 390

BALTIMORE, MARYLAND. 034, 266, 411, 708, 830

BALTIMORE COUNTY, MARYLAND. 235, 411

BANE, FRANK. 389, 470, 767

BANKS, JOHN C. 016

BANOVETZ, JAMES M. 017, 018

BARDEN, CHARLES. 238

BARNES, PHILIP W. 019

BARRINGTON BOROUGH, NEW JERSEY. 201

BARTLES, WILLIAM H. 525

BASCHE, NANCY. 020

BATON ROUGE, LOUISIANA. 075, 143, 155, 199, 270, 364, 468, 639, 736, 803, 818, 833

BATTERTON, RICHARD Y. 767

INDEX

BATTLE CREEK, MICHIGAN. 100, 607

BAUER, WILLIAM J. 222

BAY AREA TRANSPORTATION STUDY COMMISSION. 063, 707

BEADES, JOHN J. 104

BEAVER COUNTY, PENNSYLVANIA. 582

BEBEE, MAYNARD. 390

BEBOUT, JOHN E. 476, 760

BEEBE, JAMES L. 432

BEHRENS, MANLEY L. 525

BEILBY, EBER. 058

BELL, GEORGE A. 044

BELL, JAMES R. 047, 204

BELLMAWR BOROUGH, NEW JERSEY. 201

BELLUSH, JEWELL L. 047, 204

BEMIS, GEORGE W. 020

BENNINGHOVEN, DONALD. 064

BENSON, CHARLES. 670

BENSON, GEORGE C.S. 760

BENTLEY, ALVIN M. 761

BENTON, W.E. 243

BENTON COUNTY, WASHINGTON. 464

BENTON HARBOR, MICHIGAN. 608

BERGEN, H.E. 065

BERNALILLO COUNTY, NEW MEXICO. 107

BERNARD, WILLIAM CHARLES. 021

BERRY, DEAN L. 022

BERRY, DONALD S. 428

REFORM OF LOCAL GOVERNMENT STRUCTURES IN THE UNITED STATES: 1945-1971.

BERTRAND, A.L. 388

BEST, WALLACE H. 047, 204

BIBLE, ALAN. 765

BIGGER, RICHARD. 047, 204, 379, 380, 381

BILLS (FRANK J.) AND ASSOCIATES. 023

BINGHAM, DAVID A. 024, 025

BIRD, FREDERICK L. 026

BIRKHEAD, GUTHERIE S. 027, 175, 498, 760

BIRMINGHAM, ALABAMA. 152, 235

BISHOP, WARREN A. 321

BLACK, FRANCIS J. 759

BLACK, GUY. 028

BLAIR, GEORGE S. 029, 828

BLAISDELL, NEAL. 767

BLAKEMAN, T. LEDYARD. 104

BLASER, LEE. 798

BLESSING, CHARLES. 222

BLOOM, LEON. 525

BLUE EARTH COUNTY, MINNESOTA. 030

BLUE EARTH COUNTY COUNCIL ON INTERGOVERNMENTAL RELATIONS (MINNESOTA). 030

BOD, ALEXANDER. 670

BOGUE, DONALD J. 222

BOLLENS, JOHN. 031, 047, 204, 667, 669, 743

BONELLI, FRANK G. 068

BOOTH, DAVID A. 032, 033, 225

BOSSELMAN, FRED. 720

BOSSERT, H. DALE. 390

INDEX

BOSTON, MASSACHUSETTS. 104, 145, 155, 235, 266, 414, 415

BOSTON COLLEGE. BUREAU OF PUBLIC AFFAIRS. 032, 225, 277, 547

BOSTON COLLEGE. COLLEGE OF BUSINESS ADMINISTRATION. 104

BOSTON METROPOLITAN DISTRICT COMMISSION. 145

BOWDEN, ELBERT V. 238

BOWDEN, KATHLEEN. 061

BOWEN, DON L. 034

BOWEN, HOWARD. 767

BOWIE, MARYLAND. 437

BRADFORD, ROBERT B. 231

BRAMAN, JAMES D. 471

BRANIGAN, EDWARD. 144

BRAY, ARTHUR. 768

BRAZER, HARVEY E. 027

BRAZIER, GARY. 315

BREAK, GEORGE. 670

BRENNAN, S.C. 798

BRICKMAN, DAVID. 104

BRIDGE, FRANKLIN M. 035, 508

BRILEY, BEVERLY. 036, 158, 468

BRINER, WILLIAM S. 058

BRISBANE, CALIFORNIA. 001

BRISBANE IMPROVEMENT ASSOCIATION. 001

BROCKETTE, M.L. 238

BROMAGE, ARTHUR W. 037, 038, 830

BROOKFIELD, MISSOURI. 620

BROWARD COUNTY, FLORIDA. 212

REFORM OF LOCAL GOVERNMENT STRUCTURES IN THE UNITED STATES: 1945-1971.

BROWDER, GORDON. 772

BROWN, BERNARD G. 039

BROWN, EDMUND G. 068

BROWN, JOE F. 238

BROWN, MARGERY H. 772

BROWN, WILLIE L. 743

BROWN COUNTY, WISCONSIN 573

BRUGMAN, BRUCE. 670

BRYAN, JAMES E. 493

BRYANT, STEWART. 670

BUCHANAN COUNTY, MISSOURI. 454

BUCHHOLZ, MRS. WERNER. 525

BUECHE, KENNETH G. 040

BUECHNER, JOHN C. 041, 042

BUREAU OF GOVERNMENTAL RESEARCH (NEW ORLEANS). 631

BUREAU OF GOVERNMENTAL RESEARCH AND SERVICES (SEATTLE, WASHINGTON). 070

BUREAU OF MUNICIPAL RESEARCH (SYRACUSE, NEW YORK). 043

BUREAU OF MUNICIPAL RESEARCH (TORONTO). 233

BURGESS, JAMES V. 044

BURKHEAD, JESSE. 175

BURNS, JOHN J. 390

BURNS, RALPH M. 468

BURTON, JOHN E. 389

BYRD, G.F. 798

CAHN, MRS. RICHARD. 231

CALHOUN COUNTY, MICHIGAN. 607

INDEX

CALIFORNIA. 001, 006, 011, 020, 031, 045, 046, 047, 048, 049, 050, 051, 052, 053, 054, 055, 056, 057, 058, 059, 060, 061, 062, 063, 064, 065, 066, 067, 068, 098, 108, 110, 142, 143, 145, 146, 151, 155, 158, 159, 160, 174, 184, 187, 204, 223, 229, 231, 234, 235, 236, 253, 255, 266, 311, 333, 335, 336, 337, 338, 345, 349, 359, 360, 364, 373, 374, 377, 379, 380, 381, 384, 386, 391, 392, 393, 394, 397, 410, 417, 419, 424, 432, 444, 468, 472, 498, 571, 606, 612, 615, 616, 646, 647, 648, 649, 650, 651, 652, 653, 654, 655, 656, 657, 658, 665, 666, 667, 668, 669, 670, 672, 673, 674, 684, 692, 707, 743, 758, 787, 793, 795, 818, 834, 835, 836

CALIFORNIA. COORDINATING COUNCIL ON URBAN POLICY. 045

CALIFORNIA. COUNCIL ON INTERGOVERNMENTAL RELATIONS. 046

CALIFORNIA. GOVERNOR'S COMMISSION OF METROPOLITAN AREA PROBLEMS. 047, 056, 059, 204, 666, 669

CALIFORNIA. INTERGOVERNMENTAL COUNCIL ON URBAN GROWTH. 048, 049

CALIFORNIA. LEGISLATURE. ASSEMBLY. INTERIM COMMITTEE ON CONSERVATION, PLANNING, AND PUBLIC WORKS. SUBCOMMITTEE ON PLANNING. 050

CALIFORNIA. LEGISLATURE. ASSEMBLY. INTERIM COMMITTEE ON MUNICIPAL AND COUNTY GOVERNMENT. 051, 052, 053, 054, 055, 056, 057, 058, 059, 060

CALIFORNIA. LEGISLATURE. ASSEMBLY. MUNICIPAL AND COUNTY GOVERNMENT COMMITTEE. 061

CALIFORNIA. LEGISLATURE. JOINT COMMITTEE ON BAY AREA REGIONAL ORGANIZATION. 062

CALIFORNIA. LEGISLATURE. SENATE. COMMITTEE OF GOVERNMENTAL EFFICIENCY. 063

CALIFORNIA. LEGISLATURE. SENATE. COMMITTEE ON LOCAL GOVERNMENT. 064

CALIFORNIA. LEGISLATURE. SENATE. FACT FINDING COMMITTEE ON LOCAL GOVERNMENT. 066

CALIFORNIA. LEGISLATURE. SENATE. INTERIM COMMITTEE ON BAY AREA PROBLEMS. 067

CALIFORNIA. LEGISLATURE. SENATE. SUBCOMMITTEE OF THE SENATE COMMITTEE ON LOCAL GOVERNMENT. 065

CALIFORNIA. STATE ADVISORY COMMISSION ON INTERGOVERNMENTAL RELATIONS. 066

CALIFORNIA. UNIVERSITY. BUREAU OF GOVERNMENTAL RESEARCH. 183

CALIFORNIA. UNIVERSITY. BUREAU OF PUBLIC ADMINISTRATION. 419, 571, 665, 666, 671, 672

REFORM OF LOCAL GOVERNMENT STRUCTURES IN THE UNITED STATES: 1945-1971.

CALIFORNIA. UNIVERSITY. CENTER FOR PLANNING AND DEVELOPMENT RESEARCH, INSTITUTE OF URBAN AND REGIONAL DEVELOPMENT. 182

CALIFORNIA. UNIVERSITY. DEPARTMENT OF POLITICAL SCIENCE. 384

CALIFORNIA. UNIVERSITY. INSTITUTE OF GOVERNMENT AND PUBLIC AFFAIRS. 187, 223, 253, 272, 684, 692, 743

CALIFORNIA. UNIVERSITY. INSTITUTE OF GOVERNMENTAL AFFAIRS. 108, 174, 377, 787

CALIFORNIA. UNIVERSITY. INSTITUTE OF GOVERNMENTAL STUDIES. 142, 146, 336, 337, 667, 670, 674

CALIFORNIA. UNIVERSITY. INSTITUTE OF URBAN AND REGIONAL DEVELOPMENT. 210

CALIFORNIA CONTRACT CITIES ASSOCIATION. 068

CALKINS, HOWARD A. 733

CALVERT COUNTY, MARYLAND. 411

CALWA-MALAGA AREA, CALIFORNIA. 836

CALWA-MALAGA DEVELOPMENT ASSOCIATION. 836

CAMBRIDGE, MARYLAND. 276

CAMERON, GORDON K. 525

CAMPBELL, CLIFFORD J. 427

CAMPBELL, ERNEST HOWARD. 069, 070, 321

CAMPBELL, O.W. 166, 432, 470, 759

CAMPEN, HOWARD W. 204

CANADA. 127, 143, 145, 155, 235, 362, 364, 373, 374, 432, 444, 445, 470, 532, 638, 639, 667, 803, 818, 830, 833

CANTERBURY, CHARLES T. 704

CAPE, WILLIAM H. 071, 072, 073, 074, 156

CARBERT, LESLIE E. 142

CARDWELL, ROSSON L. 222

CARHART, BARTLEY R. 490

CARLMAN, LEONARD. 427

INDEX

CARLSON, THOMAS M. 231

CAROLINE COUNTY, MARYLAND. 411

CARPENTER, RICHARD. 231, 432

CARR, FRANCIS J. 231

CARROLL, J. DOUGLAS. 222, 428

CARROLL COUNTY, MARYLAND. 411

CARTER, RICHARD FRANK. 064

CASS, CHARLES. 238

CASSELLA, WILLIAM N. 075, 158

CATOOSA COUNTY, GEORGIA. 629, 630

CEASE, RONALD C. 464

CECIL COUNTY, MARYLAND. 076, 411

CECIL COUNTY, MARYLAND. GOVERNMENTAL STUDY COMMISSION. 076

CHADMAN, S.B. 468

CHAMBER OF COMMERCE OF THE UNITED STATES. 077

CHAMBERLAIN, CLARENCE. 525

CHAMBERLIN, JOSEPH E. 078

CHAMPAIGN, ILLINOIS. 461

CHANDLER, L.E. 079

CHAPEL HILL, NORTH CAROLINA. 004

CHAPIN, F. STUART. 765

CHAOMAN, JERRY. 238

CHAPMAN, RICHARD D. 104

CHAPPELL, GREGG. 238

CHARLES COUNTY, MARYLAND. 411

CHARLESTON, SOUTH CAROLINA. 080, 081, 082, 354, 627, 697

CHARLESTON, SOUTH CAROLINA. UNIFICATION STUDY BOARD. 080

REFORM OF LOCAL GOVERNMENT STRUCTURES IN THE UNITED STATES: 1945-1971.

CHARLESTON, WEST VIRGINIA. 004, 691

CHARLESTON, WEST VIRGINIA. MUNICIPAL PLANNING COMMISSION. 691

CHARLESTON COUNTY, SOUTH CAROLINA. 081, 082

CHARLESTON COUNTY, SOUTH CAROLINA. CHARTER COMMISSION. 081, 082

CHARLESTON CHAMBER OF COMMERCE (SOUTH CAROLINA). 627

CHARTERS. 005, 015, 016, 024, 031, 036, 038, 041, 074, 076, 081, 082, 084, 087, 092, 093, 107, 136, 149, 158, 163, 164, 171, 196, 208, 214, 235, 250, 261, 262, 264, 274, 301, 324, 325, 328, 340, 346, 353, 391, 392, 395, 404, 422, 423, 425, 459, 462, 465, 474, 476, 477, 488, 490, 494, 497, 501, 502, 505, 506, 524, 528, 529, 547, 550, 551, 563, 564, 567, 584, 588, 597, 621, 623, 628, 632, 634, 644, 650, 651, 652, 653, 654, 655, 694, 704, 716, 722, 723, 732, 738, 739, 744, 792, 833

CHATHAM COUNTY, GEORGIA. 083

CHATHAM COUNTY, GEORGIA. LOCAL GOVERNMENT STUDY COMMISSION. 083

CHATTANOOGA, TENNESSEE. 629, 630, 729

CHATTANOOGA AREA REGIONAL COUNCIL OF GOVERNMENTS. 630

CHATTERS, CARL H. 539

CHERINGTON, CHARLES R. 145

CHICAGO, ILLINOIS. 007, 017, 018, 116, 213, 222, 235, 266, 301, 302, 303, 425, 426, 427, 428, 429, 538, 539, 541, 542, 544, 552, 683, 709

CHILDS, RICHARD S. 084

CHO, YONG H. 085

CHOCTAWHATCHEE REGION, ALABAMA. 268

CHOCTAWHATCHEE REGIONAL LIBRARY. 268

CHRISTENSEN, FRED. 468

CHRISTOPHER, GEORGE. 204

CHUTE, CHARLTON, F. 760

CINCINNATI, OHIO. 264, 265, 626

CINCINNATI. UNIVERSITY. INSTITUTE OF GOVERNMENTAL RESEARCH. 264

CINCINNATI BUREAU OF GOVERNMENTAL RESEARCH. 086

INDEX

CITIZEN PARTICIPATION. 002, 011, 016, 054, 088, 089, 092, 104, 105, 114, 124, 126, 137, 141, 182, 185, 202, 205, 209, 210, 223, 226, 254, 257, 259, 262, 263, 266, 270, 271, 294, 304, 312, 323, 330, 334, 368, 376, 390, 391, 392, 418, 435, 442, 456, 457, 471, 473, 478, 546, 575, 600, 611, 625, 652, 653, 662, 663, 670, 675, 678, 682, 709, 712, 734, 743, 748, 769, 770, 771, 798, 832

CITIZENS BUDGET COMMISSION. 634

CITIZENS COMMITTEE FOR METROPOLITAN GOVERNMENT (NASHVILLE, TENNESSEE). 087

CITIZENS' CONFERENCE FOR GOVERNMENTAL COOPERATION (OREGON). 088

CITIZEN'S COUNCIL ON CITY PLANNING. 089

CITIZENS' HOUSING AND PLANNING COUNCIL OF NEW YORK. 327

CITIZENS LEAGUE (MINNEAPOLIS, MINNESOTA). 090, 091

CITIZENS LEAGUE OF MINNEAPOLIS AND HENNEPIN COUNTY. 092, 093

CITIZENS RESEARCH COUNCIL OF MICHIGAN. 037, 075, 094, 095, 096, 097, 098, 099, 100, 101, 102, 103

CITIZENS UNION OF THE CITY OF NEW YORK. 327

CITIZENS UNION RESEARCH FOUNDATION. 084, 105

CITY CLUB OF PORTLAND. 106

CITY-COUNTY CHARTER COMMITTEE, ALBUQUERQUE, NEW MEXICO. 107

CITY PLANNING AND ARCHITECTURAL ASSOCIATES. 209

CLACKAMAS COUNTY, OREGON. 362, 562, 597, 599

CLARK, JAMES L. 108

CLARK, JOSEPH S. 765

CLARK COUNTY, NEVADA. 023

CLARK COUNTY, OREGON. 597

CLAUNCH, JOHN M. 109

CLAY COUNTY, MISSOURI. 453

CLAYTON, ROSS. 183

CLEARWATER, FLORIDA. 593

CLEVELAND, HARLAN. 389

REFORM OF LOCAL GOVERNMENT STRUCTURES IN THE UNITED STATES: 1945-1971.

CLEVELAND, OHIO. 110, 111, 113, 114, 115, 161, 235, 266, 275, 339, 545

CLEVELAND BUREAU OF GOVERNMENTAL RESEARCH. 110, 111, 112

CLEVELAND METROPOLITAN SERVICES COMMISSION. 113, 242, 274, 275

CLEVELAND METROPOLITAN SERVICES COMMISSION. STUDY GROUP ON GOVERNMENT ORGANIZATION. 114

CLEVELAND METROPOLITAN SERVICES COMMISSION. STUDY GROUP ON LAND USE AND DEVELOPMENT. 115

CLINTON, GORDON S. 761

COCHRAN, DAVE. 238

COFFEE, RICHARD J. 618

COHN, RUBIN G. 116

COKE, JAMES G. 117, 828

COLEMAN, WILLIAM G. 119, 146, 468, 684, 766

COLLEGE PARK, MARYLAND. 437

COLLIER, JAMES M. 118

COLORADO. 016, 021, 035, 040, 041, 042, 078, 120, 121, 122, 123, 157, 184, 314, 363, 364, 386, 445, 472, 758, 804

COLORADO. DIVISION OF LOCAL GOVERNMENT. 120

COLORADO. GOVERNOR'S LOCAL AFFAIRS STUDY COMMISSION. 121, 122

COLORADO. STATE PLANNING COMMISSION. 123

COLORADO. UNIVERSITY. BUREAU OF GOVERNMENTAL RESEARCH AND SERVICE. 021, 035, 040, 041, 042

COLORADO. UNIVERSITY. BUREAU OF STATE AND COMMUNITY SERVICE. 157

COLORADO CONFERENCE FOR THE STUDY OF URBAN AND COMMUNITY PROBLEMS. 123

COLORADO SPRINGS, COLORADO. 078, 364

COLORADO SPRINGS, COLORADO. OFFICE OF THE CITY MANAGER. 078

COLORADO STATE ASSOCIATION OF COUNTY COMMISSIONERS. 157

COLQUITT COUNTY, GEORGIA. 124

INDEX

COLQUITT COUNTY COUNCIL ON INTERGOVERNMENTAL RELATIONS (GEORGIA). 124

COLUMBIA, SOUTH CAROLINA. 352

COLUMBIA COUNTY, OREGON. 562, 597

COLUMBIAN RESEARCH INSTITUTE (PORTLAND, OREGON). 464

COLUMBIANA COUNTY, OHIO. 548

COMMISSION GOVERNMENT. 048, 071, 079, 106, 109, 118, 119, 136, 139, 140, 196, 197, 213, 215, 226, 249, 269, 273, 274, 314, 320, 325, 326, 350, 352, 375, 398, 399, 404, 435, 488, 592, 593, 622, 681, 705, 708, 727, 738, 744, 785, 790, 796, 822

COMMITTEE FOR ECONOMIC DEVELOPMENT. 125, 126, 127

COMMITTEE OF ONE HUNDRED. 128

COMMITTEE OF 100 FOR PULASKI COUNTY. GOVERNMENT OPERATIONS COMMITTEE. 129

COMMUNITY CONTROL. 020, 105, 125, 127, 137, 175, 182, 210, 323, 327, 376, 391, 456, 573, 575, 603, 653, 670, 770, 773

COMMUNITY RESEARCH (DAYTON). 130, 131, 132, 133, 134, 135, 136

COMMUNITY SERVICE, INCORPORATED (YELLOW SPRINGS, OHIO). 137

COMMUNITY SERVICES COMMISSION FOR DAVIDSON COUNTY AND THE CITY OF NASHVILLE (TENNESSEE). 138

COMMUNITY STUDIES (KANSAS CITY, MISSOURI). 139

CONDON, GEORGE A. 140

CONFERENCE OF METROPOLITAN AREA PROBLEMS, EMORY UNIVERSITY, 1961. 141

CONFERENCE ON BAY AREA REGIONAL ORGANIZATION, 1970. 142

CONFERENCE ON CURRENT GOVERNMENTAL PROBLEMS, 10TH, UNIVERSITY OF MASSACHUSETTS, 1950. 144

CONFERENCE ON GOVERNMENT OF METROPOLITAN AREAS, UNIVERSITY OF PENNSYLVANIA, 1957. 145

CONFERENCE ON INTERGOVERNMENTAL RELATIONS, BERKELEY, CALIFORNIA, 1966. 146

CONFERENCES ON COMMUNITY PLANNING, 1967-1968. 143

CONKLING, GEORGE J. 768

CONLEY, JUDY B. 068

REFORM OF LOCAL GOVERNMENT STRUCTURES IN THE UNITED STATES: 1945-1971.

CONNECTICUT. 147, 148, 149, 172, 184, 225, 235, 248, 315, 378, 382, 383, 385, 413, 472, 714, 715, 716, 717, 758, 797

CONNECTICUT. COMMISSION TO STUDY THE NECESSITY AND FEASIBILITY OF METROPOLITAN GOVERNMENT. 147

CONNECTICUT. UNIVERSITY. INSTITUTE OF PUBLIC SERVICE. 148, 382, 383, 714, 715, 716, 717, 797

CONNECTICUT. UNIVERSITY. INSTITUTE OF URBAN RESEARCH. 385

CONNECTICUT PUBLIC EXPENDITURE COUNCIL. 149

CONNERY, JOSEPH S. 065

CONNERY, ROBERT H. 150

CONNOR, EDWARD. 767, 830

CONROY, HAROLD. 390

CONSTANDSE, A.K. 388

CONTRA COSTA COUNTY, CALIFORNIA. 151, 359

CONTRA COSTA COUNTY, CALIFORNIA. OFFICE OF THE COUNTY ADMINISTRATOR. 151

COOK COUNTY, ILLINOIS. 017, 213, 302, 539

COOKE, FRANK J. 768

COOPER, WELDON. 152

COPE, ORIN K. 381

CORCORAN, PAUL R. 104

CORMAN, JAMES. 204

CORZINE, JOHN. 674

COSMAN, BURT. 525

COUNCIL GOVERNMENT. 009, 090, 091, 114, 367, 370, 433, 687, 830

COUNCIL OF STATE GOVERNMENTS. 153, 154, 155, 239

COUNCIL-MANAGER GOVERNMENT. 015, 038, 041, 042, 072, 076, 119, 179, 190, 208, 215, 218, 227, 230, 249, 266, 269, 273, 276, 320, 325, 326, 334, 348, 350, 368, 404, 405, 459, 475, 488, 536, 563, 592, 594, 614, 620, 623, 624, 636, 639, 648, 681, 708, 710, 714, 715, 716, 718, 727, 732, 738, 790, 796, 797, 799, 822

INDEX

COUNCILS OF GOVERNMENT. 011, 018, 019, 021, 062, 066, 068, 120, 128, 133, 135, 142, 143, 146, 156, 182, 187, 209, 238, 255, 256, 257, 265, 291, 305, 311, 337, 369, 410, 418, 424, 430, 437, 440, 449, 464, 468, 469, 478, 479, 480, 482, 483, 532, 548, 597, 610, 629, 630, 660, 667, 681, 698, 711, 734, 745, 781

COUNTY COMMISSIONERS CONFERENCE, 5TH, BOULDER, COLORADO, 1958. 157

COUNTY GOVERNMENT. 010, 017, 020, 022, 023, 025, 032, 034, 035, 037, 053, 065, 069, 071, 072, 076, 079, 081, 082, 083, 109, 110, 113, 114, 118, 120, 121, 122, 123, 129, 140, 152, 156, 157, 159, 173, 175, 176, 177, 178, 179, 185, 186, 189, 193, 194, 195, 199, 206, 212, 213, 226, 229, 274, 278, 281, 291, 292, 297, 298, 299, 300, 302, 303, 308, 310, 318, 321, 330, 332, 335, 343, 351, 363, 365, 371, 372, 382, 387, 398, 402, 408, 409, 411, 432, 447, 448, 452, 468, 484, 485, 487, 489, 490, 491, 505, 509, 533, 538, 546, 550, 553, 555, 559, 568, 571, 581, 583, 595, 605, 611, 613, 617, 618, 631, 637, 688, 698, 699, 701, 702, 703, 708, 719, 720, 726, 731, 736, 758, 778, 783, 785, 795, 804, 806, 811, 812, 813, 814, 815, 816, 817, 821, 831

COUNTY GOVERNMENT INSTITUTE. 036

COUNTY HOME RULE CONGRESS, NEW YORK, 1962. 158

COUNTY SUPERVISORS ASSOCIATION OF CALIFORNIA. 059, 159, 229

COURTNEY, JOSEPH P. 277

COVEY, C.D. 388

CRAWFORD, FRED G. 160

CROMARTY, ARTHUR. 768

CRONIN, ARTHUR D. 104

CROUCH, WINSTON W. 047, 145, 204, 432, 721

CROW, CHARLES. 238

CULLEN, RICHARD. 468

CULVER, LOWELL W. 143

CULVER, WILLIS. 671

CUMBERLAND, MARYLAND. 622

CUMMINGS, CHARLES. 064

CURRAN, MICHAEL P. 225, 277

CURRY, DAVID A. 065

REFORM OF LOCAL GOVERNMENT STRUCTURES IN THE UNITED STATES: 1945-1971.

CURRY, JOHN E. 618

CURTIN, DANIEL J. 047, 204

CUTLER, RICHARD. 819, 820

CUYAHOGA COUNTY, OHIO. 110, 161

CUYAHOGA COUNTY, OHIO. CHARTER COMMISSION. 161

DADE COUNTY, FLORIDA. 075, 143, 162, 163, 164, 165, 166, 167, 168, 169, 314, 333, 339, 362, 364, 373, 432, 444, 445, 468, 532, 605, 628, 639, 680, 694, 759, 803, 818, 825, 833

DADE COUNTY, FLORIDA. BUDGET DEPARTMENT. 162

DADE COUNTY, FLORIDA. CHARTER. 163

DADE COUNTY, FLORIDA. HOME RULE AMENDMENT. 164

DADE COUNTY, FLORIDA. METROPOLITAN DADE COUNTY PLANNING DEPARTMENT. 165

DADE COUNTY, FLORIDA. OFFICE OF COUNTY MANAGER. 166, 167, 168

DADE COUNTY RESEARCH FOUNDATION (FLORDIA). 169

DAIL, CHARLES C. 204

DALAND, ROBERT T. 170

DALEY, RICHARD. 428, 429, 470

DALLAS, TEXAS. 109, 266, 733

DALLAS COUNTY, TEXAS. 109

DALRYMPLE, TATE. 428

DALY, CASSIUS H. 768

DAUER, MANNING J. 171

DAVENPORT, DONALD H. 508

DAVIDSON COUNTY, TENNESSEE. 033, 036, 087, 138, 143, 158, 195, 202, 333, 364, 410, 465, 466, 532, 639, 818, 833

DAVIES, AUDREY M. 172

DAVIS, CHESTER R. 222, 426

INDEX

DAVIS, HARMER. 743

DAVIS, HOWARD. 832

DAVIS, J. WILLIAM. 173

DAVIS, RAYMOND G. 174

DAYTON, OHIO. 130, 131, 132. 133, 134, 135

DAYTON, OHIO. DIVISION OF HEALTH. 132

DEAN, GEORGE M. 231

DEAVER, CHESTER. 058

DEBS, ERNEST E. 068

DECATUR, GEORGIA. 176, 177

DECENTRALIZATION. 006, 020, 028, 090, 091, 105, 127, 233, 272, 327, 376, 601, 647

DE KALB, GEORGIA. 176, 177

DE KALB COUNTY, GEORGIA. LOCAL GOVERNMENT COMMISSION. 176, 177, 178

DELAKE, OREGON. 565

DELAWARE. 117, 179, 184, 244, 410, 472, 576, 577, 578, 579, 580, 586, 590, 742, 758

DELAWARE. GOVERNOR'S COMMITTEE ON REORGANIZATION OF THE GOVERNMENT OF NEW CASTLE COUNTY, DELAWARE. 179

DE LONE, DON E. 231

DEMING, GEORGE H. 180, 390, 571, 733, 760

DENKER, U.A. 798

DENNEY, HUGH, 773

DENT, ROBERT C. 204

DENTON, EUGENE H. 181

DENVER, COLORADO. 021, 035, 122, 314, 364, 386

DENVER. UNIVERSITY. DEPARTMENT OF GOVERNMENT MANAGEMENT. 397

DENVER COUNTY, COLORADO. 021, 035

REFORM OF LOCAL GOVERNMENT STRUCTURES IN THE UNITED STATES: 1945-1971.

DES MOINES, IOWA. 687

DETROIT, MICHIGAN. 235, 266, 303, 323, 417, 418, 431, 443, 608, 830

DEUTSCH, KARL W. 182

DEVENDORF, EARL. 389

DEWART, WILLIAM. 064

DEYO, ALDEN. 238

DILWORTH, RICHARDSON. 761, 765

DINERMAN, BEATRICE. 183

DISTRICT GOVERNMENT. 013, 020, 021, 050, 105, 121, 232, 327, 386, 403, 436, 596, 607, 645

DISTRICT OF COLUMBIA. 014, 205, 235, 255, 256, 265, 410, 417, 437, 498, 575, 643, 758, 764

DIXON, ROBERT G. 184

DOBLER, CLIFFORD I. 468

DOHM, RICHARD R. 156

DONNENWIRTH, CLAIR. 767

DONOGHUE, JAMES R. 185, 186

DORCHESTER COUNTY, MARYLAND. 411

DORN, WARREN. 432

DOSS, JIM. 238

DOUGLAS, PETER. 187

DOUGLASS, PAUL. 638

DOUTHIT, ANCIL M. 238

DOVELL, J.E. 188, 189

DOWDEN, JAMES. 238

DOWLING, EDWARD T. 190

DOWNS, JAMES C. 733

DOYLE, JOHN. 238

INDEX

DRURY, JAMES W. 191

DUKE, RICHARD D. 471

DUMAS, WOODROW W. 143

DUNCAN, JOHN PAUL. 192, 193, 194

DUNCAN, WILLIAM E. 064

DUNCOMBE, HERBERT SYDNEY. 195, 468, 601

DUNN, FRANCIS. 231

DUNNUM, CARROLL M. 068

DURHAM, NORTH CAROLINA. 196, 197, 537

DURHAM CITY-COUNTY CHARTER COMMISSION (NORTH CAROLINA). 196, 197

DURHAM COUNTY, NORTH CAROLINA. 196, 197

DUTTON, W.C. 471

DUVAL COUNTY, FLORIDA. 077, 211, 639, 818

DYCKMAN, JOHN W. 670

DYER, JOHN A. 218, 268

DYERSBURG, TENNESSEE. 198

DYERSBURG REGIONAL PLANNING COMMISSION (TENNESSEE). 198

DYGERT, PAUL. 670

EAST BATON ROUGE PARISH COUNCIL, LOUISIANA. 199

EAST BATON ROUGE PARISH COUNTY, LOUISIANA. 199

EAST BAY REGIONAL PARK DISTRICT (SAN FRANCISCO). 707

EAST ST. LOUIS, ILLINOIS. 705, 706

EATON, JOE. 759

EBERLE, FREDERICK. 638

EBY, MARTIN K. 798

EDELMAN, SIDNEY. 200

REFORM OF LOCAL GOVERNMENT STRUCTURES IN THE UNITED STATES: 1945-1971.

EDWARDS, WILLIAM. 832

EFFROSS, HARRIS E. 201

EICHLER, JOSEPH L. 231

EISNER, LESTER. 390

ELAZAR, DANIEL J. 010, 202

EL CAJON VALLEY, CALIFORNIA. 379

ELISON, LARRY M. 772

ELK RIVER BASIN AREA, ALABAMA. 268

ELK RIVER DEVELOPMENT ASSOCIATION. 268

ELKIN, NORMAN N. 425

ELKINS, EUGENE R. 203

EMERSON, HAVEN. 144

EMMERICH, HERBERT. 470

EMORY UNIVERSITY. INSTITUTE OF CITIZENSHIP. 141

ENGELBERT, ERNEST A. 047, 204

ENGLAND. 833

ERBER, ERNEST. 490

ERIC HILL ASSOCIATES. 629

ERICSON, ELMER. 427

ESCAMBIA COUNTY, FLORIDA. 211, 639

ESCHWEILER, PETER Q. 720

EUBANKS, SAM B. 231

EUGENE, OREGON. 566

EURMAN, STUART. 205

EVANS, ARTHUR. 759

EVANS, I.W. 772

EVERS, K.T. 830

INDEX

EWALD, WILLIAM R. 206

EWING TOWNSHIP, NEW JERSEY. 201

FAIN, JAMES. 158

FAIRFAX, VIRGINIA. 208, 437

FAIRFAX COUNTY, VIRGINIA. 207, 208, 437, 611, 785, 786

FAIRFAX COUNTY, VIRGINIA. BOARD OF COUNTY SUPERVISORS. 207

FAIRFAX COUNTY, VIRGINIA. COMMISSION ON URBAN COUNTY GOVERNMENT. CHARTER COMMITTEE. 208

FAIRVIEW PARK, OHIO. 112

FALES, JAMES M. 419

FARGO, NORTH DAKOTA. 551

FASCELL, DANTE B. 761

FEDERATION. 045, 047, 049, 119, 124, 125, 126, 127, 133, 145, 146, 152, 153, 155, 166, 182, 183, 204, 205, 216, 232, 235, 258, 265, 267, 272, 282, 313, 315, 321, 329, 331, 333, 339, 366, 373, 406, 445, 464, 467, 473, 548, 607, 608, 626, 648, 661, 667, 678, 681, 747

FEENY, JOHN. 508

FEISS, CARL. 209, 638, 761

FELLIN, PHILLIP A. 678

FELT, JAMES. 390

FERGUSON, SALLY. 706

FERGUSON, WARREN. 068

FERRELL, JOSEPH S. 536

FICKLIN, JOHN R. 146, 684

FISCHER, CLAUDE S. 210

FLANNERY, JAMES J. 212

FLEMMING, ROBERT. 238

FLINT, MICHIGAN. 608

FLORIDA. 075, 077, 143, 162, 163, 164, 165, 166, 167, 168, 169, 171, 184, 188, 189, 205, 211, 212, 235, 246, 260, 269, 314, 333, 339, 362, 364, 373, 374, 414, 432, 438, 444, 445, 468, 470, 472, 532, 553, 593, 605, 628, 638, 639, 667, 680, 694, 736, 758, 759, 803, 818, 825, 833

FLORIDA. LEGISLATIVE SERVICE. 211

FLORDIA. STATE UNIVERSITY. BUREAU OF GOVERNMENTAL RESEARCH AND SERVICE. 212

FLORIDA. UNIVERSITY. BUREAU OF BUSINESS AND ECONOMIC RESEARCH. 825

FLORIDA. UNIVERSITY. PUBLIC ADMINISTRATION CLEARING SERVICE. 171, 188, 189, 246, 260, 333, 635, 680

FLORO, GEORGE K. 710

FLYNN, JOHN E. 768

FORDE, KEVIN M. 213

FORDHAM, JEFFERSON B. 158, 214, 721, 760

FORSYTH COUNTY, NORTH CAROLINA. 004

FORT WORTH, TEXAS. 733

FORTENBERRY, CHARLES N. 269

FOSSEY, RALPH. 759

FRANCIS, CLARENCE. 523

FRANCOIS, FRANCIS. 720

FRANKLIN COUNTY, WASHINGTON. 464

FRANZEN, JAMES J. 058

FREDERICK COUNTY, MARYLAND. 411

FREEMAN, ROY. 493

FREMONT, CALIFORNIA. 616

FRESNO, CALIFORNIA. 835, 836

FRESNO, CALIFORNIA. METROPOLITAN STUDY COMMITTEE. 835

FRIEDELBAUM, STANLEY H. 215

FRIEDEN, BERNARD J. 216

INDEX

FRIEDLAND, LOUIS L. 791

FRIEDMAN, ROBERT S. 034, 278

FRIESEMA, H. PAUL 217, 688

FRISINA, MARY. 060

FRONTENAC, MISSOURI. 237

FROSH, STANLEY B. 158

FRYE, JOHN C. 423

FRYE, ROBERT J. 218

FRYER, ROBERT E. 219, 791

FUGIEL, PETER J. 017

FULTON COUNTY, GEORGIA. 220, 221, 364

FULTON COUNTY, GEORGIA. LOCAL GOVERNMENT COMMISSION. 220, 221

FULTON-DE KALB HOSPITAL AUTHORITY. 221

GALEGAR, WILLIAM C. 238

GALLAGHER, JOHN F. 223

GALLAS, EDWARD C. 468

GALLOWAY, JAMES L. 224

GARDINER, FREDERICK G. 145, 470

GARDNER, JAMES L. 798

GARDNER, JOHN W. 743

GARDNER, NEELY D. 146

GARRETT COUNTY, MARYLAND. 411

GARVEY, JOHN. 766

GASTONIA, NORTH CAROLINA. 004

GAUS, JOHN M. 389

GEORGE WASHINGTON UNIVERSITY. PROGRAM OF POLICY STUDIES IN SCIENCE AND TECHNOLOGY. 028

GEORGIA. 044, 083, 124, 141, 176, 177, 184, 220, 221, 227, 235, 269, 329, 364, 410, 430, 472, 629, 630, 758, 771

GEORGIA. UNIVERSITY. BUREAU OF PUBLIC ADMINISTRATION. 227

GEORGIA. UNIVERSITY. INSTITUTE OF COMMUNITY AND AREA DEVELOPMENT AND INSTITUTE OF LAW AND GOVERNMENT. 044

GEORGIA-TENNESSEE REGIONAL HEALTH COMMISSION. 630

GERARD, ROY. 720

GERE, EDWIN ANDRUS. 225

GETTING, VLADO A. 144

GIBSON, FRANK K. 226, 227

GILL, JOSEPH C. 060

GILLESPIE, JOHN. 228

GILLIAM, HAROLD. 743

GILLIES, JAMES. 047, 204

GLADFELDER, JANE. 229

GLOUCESTER CITY, NEW JERSEY. 201

GODDARD, JAMES E. 428

GOFF, CHARLES D. 230

GOLDEN GATE AUTHORITY COMMISSION. 231

GOODBREAD, VERNE. 246

GOODLET, JAMES. 759

GOODLOE, THOMAS. 064

GOODMAN, ROY M. 523

GOODWIN, GEORGE. 144, 232

GORYNSKI, JULIUSZ. 233

GOURLEY, FRANZE. 238

INDEX

GOVE, SAMUEL K. 010, 234

GOVERNMENT AFFAIRS FOUNDATION. 235, 470

GOVERNMENT RESEARCH INSTITUTE (ST. LOUIS, MISSOURI). 236, 237

GOVERNMENTAL CONSOLIDATION. 001, 006, 018, 023, 033, 035, 036, 051, 052, 054, 066, 075, 077, 080, 081, 083, 086, 095, 099, 100, 101, 103, 111, 112, 122, 132, 133, 139, 143, 149, 151, 152, 155, 167, 171, 188, 192, 196, 197, 200, 202, 205, 206, 212, 216, 221, 227, 228, 237, 241, 251, 254, 258, 260, 264, 272, 283, 293, 302, 304, 306, 308, 309, 329, 331, 332, 333, 339, 350, 361, 362, 363, 364, 366, 369, 375, 384, 396, 401, 407, 409, 413, 420, 422, 423, 425, 436, 444, 445, 461, 464, 465, 466, 467, 473, 485, 487, 510, 532, 538, 543, 548, 554, 557, 559, 565, 572, 585, 597, 599, 606, 607, 608, 632, 640, 649, 667, 678, 681, 692, 694, 695, 697, 698, 729, 735, 747, 779, 780, 781, 783, 784, 788, 789, 799, 817, 825, 831

GOVERNMENTAL SEPARATION. 014, 075, 133, 151, 155, 212, 216, 241, 302, 339, 362, 364, 366, 396, 403, 445, 464, 467, 538, 543, 607, 681, 683, 747, 781, 788

GOVERNOR'S INTERGOVERNMENTAL RELATIONS AND REGIONAL PLANNING WORKSHOP, 4TH, AUSTIN, TEXAS, 1969. 238

GRADY, J.H. 830

GRAHAM, DONALD M. 104

GRANAHAN, KATHRYNE. 761

GRAND FORKS, NORTH DAKOTA. 551

GRAND RAPIDS, MICHIGAN. 365, 604

GRANITE CITY, ILLINOIS. 405

GRANT, DANIEL. 235

GRAVES, FRANK. 768

GRAVES, GENE H. 017

GRAVES, LEON B. 073

GRAVES, W. BROOKE. 239, 240

GREELEY, SAMUEL A. 539

GREEN, PHILIP. 536

GREENBELT, MARYLAND. 437

REFORM OF LOCAL GOVERNMENT STRUCTURES IN THE UNITED STATES: 1945-1971.

GREENBERG, MILTON. 241, 242

GREENE, LEE S. 243, 760

GREENVILLE, TENNESSEE. 728

GREER, SCOTT. 027

GRIER, GEORGE W. 244

GRIFFENHAGEN AND ASSOCIATES. 177

GRIFFENHAGEN-KROEGER. 245

GRIFFITHS, MARTHA W. 761

GRIGGS, BERTRAM S. 146

GROBMAN, HULDA. 246

GROSS, BERTRAM M. 418

GROSSE POINT, MICHIGAN. 095

GRUBB, HERBERT. 238

GRUEN, VICTOR. 733

GRUMM, JOHN G. 243

GRUNWALD, ROBERT. 834

GRYGOTIS, ANNA. 493

GUGIN, DAVID A. 247

GUILFORD COUNTY, NORTH CAROLINA. 194

GULICK, LUTHER. 141, 145, 248, 389, 470, 571

GUNLOCK, VIRGIL E. 539

GUNTHER, JOHN J. 766

GUSTAFSON, NEIL. 772

GUTHEIM, FREDERICK. 765

HAAG, JAMES J. 249, 250

HAAR, CHARLES. 721

INDEX

HACKETT, JAMES E. 222

HAEFELE, E.T. 426

HAGENSICK, A. CLARKE. 251, 252

HAGERSTOWN, MARYLAND. 623

HAGMAN, DONALD G. 253, 684

HAIGHT, ALFRED W. 508

HAINES, FRANK W. 617

HALL, CHARLES. 468

HAM, ELTON W. 254

HAMILTON, RANDY. 670, 773

HAMILTON, THOMAS H. 389

HAMILTON COUNTY, OHIO. 264, 626

HAMILTON COUNTY, TENNESSEE. 629, 630, 729

HAMILTON COUNTY RESEARCH FOUNDATION (OHIO). 266

HAMMOCK, TED L. 227

HAMPTON, VIRGINIA. 235, 784

HANNAH, JOHN A. 470

HANSON, ROYCE. 255, 256, 469

HANTEN, EDWARD. 085

HARFORD COUNTY, MARYLAND. 411

HARMON, JAMES. 379, 380

HARRAL, HENRY. 828

HARRIS, BRITTON. 721

HARRIS, CHARLES W. 257

HARRIS, DALE. 772

HARRIS, SEYMOUR. 104

HARRIS COUNTY, TEXAS. 039, 258, 724

REFORM OF LOCAL GOVERNMENT STRUCTURES IN THE UNITED STATES: 1945-1971.

HARRIS COUNTY, TEXAS. HOME RULE COMMISSION. 258

HARRISS, C. LOWELL. 523

HART, W. 830

HARTKE, VANCE. 765

HARTLEY, REX. 259

HARTMAN, GEORGE W. 222, 428

HARTMAN, RICHARD C. 478

HARWELL, JIM. 238

HARWOOD, ROBERT. 601

HATCH, STANLEY C. 058

HAUPTMANN, JERZY. 156

HAVARD, WILLIAM C. 260

HAWAII. 261, 346, 362, 472, 613, 758

HAWAII. LEGISLATIVE REFERENCE BUREAU. 261

HAWAII. UNIVERSITY. LEGISLATIVE REFERENCE BUREAU. 346

HAWKINS, BRETT W. 262

HAWLEY, WILLIS D. 146

HAYES, FRED O'R. 429

HAYMAN, DONALD. 536

HAYWARD, CALIFORNIA. 616

HAZELTON, PENNSYLVANIA. 375, 585

HEATON, MRS. GEORGE. 064

HEDGES, CHARLES W. 104, 468

HEIKOFF, JOSEPH. 427

HEIN, CLARENCE J. 388, 603

HEISSENBUTTEL, HENRY. 525

HENIG, HOWARD. 390

INDEX

HENNEPIN COUNTY, MINNESOTA. 091, 092, 093, 328

HENNIGAN, ROBERT D. 390, 508

HENRICO COUNTY, VIRGINIA. 194, 236, 632

HENRY, F. PATRICK. 835

HENRY COUNTY, INDIANA. 263

HENRY COUNTY, INDIANA. COUNCIL ON INTERGOVERNMENTAL RELATIONS. 263

HERMAN, HAROLD. 175

HERMAN, HERBERT. 175

HERMAN, M. JUSTIN. 670

HERRELL, CLIFF. 759

HERRICK, JOSEPH C. 468

HERRING, FRANCIS W. 047, 204

HESSLER, IOLA O. 264, 265, 266

HETLAND, JAMES L. 142

HETRICK, CHARLES B. 224, 267, 570, 587

HEWITT, G. WILFRED. 231

HEYMAN, IRA M. 743

HICKEY, JAMES. 670

HIGGINS, DANIEL J. 064

HIGHSAW, ROBERT B. 268, 269

HILL, FRANCIS. 830

HILLENBRAND, BERNARD F. 143, 158, 429, 761, 766

HILLERY, GEORGE A. 270

HILLSBOROUGH COUNTY, FLORIDA. 211, 212, 639

HINDMAN, JO. 271

HIRSCH, WERNER Z. 272

HIRSTEIN, WILLIAM. 058

REFORM OF LOCAL GOVERNMENT STRUCTURES IN THE UNITED STATES: 1945-1971.

HOBBS, EDWARD H. 273

HOLDEN, MATTHEW. 274, 275

HOLJEVAC, V. 830

HOLLANDS, ROGER G. 276

HOLLIMAN, WILLIAM. 064

HOLLINGER, L.S. 468

HOLMGREN, R. BRUCE. 539

HOLTMAN, WALTER P. 047, 204

HOME RULE. 003, 009, 010, 024, 037, 041, 055, 068, 069, 074, 075, 076, 082, 086, 088, 097, 098, 102, 116, 119, 121, 122, 138, 142, 149, 154, 158, 161, 164, 191, 192, 203, 211, 214, 219, 224, 225, 227, 236, 247, 252, 258, 277, 287, 293, 325, 331, 333, 340, 342, 346, 365, 378, 386, 396, 404, 413, 414, 416, 419, 431, 439, 440, 441, 446, 455, 462, 495, 499, 501, 506, 514, 526, 532, 547, 551, 567, 570, 581, 584, 587, 588, 593, 609, 622, 624, 625, 642, 668, 670, 682, 686, 698, 708, 724, 730, 738, 739, 772, 777, 778, 790, 815, 816

HOMER, PORTER WYMAN. 143

HONIKMAN, A.H. 830

HONOLULU, HAWAII. 362, 613

HONOLULU COUNTY, HAWAII. 362

HORNE, CHARLES F. 068

HORONJEFF, ROBERT. 670

HORTON, ROBERT A. 143

HOUSTON, TEXAS. 039, 258, 266, 724, 733

HOWARD, L. VAUGHAN. 278

HOWARD, S. KENNETH. 536

HOWARD COUNTY, MARYLAND. 411

HOWARDS, IRVING. 010, 279

HOWSON, LOUIS R. 539

HOYT, JOHN S. 280

INDEX

HUDSON, TOM. 058

HUGHES, JOHN H. 389

HUGHS, RICHARD J. 768

HULTON, CHARLES. 670

HUMMEL, DON. 767

HUMPHREY, HUBERT H. 469

HUNGER, JOHN M. 281

HUNNICUTT, WARREN P. 246

HUNTER, DWIGHT K. 598

HUNTER, FAY. 670

HUNTLEIGH VILLAGE, MISSOURI. 237

HURD, T. NORMAN. 389, 390

HURF, GEORGE B. 246

HUTCHISON, CLAUDE B. 204, 231

HUTCHISON, THEODORE M. 282

HUTH, ORA. 142

HYDE, VICTOR. 427

ICABONI, ANGELO. 204

ICE, ALTEN. 238

IDAHO. 184, 195, 283, 472, 530, 601, 642, 758

IDAHO. LEGISLATIVE COUNCIL. COMMITTEE ON LOCAL GOVERNMENT. 283

IDAHO. UNIVERSITY. BUREAU OF PUBLIC AFFAIRS RESEARCH. 530, 601, 642

IHNER, RUTH. 143

REFORM OF LOCAL GOVERNMENT STRUCTURES IN THE UNITED STATES: 1945-1971.

ILLINOIS. 007, 010, 017, 018, 116, 184, 213, 222, 224, 234, 235, 266, 267, 279, 284, 285, 286, 287, 288, 289, 290, 291, 292, 293, 294, 295, 296, 297, 298, 299, 300, 301, 302, 303, 405, 425, 426, 427, 428, 429, 472, 538, 539, 540, 541, 542, 543, 544, 552, 570, 587, 683, 705, 706, 709, 758

ILLINOIS. CITIES AND VILLAGES MUNICIPAL PROBLEMS COMMISSION. 284, 285, 286, 287, 288, 289

ILLINOIS. COMMISSION ON INTERGOVERNMENTAL COOPERATION. 290

ILLINOIS. COMMISSION ON LOCAL GOVERNMENT. 291

ILLINOIS. COMMISSION ON URBAN AREA GOVERNMENT. 292, 293

ILLINOIS. CONSTITUTIONAL CONVENTION, 1969-1970. COMMITTEE ON LOCAL GOVERNMENT. 294, 295, 296

ILLINOIS. COUNTY PROBLEMS COMMISSION. 297, 298, 299

ILLINOIS. COUNTY STUDY AND SURVEY COMMISSION. 300

ILLINOIS. LEGISLATIVE COUNCIL. 301, 302

ILLINOIS. UNIVERSITY. INSTITUTE OF GOVERNMENT AND PUBLIC AFFAIRS. 007, 010, 116, 234, 461, 540

ILLINOIS CITY MANAGERS' ASSOCIATION. STUDY COMMITTEE ON MERTROPOLITAN GOVERNMENT. 303

ILLINOIS MUNICIPAL LEAGUE. COMMITTEE ON HOME RULE. 010

INCORPORATION. 006, 014, 016, 025, 040, 051, 055, 059, 065, 097, 099, 102, 107, 130, 154, 181, 204, 206, 208, 214, 221, 227, 234, 241, 245, 250, 253, 293, 324, 341, 357, 377, 379, 380, 381, 384, 394, 397, 404, 452, 488, 538, 543, 549, 599, 602, 609, 615, 626, 646, 664, 665, 666, 727, 779, 786, 787, 790, 793, 802, 836

INDIAN NATIONS, OKLAHOMA. 745

INDIANA. 004, 184, 235, 263, 304, 305, 306, 307, 308, 309, 310, 347, 366, 371, 407, 472, 637, 712, 758

INDIANA. COMMISSION TO STUDY THE OVERLAPPING OF FUNCTIONS OF PUBLIC OFFICIALS AND GOVERNING BODIES IN INDIANAPOLIS AND MARION COUNTY. 304

INDIANA. DEPARTMENT OF COMMERCE. DIVISION OF PLANNING. 305, 306

INDIANA. LEGISLATIVE ADVISORY COMMISSION. MUNICIPAL PROBLEMS STUDY COMMITTEE. 307

INDIANA. METROPOLITAN AREA STUDY COMMISSION OF MARION COUNTY. 308

INDEX

INDIANA. UNIVERSITY. DEPARTMENT OF GOVERNMENT. 347

INDIANA CITIZENSHIP CLEARING HOUSE. 347

INDIANAPOLIS, INDIANA. 235, 304, 305, 308, 309, 310, 366, 407, 637

INDIANAPOLIS CHAMBER OF COMMERCE. GOVERNMENTAL AFFAIRS DEPARTMENT. 309

INDIANAPOLIS CHAMBER OF COMMERCE. GOVERNMENTAL RESEARCH DEPARTMENT. 310

INGHAM COUNTY, MICHIGAN. 603

INGRAM, PETER. 058

INSITUTE FOR LOCAL SELF GOVERNMENT (CALIFORNIA). 311, 312

INSTITUTE FOR RURAL AMERICA. 313

INSTITUTE OF ADMINISTRATION. 172

INSTITUTE OF PUBLIC ADMINISTRATION. 150

INTER-COUNTY REGIONAL PLANNING COMMISSION (DADE COUNTY, FLORIDA). 314

INTERGOVERNMENTAL COOPERATION. 010, 018, 023, 025, 029, 030, 044, 045, 046, 047, 048, 049, 052, 053, 054, 056, 060, 066, 068, 070, 083, 088, 095, 096, 102, 109, 111, 121, 124, 127, 128, 133, 135, 137, 143, 144, 146, 153, 156, 170, 216, 217, 234, 238, 239, 240, 246, 255, 259, 263, 268, 275, 276, 279, 282, 290, 294, 306, 316, 317, 319, 320, 344, 351, 359, 360, 364, 375, 376, 383, 385, 389, 390, 401, 406, 417, 420, 437, 442, 453, 454, 480, 491, 492, 498, 504, 507, 510, 511, 513, 514, 515, 516, 517, 518, 530, 532, 542, 544, 561, 562, 595, 598, 604, 613, 658, 670, 699, 705, 707, 711, 712, 749, 750, 751, 752, 753, 754, 759, 760, 762, 763, 766, 767, 800, 801, 802, 803, 804, 805, 811, 823, 824

INTERGOVERNMENTAL COOPERATION COUNCIL (OREGON). 316, 317

INTERPLAN CORPORATION. 209

IOWA. 184, 217, 318, 319, 320, 472, 636, 686, 687, 688, 710, 713, 718, 758

IOWA. STATE UNIVERSITY. INSTITUTE OF PUBLIC AFFAIRS. 636, 713

IOWA. UNIVERSITY. INSTITUTE OF PUBLIC AFFAIRS. 217, 318, 319, 320, 686, 687, 688, 718, 773

IRION, FREDERICK C. 243

ITTNER, RUTH. 321, 322

REFORM OF LOCAL GOVERNMENT STRUCTURES IN THE UNITED STATES: 1945-1971.

JACKSON, PENROSE B. 212

JACKSON, SAMUEL C. 479

JACKSON, MICHIGAN. 101

JACKSON COUNTY, MICHIGAN. 101

JACKSONVILLE, FLORIDA. 077, 639, 818

JACOBSON, NORMAN. 670

JAMES COUNTY, VIRGINIA. 799

JAMISON, ROBERT. 238

JANOWITZ, MORRIS. 323

JANS, RALPH T. 324

JAVITS, JACOB, 523

JEFFERSON COUNTY, ALABAMA. 152

JEFFERSON COUNTY, KENTUCKY. 387

JEFFERSON PARISH, LOUISIANA. 278

JERSEY CITY, NEW JERSEY. 325

JERSEY CITY. CHARTER COMMISSION OF THE CITY OF JERSEY CITY. 325

JESPERSON, NORVELL. 238

JOHNSON, ARTHUR S. 405

JOHNSON, JAMES C. 684

JOHNSON COUNTY, KANSAS. 139

JOHNSTON, WAYNE A. 222

JOINER, CHARLES A. 326

JOINT COMMITTEE OF THE CITIZENS UNION AND CITIZENS HOUSING AND PLANNING COUNCIL OF NEW YORK CITY. 327

JOINT COMMITTEE ON BAY AREA REGIONAL ORGANIZATION (SAN FRANCISCO). 063

JOINT COMMITTEE ON CHARTER REVIEW (MINNEAPOLIS, MINNESOTA). 328

JOINT COMMITTEE ON METROPOLITAN GROWTH OF THE LEAGUE OF WOMEN VOTERS OF ATLANTA AND OF DE KALB COUNTY. 329

INDEX

JOJKIC, D. 830

JONES, MURRAY. 539, 830

JONES, RON. 238

JONES, VICTOR. 146, 539, 571, 670, 721, 834

JORDAN, C.H. 388

JOSEPH, WILLIAM E. 493

JUNZ, SOPHIE. 706

KAGO, HERBERT M. 175

KAHN, ALFRED J. 471

KAISER, EDGAR F. 231

KALAMAZOO, MICHIGAN. 241, 254, 608, 640, 641

KALAMAZOO COUNTY, MICHIGAN. 241, 330, 331, 332, 640, 641

KALAMAZOO COUNTY CITIZENS STUDY COMMITTEE ON COMMUNITY SERVICES. 241, 330, 331, 332, 640, 641

KAMMERER, GLADYS M. 333

KAMP, MAURICE. 468

KANSAS. 071, 072, 073, 139, 181, 184, 191, 243, 398, 399, 472, 592, 710, 758, 796, 798

KANSAS. UNIVERSITY. GOVERNMENTAL RESEARCH CENTER. 071, 072, 073, 181, 191, 398, 399, 592, 710, 796

KANSAS CITY, KANSAS. 398

KANSAS CITY, MISSOURI. 205, 235, 266, 450, 453

KANTER, DONALD L. 222

KEAN, R. GORDON. 468

KEATING, KENNETH. 765

KEHEW, ROGER. 064

KEITH, GEORGE D. 156

REFORM OF LOCAL GOVERNMENT STRUCTURES IN THE UNITED STATES: 1945-1971.

KEITHLEY, JEROME. 064

KELLER, LEWIS. 047, 059, 204, 665, 669

KELLEY, KENNETH J. 104

KELLY, AUGUSTIN J. 493

KELLY, DON. 238

KELSO, PAUL. 334

KENNEDY, DAVID M. 222

KENNEDY, EDWARD. 315

KENNEDY, HAROLD W. 068, 204, 335, 432, 468

KENNEDY, W. NORMAN. 047, 571

KENT, T.J. 336, 337, 338

KENT COUNTY, MARYLAND. 411

KENT COUNTY, MICHIGAN. 365

KENTUCKY. 004, 184, 235, 269, 339, 340, 341, 342, 343, 387, 472, 758, 777

KENTUCKY.   LEGISLATIVE RESEARCH COMMISSION. 339, 340, 341, 342, 343, 777

KEPNER, KATHLEEN R. 806

KERR, CLARK. 571

KERSTETTER, JOHN R. 184, 344

KESTENBAUM, MEYER. 470

KIKER, JOHN E. 246

KILPATRICK, WYLIE. 246

KINCAID, JOHN I. 238

KING, JAMES S. 428

KING COUNTY, WASHINGTON. 321, 367, 370, 433, 434

KINGSPORT, TENNESSEE. 531

KINSTON, NORTH CAROLINA. 004

KLAMATH FALLS, OREGON. 566

INDEX

KLEIJN, A. 830

KLOSS, HENRY. 345

KNEIER, CHARLES M. 010

KNOX, JOHN T. 142, 670

KNOX COUNTY, TENNESSEE. 351

KNOXVILLE, TENNESSEE. 339, 351

KORNHAUSER, WILLIAM. 670

KOSAKI, RICHARD H. 346

KOVAR, EDWARD B. 104

KRAMER, FRED. 429

KRAMER, LEONARD J. 347

KRANENBERG, GEORGE. 427

KREGG, GEORGE W. 390

KRETEK, GERMAINE. 761, 765

KUNZ, ARTHUR. 720

KWEDER, B. JAMES. 348

LADUE, MISSOURI. 237

LAGRANGE, GEORGIA. 227

LAKE TAHOE, CALIFORNIA. 174, 349

LAKE TAHOE, NEVADA. 174, 349

LAKE TAHOE JOINT STUDY COMMITTEE. 349

LAKEWOOD, CALIFORNIA. 006, 054, 234, 335, 380, 410, 432, 444, 468, 787, 793, 818

LAMB, JOHN S. 350

LAMBERT, WALTER N. 351

LA MESA, CALIFORNIA. 381

REFORM OF LOCAL GOVERNMENT STRUCTURES IN THE UNITED STATES: 1945-1971.

LANHAM, FRITZ. 238

LANSING, MICHIGAN. 603

LANTES, THOMAS. 231

LARSEN, CHRISTIAN L. 352, 353, 354

LARSON, DONALD R. 470, 761

LASCELLES, G.A. 432

LAS VEGAS, NEVADA. 023

LATAH COUNTY, IDAHO. 195

LAUBER, JOHN G. 468

LAVERNE, THOMAS. 525

LAWNDALE, CALIFORNIA. 410

LAWRENCE, H. BEMIS. 468

LAWSON, WILLIAM. 238

LAZZARA, JOSEPH. 768

LEADLEY, SAMUEL M. 355

LEAGUE OF ARIZONA CITIES AND TOWNS. 356, 357, 358

LEAGUE OF CALIFORNIA CITIES. 059, 359, 360

LEAGUE OF IOWA MUNICIPALITIES. 319, 636, 713

LEAGUE OF VIRGINIA COUNTIES. 226

LEAGUE OF VIRGINIA MUNICIPALITIES. COMMITTEE ON CONSOLIDATION OF LOCAL GOVERNMENTS. 361

LEAGUE OF WOMEN VOTERS OF ATLANTA COUNTY. 329

LEAGUE OF WOMEN VOTERS OF BEAVERTON, MILWAUKEE, OSWEGO, AND PORTLAND (OREGON). 362

LEAGUE OF WOMEN VOTERS OF COLORADO. COMMITTEE FOR THE STUDY OF GOVERNMENTAL RELATIONSHIPS. 363, 364

LEAGUE OF WOMEN VOTERS OF DE KALB COUNTY. 329

LEAGUE OF WOMEN VOTERS OF GRAND RAPIDS, MICHIGAN. 365

INDEX

LEAGUE OF WOMEN VOTERS OF INDIANAPOLIS. 366

LEAGUE OF WOMEN VOTERS OF KING COUNTY (SEATTLE). 367

LEAGUE OF WOMEN VOTERS OF MONTGOMERY COUNTY, MARYLAND. LOCAL GOVERNMENT COMMITTEE. 368

LEAGUE OF WOMEN VOTERS OF PORTLAND AND EAST MULTNOMAH COUNTY (OREGON). 369

LEAGUE OF WOMEN VOTERS OF SEATTLE-BELLEVUE-RENTION HIGHLINE. 370

LEAGUE OF WOMEN VOTERS OF TERRE HAUTE, INDIANA. 371

LEAGUES OF WOMEN VOTERS OF WEST VIRGINIA. 372

LEASK, SAMUEL. 373, 374

LEBANON COUNTY, PENNSYLVANIA. 582

LEDUE, EDGAR C. 375

LEE, CARTER. 277

LEE, EUGENE. 142, 231, 479, 670

LEE, RICHARD C. 104

LEE, ROBERT D. 375

LEE, WALTER. 144

LEEMANS, A.F. 376

LEGG, HERBERT H. 069

LE GROTTE, JIM. 238

LE GUTES, RICHARD T. 377

LEHMAN, MAXWELL. 378

LEHMANN, RICHARD. 819, 820

LEIFFER, DON B. 379, 380, 381

LEIPZIGER-PEARCE, HUGO. 733

LEON COUNTY, FLORIDA. 212

LEVENSON, ROSALINE. 382, 383

LEVITT, ARTHUR. 389

REFORM OF LOCAL GOVERNMENT STRUCTURES IN THE UNITED STATES: 1945-1971.

LEVY, JOHN. 720

LEWIS, HENRY. 536

LEWIS, ROBERT L. 238

LEXINGTON, KENTUCKY. 004

LICHTERMAN, MARTIN. 315

LINCOLN, NEBRASKA. 004

LINCOLN COUNTY, OREGON. 565, 566

LINDEEN, GORDON. 064

LINDSAY, JOHN V. 523

LIPMAN, WILLIAM F. 047, 204

LIPPMAN, JACK. 525

LITTLE, RICHARD. 384

LITTLE CITY HALLS. 327, 391, 771

LITTLEFIELD, NEIL O. 385, 386

LIVINGSTON, LAWRENCE. 231

LLOYD, GERALD. 525, 720

LLOYD, RAYMOND. 146

LOCAL GOVERNMENT IMPROVEMENT COMMITTEE, JEFFERSON COUNTY, KENTUCKY. 387

LOCAL GOVERNMENT WORKSHOP. STATE UNIVERSITY COLLEGE OF EDUCATION AT ALBANY, 1960. 389

LOCKARD, DUANE. 617

LOEB, AL M. 146

LOGAN, JOHN A. 222, 427

LOHMAN, JOSEPH. 670

LONDON, ENGLAND. 833

LONG, NORTON. 222, 773

LONG BEACH, CALIFORNIA. 793

INDEX

LOS ANGELES, CALIFORNIA. 006, 020, 031, 053, 054, 145, 160, 235, 266, 333, 373, 384, 391, 392, 393, 394, 410, 419, 432, 692, 787, 818

LOS ANGELES. CITY CHARTER COMMISSION. 391

LOS ANGELES. OFFICE OF CITY ADMINISTRATIVE OFFICER. 373

LOS ANGELES (CITY). TOWN HALL. 031

LOS ANGELES CHAMBER OF COMMERCE. 432

LOS ANGELES COUNTY, CALIFORNIA. 006, 020, 053, 054, 066, 110, 145, 158, 234, 333, 335, 359, 364, 384, 392, 393, 394, 410

LOS ANGELES COUNTY. CHARTER STUDY COMMISSION. 392

LOS ANGELES COUNTY. CHIEF ADMINISTRATIVE OFFICE. 393

LOS ANGELES COUNTY. CHIEF ADMINISTRATIVE OFFICE. COUNTY-CITY SERVICES SECTION. 394

LOUDOUN COUNTY, VIRGINIA. 437

LOUISIANA. 075, 079, 143, 155, 199, 235, 269, 270, 278, 364, 395, 468, 472, 631, 639, 736, 758, 803, 818, 833

LOUISIANA. LEGISLATIVE COUNCIL. 395

LOUISIANA. STATE UNIVERSITY. AGRICULTURAL EXPERIMENT STATION. AGRICULTURAL AND MECHANICAL COLLEGE. 270

LOUISIANA. STATE UNIVERSITY. DEPARTMENT OF AGRICULTURAL ECONOMICS AND AGRIBUSINESS. 388

LOUISVILLE, KENTUCKY. 387

LOVELACE, ROBERT A. 420

LOWER FOX RIVER VALLEY, WISCONSIN. 711

LOWER PENINSULAR, VIRGINIA. 784

LOWER RIO GRANDE VALLEY DEVELOPMENT COUNCIL. 737

LOYOLA UNIVERSITY. CENTER FOR RESEARCH IN URBAN GOVERNMENT. 017, 018, 213, 683, 709

LUBIN, JERRY. 670

LUKENS, MATTHIAS. 768

LUND, JOSEPH W. 104

REFORM OF LOCAL GOVERNMENT STRUCTURES IN THE UNITED STATES: 1945-1971.

LUSTIS, MORTON. 828

LUTZ, STUART E. 390

LYFORD, JOSEPH. 670

LYON, LEVERETT S. 539

LYON, LOUIS. 238

McALLEN, TEXAS. 735

McBEATH, GRETCHEN. 548

McBRIEN, J.P. 065

McCANN, WILLIAM J. 060

McCLURE, WESLEY. 204

MacCORKEL, STUART A. 396

MacDONALD, J.K. 058

MacDOUGALL, WILLIAM R. 058, 158, 231, 468

McELLIGOTT, MICHAEL. 598

McELLIGOTY, PEGGY L. 058

McGEE, CUSHMAN. 389

McGEE, VERNON. 238

McGINLEY, GORDON W. 060

McGINNIS, PATRICK B. 104

McGOLDRICK, JOSEPH. 523

McGRATH, THOMAS F. 508

McGREW, JAMES WILSON. 397

McHANEY, POWELL B. 470

McHUGH, JOHN. 618

McINNIS, JOHN F. 060, 068, 670

McKENNA, JOSEPH M. 398, 399

INDEX

McKINLEY, DORIS E. 493

MacLAUGHLIN, FRANCIS M. 058

McMAHON, ALICE. 638

McMAHON, DANIEL. 768

McMORRAN, J. BURCH. 389

McNAIR, ROBERT E. 478

MACOMB COUNTY, MICHIGAN. 096, 443

McPHEETERS, HAROLD L. 508

MacRAE, ROBERT. 539

MACY, JOHN W. 146

MADDOX, ROBERT C. 768

MADDOX, RUSSELL WEBBER. 400

MADISON, SOUTH DAKOTA. 710

MAHAR, RALPH C. 144

MAIHL, VIOLA R. 493

MAINE. 184, 225, 249, 250, 315, 382, 401, 402, 413, 472, 758

MAINE. INTERGOVERNMENTAL RELATIONS COMMISSION. 401, 402

MAINE. UNIVERSITY. BUREAU OF PUBLIC ADMINISTRATION. 249, 251

MANKATO, MINNESOTA. 030

MAKIELSKI, S.J. 403

MALONE, WILLIAM M. 231

MALTESTON, JACK D. 231

MANN, DEAN E. 025

MANN, MAVIS ANDREE. 404

MANN, SEYMOUR Z. 405

MANVEL, ALLEN D. 406, 758

MARCOU, GEORGE. 427

REFORM OF LOCAL GOVERNMENT STRUCTURES IN THE UNITED STATES: 1945-1971.

MARIN COUNTY, CALIFORNIA. 359

MARINER, ELWYN E. 144

MARINETTE, WISCONSIN. 230

MARION COUNTY, INDIANA. 304, 308, 309, 310, 366, 407, 637

MARION COUNTY, OREGON. 088, 316, 317, 610

MARION COUNTY GOVERNMENT STUDY COMMITTEE (INDIANA). 407

MARPLE, GARLAND. 390

MARS, DAVID. 143, 408

MARSHALL, JOHN E. 144

MARTENS, SHARON WILSON. 409

MARTIN, JUNE. 390, 508

MARTIN, PARK H. 470

MARTIN, ROSCOE C. 146, 175, 410, 772

MARYLAND. 004, 014, 034, 076, 098, 184, 195, 235, 256, 266, 353, 368, 411, 437, 472, 621, 622, 623, 624, 625, 643, 708, 758, 830

MARYLAND. STATE PLANNING DEPARTMENT. 411

MARYLAND. UNIVERSITY. COLLEGE OF BUSINESS AND PUBLIC ADMINISTRATION. BUREAU OF GOVERNMENT RESEARCH. 034, 708

MARYLAND. UNIVERSITY. COLLEGE OF BUSINESS AND PUBLIC ADMINISTRATION. BUREAU OF PUBLIC ADMINISTRATION. 353, 621, 624, 625

MARYLAND. UNIVERSITY. COLLEGE OF BUSINESS AND PUBLIC ADMINISTRATION. DEPARTMENT OF GOVERNMENT AND POLITICS. 622, 623

MARYLAND. UNIVERSITY. COLLEGE OF BUSINESS AND PUBLIC ADMINISTRATION. MARYLAND TECHNICAL ADVISORY SERVICE. BUREAU OF GOVERNMENTAL RESEARCH. 276

MARYLAND NATIONAL CAPITAL PARK AND PLANNING COMMISSION. 621, 643

MASON CITY, IOWA. 710

MASSACHUSETTS. 032, 104, 144, 145, 155, 184, 190, 225, 232, 235, 266, 277, 315, 382, 412, 413, 414, 415, 416, 472, 547, 758

MASSACHUSETTS. EXECUTIVE OFFICE FOR ADMINISTRATION AND FINANCE. OFFICE OF PLANNING AND PROGRAM COORDINATION. 412

INDEX

MASSACHUSETTS. LEGISLATIVE RESEARCH COUNCIL. 413, 414

MASSACHUSETTS. SPECIAL COMMISSION TO STUDY THE ORGANIZATION AND OPERATION OF THE METROPOLITAN DISTRICT COMMISSION. 415

MASSACHUSETTS. UNIVERSITY. BUREAU OF GOVERNMENTAL RESEARCH. 032, 190, 225, 232, 315, 416, 547

MASSACHUSETTS. UNIVERSITY. BUREAU OF PUBLIC ADMINISTRATION. 144

MATHEWS, STEVE. 238

MATHEWSON, KENT. 417, 418

MATTHEWS, DEAN S. 238

MAUER, THEODORE. 525

MAXON, DONALD L. 064

MAY, SAMUEL C. 419

MAYOR-COUNCIL GOVERNMENT. 015, 031, 035, 106, 119, 150, 160, 215, 227, 249, 266, 269, 273, 276, 320, 325, 328, 350, 352, 353, 371, 391, 404, 435, 455, 488, 536, 553, 564, 592, 614, 625, 681, 704, 708, 714, 715, 716, 722, 723, 727, 728, 738, 744, 790, 797, 822, 830

MAYS, CARL J. 525

MEDFORD, OREGON. 566

MEIER, RICHARD L. 182

MEISENHELDER, EDWARD W. 420

MELTZER, JACK. 426

MEMPHIS, TENNESSEE. 421, 422, 423

MEMPHIS AND SHELBY COUNTY PLANNING COMMISSION (TENNESSEE). 421, 422, 423

MENDELSON, ROBERT. 706

MENOMONEE FALLS, WISCONSIN. 822

MERCHANTVILLE BOROUGH, NEW JERSEY. 201

MERELMAN, JACK M. 146, 424

MERRIAM, ROBERT E. 425

MERRILL, MALCOLM H. 047, 204

REFORM OF LOCAL GOVERNMENT STRUCTURES IN THE UNITED STATES: 1945-1971.

METROPOLITAN AREA PLANNING CONFERENCE. 426, 427, 428, 429

METROPOLITAN ATLANTA COUNCIL OF LOCAL GOVERNMENTS. 430

METROPOLITAN DADE COUNTY TRANSIT AUTHORITY. 168

METROPOLITAN FUND. 096, 257, 418, 431

METROPOLITAN GOVERNMENT SYMPOSIUM, LOS ANGELES. 1958. 432

METROPOLITAN PLANNING COMMISSION (ATLANTA, GEORGIA). 221

METROPOLITAN PROBLEMS ADVISORY COMMITTEE (SEATTLE, WASHINGTON). 433, 434

METROPOLITAN REGIONAL COUNCIL. 378

METROPOLITAN ST. LOUIS SURVEY (MISSOURI). 435, 436

METROPOLITAN WASHINGTON COUNCIL OF GOVERNMENTS. 143, 437, 469

METZGER, KARL E. 768

MEYER, ORVILLE. 428

MEYERSON, MARTIN. 760

MIAMI, FLORIDA. 162, 165, 166, 167, 168, 169, 205, 235, 314, 333, 339, 362, 373, 374, 432, 438, 444, 470, 532, 605, 628, 639, 667, 680, 694, 736, 759, 803, 818, 825, 833

MIAMI, FLORIDA. CITY PLANNING BOARD. 438

MIAMI BEACH, FLORIDA. 167

MIAMI VALLEY, OHIO. 134, 135, 548

MIAMI VALLEY REGIONAL PLANNING COMMISSION. 134

MICHAEL, JAY. 060

MICHAELIAN, EDWIN G. 143, 390, 468, 768

MICHAELS, BURTON M. 073

MICHIGAN. 022, 037, 075, 094, 095, 096, 097, 098, 099, 100, 101, 102, 103, 128, 184, 219, 235, 241, 254, 266, 303, 323, 324, 330, 331, 332, 365, 386, 414, 417, 418, 431, 439, 440, 441, 443, 463, 472, 602, 603, 604, 607, 608, 640, 641, 695, 704, 738, 739, 758, 778, 779, 791, 830

MICHIGAN. CONSTITUTIONAL CONVENTION. CITIZENS ADVISORY COMMITTEE ON LOCAL GOVERNMENT. 439

INDEX

MICHIGAN. GOVERNOR'S SPECIAL COMMISSION ON URBAN PROBLEMS. 440

MICHIGAN. GOVERNOR'S STUDY COMMISSION ON COUNTY HOME RULE. 441

MICHIGAN. GOVERNOR'S STUDY COMMISSION ON METROPOLITAN AREA PROBLEMS. 442

MICHIGAN. STATE UNIVERSITY. INSTITUTE FOR COMMUNITY DEVELOPMENT AND SERVICES. 033, 326, 602, 603, 604, 695, 778, 779

MICHIGAN. SUPERVISORS INTER-COUNTY COMMITTEE. 443

MICHIGAN. UNIVERSITY. INSTITUTE OF PUBLIC ADMINISTRATION. BUREAU OF GOVERNMENT. 219, 323, 324, 704, 738

MICHIGAN. UNIVERSITY. LAW SCHOOL. 282, 386, 596, 677, 679, 800, 801

MIDLAND, MICHIGAN. 097, 608

MIDLAND COUNTY, MICHIGAN. 097

MID WILLAMETTE VALLEY, OREGON. 088, 259, 316, 317, 410, 417, 610

MILANDER, HENRY. 759

MILEUR, JEROME M. 225

MILLER, GEORGE JOHN. 171

MILLER, HARVEY D. 536

MILLER, JOHN. 670

MILLER, WILLIAM. 617, 618, 721

MILLON, MILTON B. 468

MILLS, HARLOW. 428

MILLS, W. RAYMOND. 222

MILLSAP, CLAUDE. 468

MILNER, JAMES. 721

MILWAUKEE, WISCONSIN. 235, 661, 663, 811, 812

MILWAUKEE COUNTY, WISCONSIN. 195, 281, 811, 812, 813

MINGO, JACK. 058

MINNEAPOLIS, MINNESOTA. 018, 090, 091, 092, 093, 126, 142, 143, 266, 328, 410, 614, 746

REFORM OF LOCAL GOVERNMENT STRUCTURES IN THE UNITED STATES: 1945-1971.

MINNESOTA. 018, 030, 040, 090, 091, 092, 093, 126, 142, 143, 184, 266, 280, 328, 410, 444, 445, 446, 447, 448, 472, 614, 746, 758

MINNESOTA. COMMISSION ON MUNICIPAL ANNEXATION AND CONSOLIDATION. 444

MINNESOTA. LEGISLATIVE RESEARCH COMMITTEE. 445, 446

MINNESOTA. LEGISLATURE. INTERIM COMMISSION ON LOCAL GOVERNMENTAL FISCAL PROBLEMS. 447

MINNESOTA. LEGISLATURE. INTERIM COMMISSION TO STUDY COUNTY AND TOWNSHIP GOVERNMENTS. 448

MINNESOTA. UNIVERSITY. INSTITUTE OF AGRICULTURE. AGRICULTURAL EXTENSION SERVICE AND AGRICULTURAL EXPERIMENT STATION. 280

MISSION, TEXAS. 735

MISSISSIPPI. 184, 209, 269, 273, 449, 472, 758

MISSISSIPPI. UNIVERSITY. BUREAU OF GOVERNMENT. 273

MISSISSIPPI. UNIVERSITY. BUREAU OF PUBLIC ADMINISTRATION. 269

MISSISSIPPI-ARKANSAS-TENNESSEE COUNCIL OF GOVERNMENTS. 209, 449

MISSOURI. 075, 098, 184, 205, 235, 236, 237, 266, 339, 386, 435, 436, 450, 451, 452, 453, 454, 472, 574, 620, 644, 645, 662, 678, 758

MISSOURI. GENERAL ASSEMBLY. JOINT COMMITTEE ON LOCAL GOVERNMENT. 450

MISSOURI. GENERAL ASSEMBLY. JOINT INTERIM COMMITTEE ON GOVERNMENTAL PROBLEMS IN ST. LOUIS AND ST. LOUIS COUNTY. 451

MISSOURI. GOVERNOR'S ADVISORY COUNCIL ON LOCAL GOVERNMENT LAW. 452

MISSOURI. UNIVERSITY. KANSAS CITY. SCHOOL OF LAW. 453

MISSOURI PUBLIC EXPENDITURE SURVEY. 454

MITCHELL, RICHARD N. 525

MITCHELL, ROBERT B. 428

MOAK, LENNOX L. 455, 721

MOCINE, CORWIN. 670

MODEL CITIES. 120, 457, 769

MODESTO, CALIFORNIA. 397

INDEX

MOGULOF, MELVIN B. 456, 457, 458

MOHAMED, M.H. 830

MONPENNY, PHILIP. 461

MONROE, MICHAEL. 479

MONROE COUNTY, MICHIGAN. 096, 443

MONROE COUNTY, NEW YORK. 126, 410, 459

MONROE COUNTY, NEW YORK. CHARTER COMMISSION. 459

MONTANA. 184, 194, 195, 460, 472, 758, 772

MONTANA. LEGISLATIVE COUNCIL. 460

MONTANA. UNIVERSITY. BUREAU OF GOVERNMENT RESEARCH. 772

MONTGOMERY, ALABAMA. 004

MONTGOMERY COUNTY, MARYLAND. 195, 256, 368, 411, 437, 621

MONTGOMERY COUNTY, OHIO. 132, 134, 135, 136

MONTGOMERY COUNTY, OHIO. GENERAL HEALTH DISTRICT. 132

MONTGOMERY COUNTY, OHIO. MAYOR-MANAGERS ASSOCIATION. 134

MOONEY, G.S. 830

MOORE, FRANK C. 158, 389, 470

MORGAN, JAMES R. 814, 815, 816, 817, 819, 820

MORGAN, ROBERT. 759

MORRIS, ROBERT C. 222

MORRISON, ISADORE. 468

MORRISON, L.S. 830

MORTUEDT, ROBERT A.L. 143

MOSES, ROBERT. 389

MOTT, RODNEY L. 462

MULTNOMAH COUNTY, OREGON. 362, 369, 554, 562, 597, 599

MUNDALE, CHARLES I. 678

REFORM OF LOCAL GOVERNMENT STRUCTURES IN THE UNITED STATES: 1945-1971.

MUNDT, PAUL F. 768

MUNDY, PAUL. 017

MUNGER, FRANK J. 175

MUNICIPAL CORPORATIONS. 013, 016, 027, 070, 108, 173, 250, 260, 273, 367, 370, 397, 399, 403, 410, 434, 451, 465

MUNICIPAL GOVERNMENT. 003, 022, 025, 027, 034, 037, 085, 093, 121, 141, 173, 186, 215, 227, 243, 249, 269, 291, 292, 303, 307, 310, 318, 341, 342, 347, 363, 365, 374, 388, 395, 404, 411, 432, 437, 447, 463, 466, 470, 491, 492, 493, 501, 508, 512, 513, 514, 515, 516, 517, 518, 519, 520, 523, 525, 526, 527, 532, 534, 536, 539, 540, 545, 550, 552, 555, 571, 581, 604, 605, 606, 617, 618, 628, 633, 638, 639, 662, 675, 676, 680, 682, 684, 685, 687, 696, 718, 721, 725, 733, 736, 758, 760, 761, 762, 763, 764, 767, 768, 777, 782, 783, 787, 791, 795, 798, 803, 807, 808, 809, 818, 825, 826, 827, 828, 833

MURPHY, CHARLES. 238

MURPHY, ELLIS P. 468

MURPHY, GEORGE E. 144

MURPHY, JOSEPH H. 389

MURTHA, WILLIAM E. 766

MUSICUS, MILTON. 390

MUSKEGON, MICHIGAN. 463

MUSKEGON, MICHIGAN. GREATER MUSKEGON'S PUBLIC STUDY COMMITTEE ON CONSOLIDATION SUBCOMMITTEE ON ADMINISTRATIVE ASPECTS. 463

MUSKIE, EDMUND S. 158, 315, 469

MYLLENBECK, WESLEY L. 464

NAFTALIN, ARTHUR. 143, 767

NAHAS, ROBERT T. 231

NASHVILLE, TENNESSEE. 033, 036, 087, 138, 143, 158, 202, 235, 262, 333, 339, 364, 410, 465, 466, 468, 532, 639, 667, 736, 818, 833

NASHVILLE, TENNESSEE. METROPOLITAN GOVERNMENT CHARTER COMMISSION. 465

NASHVILLE AND DAVIDSON COUNTY PLANNING COMMISSIONS (TENNESSEE). ADVANCE PLANNING AND RESEARCH DIVISION. 466

INDEX

NATHAN, HARRIET. 142, 743

NATIONAL ASSOCIATION OF COUNTIES. 158, 195, 240, 467, 468, 689

NATIONAL CAPITAL PARK AND PLANNING COMMISSION. 643

NATIONAL CONFERENCE OF COUNCIL OF GOVERNMENTS, 1ST, WASHINGTON, D.C., 1967. 469

NATIONAL CONFERENCE ON METROPOLITAN PROBLEMS. MICHIGAN STATE UNIVERSITY. 1956. 470

NATIONAL LEAGUE OF CITIES. 471, 472, 473

NATIONAL MUNICIPAL LEAGUE. 038, 474, 475, 476

NATIONAL MUNICIPAL LEAGUE. COMMITTEE ON A GUIDE FOR CHARTER COMMISSIONS. 477

NATIONAL OPINION RESEARCH CENTER. 202

NATIONAL SERVICE TO REGIONAL COUNCILS. 478, 479, 480, 481, 482, 483, 660

NAUGATUCK VALLEY, CONNECTICUT. 148

NEBRASKA. 004, 184, 472, 484, 485, 486, 487, 712, 758

NEBRASKA. LEGISLATIVE COUNCIL. COMMITTEE ON COUNTY GOVERNMENT. 484

NEBRASKA. LEGISLATIVE COUNCIL. COMMITTEE ON COUNTY GOVERNMENT REORGANIZATION. 485

NEBRASKA. LEGISLATIVE COUNCIL. COMMITTEE ON MUNICIPAL ANNEXATION. 486

NEBRASKA. LEGISLATIVE COUNCIL. COMMITTEE ON REORGANIZATION OF COUNTY GOVERNMENT. 487

NEIGHBOR, HOWARD D. 156

NEIGHBORHOOD CONTROL. 105, 182, 391, 406, 457, 471, 543, 638, 653, 709, 771

NELSON, JOHN. 525

NELSON, MICHAEL T. 601

NESTINGEN, IVAN. 767

NETZER, DICK. 523

NEVADA. 023, 174, 184, 349, 472, 758

NEW CASTLE COUNTY, DELAWARE. 179

REFORM OF LOCAL GOVERNMENT STRUCTURES IN THE UNITED STATES: 1945-1971.

NEW ENGLAND. 225, 315, 382

NEW ENGLAND STATE PLANNING DIRECTORS. 315

NEW HAMPSHIRE. 184, 225, 315, 382, 472, 758

NEW JERSEY. 015, 117, 118, 172, 184, 201, 215, 235, 244, 248, 325, 378, 472, 488, 489, 490, 491, 492, 493, 576, 577, 578, 579, 580, 586, 590, 617, 618, 742, 744, 758, 826

NEW JERSEY. COMMISSION OF MUNICIPAL GOVERNMENT. 488

NEW JERSEY. COUNTY AND MUNICIPAL GOVERNMENT STUDY COMMISSION. 489, 490, 491, 492

NEW JERSEY. COUNTY AND MUNICIPAL LAW REVISION COMMISSION. 493

NEW JERSEY. RUTGERS UNIVERSITY. BUREAU OF GOVERNMENT RESEARCH. 015, 118, 215, 617, 618

NEW MEXICO. 107, 184, 243, 472, 633, 758

NEW MEXICO. UNIVERSITY. DIVISION OF GOVERNMENT RESEARCH. 633

NEW ORLEANS, LOUISIANA. 155, 278, 631

NEW YORK. 043, 066, 098, 105, 126, 143, 150, 155, 158, 172, 175, 184, 235, 236, 248, 327, 378, 389, 390, 410, 414, 417, 451, 459, 472, 494, 495, 496, 497, 498, 499, 500, 501, 502, 503, 504, 505, 506, 507, 508, 509, 510, 511, 512, 513, 514, 515, 516, 518, 519, 520, 521, 522, 523, 524, 525, 526, 527, 528, 634, 685, 720, 722, 723, 758, 768, 826, 833

NEW YORK (STATE). COMMISSION ON GOVERNMENTAL OPERATIONS OF THE CITY OF NEW YORK. 497

NEW YORK (STATE). DEPARTMENT OF AUDIT AND CONTROL. 498

NEW YORK (STATE). EXECUTIVE DEPARTMENT. OFFICE FOR LOCAL GOVERNMENT. 389, 390, 499, 500, 501, 502, 503, 504, 505, 506, 507, 508

NEW YORK (STATE). LEGISLATURE. JOINT COMMITTEE ON METROPOLITAN AND REGIONAL AREAS STUDIES. 521, 522, 523, 524, 525

NEW YORK (STATE). LEGISLATURE. JOINT COMMITTEE ON METROPOLITAN AREAS STUDY. 509, 510, 511, 512, 513, 514, 515, 516, 517, 518, 519, 520

NEW YORK (STATE). TEMPORARY STATE COMMISSION ON THE CONSTITUTIONAL CONVENTION. 526

NEW YORK (STATE). TEMPORARY STATE COMMISSION TO STUDY THE ORGANIZATIONAL STRUCTURE OF THE GOVERNMENT OF THE CITY OF NEW YORK. 527

INDEX

NEW YORK. STATE COLLEGE OF AGRICULTURE AND LIFE SCIENCES. 355

NEW YORK. UNIVERSITY. GRADUATE SCHOOL OF PUBLIC AFFAIRS. 833

NEW YORK, NEW YORK. 105, 143, 150, 155, 172, 327, 417, 451, 494, 495, 496, 497, 527, 528, 634, 768, 826, 833

NEW YORK (CITY). CHARTER REVISION FOR THE CITY OF NEW YORK. 494

NEW YORK (CITY). MAYOR'S TASK FORCE ON REORGANIZATION OF THE CITY OF NEW YORK GOVERNMENT. 496

NEW YORK (CITY). MAYOR'S TASK FORCE ON THE CONSTITUTIONAL CONVENTION. 495

NEW YORK CHAMBER OF COMMERCE. 528, 529

NEWPORT NEWS, VIRGINIA. 235, 784

NICHOLS, GLENN W. 530, 601

NICHOLSON, LAWRENCE E. 678

NICKELL, JAMES M. 156

NICKERSON, EUGENE H. 768

NICKS, ROY S. 531

NOEL, G. 830

NORFOLK, VIRGINIA. 013

NORRGARD, DAVID L. 532

NORTH BEND, OREGON. 245

NORTH CAROLINA. 004, 184, 194, 196, 197, 235, 269, 348, 472, 498, 533, 534, 535, 536, 537, 758

NORTH CAROLINA. LOCAL GOVERNMENT STUDY COMMISSION. 533

NORTH CAROLINA. MUNICIPAL STUDY COMMISSION. 534, 535

NORTH CAROLINA. UNIVERSITY. INSTITUTE OF GOVERNMENT. 348, 536, 537

NORTH CENTRAL TEXAS. 734

NORTH DAKOTA. 184, 409, 472, 551, 758

NORTH DAKOTA. UNIVERSITY. BUREAU OF GOVERNMENTAL AFFAIRS. 409, 551

NORTHEAST OHIO. 548

REFORM OF LOCAL GOVERNMENT STRUCTURES IN THE UNITED STATES: 1945-1971.

NORTHEASTERN ILLINOIS. 007, 222, 234, 426, 427, 428, 429, 538, 539, 540, 541, 542, 543, 544, 552

NORTHEASTERN ILLINOIS AREA PLANNING COMMISSION. 222

NORTHEASTERN ILLINOIS METROPOLITAN AREA LOCAL GOVERNMENTAL SERVICES COMMISSION. 538, 539, 540, 541, 542

NORTHEASTERN ILLINOIS METROPOLITAN AREA PLANNING COMMISSION. 426, 427, 428, 429

NORTHEASTERN ILLINOIS PLANNING COMMISSION. 543, 544

NORTHEASTERN RESOURCES COMMITTEE. 315

NORTHROP, LUCIA. 493

NORTHWEST MUNICIPAL CONFERENCE OF NORTHWEST SUBURBAN COOK COUNTY. 587

NORTHWESTERN OHIO. 548

NORTON, JAMES A. 545

NUGENT, MRS. ASHLEY BAKER. 021

NUI, ROBERT A. 468

NUQUIST, ANDREW E. 546

OAKLAND, CALIFORNIA. 419

OAKLAND COUNTY, MICHIGAN. 096, 443

OAKWOOD, OHIO. 132

OAKWOOD, OHIO. CITY HEALTH DEPARTMENT. 132

O'BRIEN, EMMET. 390

OCCARLAKE, OREGON. 565

O'CONNOR, FRANK D. 523

ODEN, WILLIAM E. 173

OGILVIE, RICHARD B. 017

O'HARE, ROBERT J.M. 277, 547

OHIO. 085, 086, 098, 110, 111, 112, 113, 114, 115, 130, 131, 132, 133, 134, 135, 136, 161, 184, 235, 242, 264, 265, 266, 274, 275, 339, 386, 414, 472, 545, 548, 549, 550, 626, 758

INDEX

OHIO. DEPARTMENT OF URBAN AFFAIRS. 548

OHIO. LEGISLATIVE SERVICE COMMISSION. 549, 550

OHIO. UNIVERSITY. CENTER FOR URBAN STUDIES. 085

OHIO-KENTUCKY-INDIANA REGIONAL PLANNING AUTHORITY. 265

OKA, KENNETH. 759

OKLAHOMA. 184, 192, 193, 194, 243, 386, 472, 745, 758

OKLAHOMA. STATE LEGISLATIVE COUNCIL. 192, 193, 194

OLSON, HOWARD. 427, 428, 539

OMAHA, NEBRASKA. 004

OMBUDSMAN. 391

OMDAHL, LLOYD B. 409, 551

ONONDAGA COUNTY, NEW YORK. 174

OPPERMAN, PAUL. 222, 426, 427, 428, 429, 552

ORANGE COUNTY, CALIFORNIA. 359

ORANGE COUNTY, FLORIDA. 211, 553, 639

ORANGE COUNTY, FLORIDA. LOCAL GOVERNMENT STUDY COMMISSION. 553

OREGON. 088, 106, 184, 235, 245, 259, 316, 317, 362, 369, 386, 410, 417, 472, 554, 555, 556, 557, 558, 559, 560, 561, 562, 563, 564, 565, 566, 567, 568, 569, 597, 598, 599, 600, 610, 758

OREGON. LEGISLATIVE ASSEMBLY. INTERIM COMMITTEE ON CITY-COUNTY CONSOLIDATION IN MULTNOMAH COUNTY. 554

OREGON. LEGISLATIVE ASSEMBLY. INTERIM COMMITTEE ON LOCAL GOVERNMENT. 555, 556, 557

OREGON. UNIVERSITY. BUREAU OF GOVERNMENTAL RESEARCH AND SERVICE. 559, 560, 711

OREGON. UNIVERSITY. BUREAU OF MUNICIPAL RESEARCH AND SERVICE. 561, 562, 563, 564, 565, 566, 567, 568

OREGON TAX RESEARCH. 569

ORLANDO, FLORIDA. 553

ORLEANS PARISH COUNTY, LOUISIANA. 278, 631

O'ROURKE, FRANCIS X. 768

O'SULLIVAN, DANIEL M. 315

O'SULLIVAN, FRANK P. 068

OVERBECK, JOHN H. 570, 587

OVERMAN, EDWARD S. 226, 531

OXLER, JOHN. 798

PACIFIC COAST CONFERENCE ON METROPOLITAN PROBLEMS, BERKELEY, CALIFORNIA, 1958. 571

PACIFIC LUTHERAN UNIVERSITY. URBAN AFFAIRS PROGRAM. 143

PACIFIC PLANNING AND RESEARCH. 050

PAGLIN, MORTON. 572

PAILLEX, ROBERT. 058

PALM BEACH COUNTY, FLORIDA. 211

PALMER, PHILIP F. 573

PANE, MICHAEL A. 618

PAPKE, JAMES. 791

PARK COLLEGE. GOVERNMENTAL RESEARCH BUREAU. 156, 574, 620

PARK RIDGE, ILLINOIS. OFFICE OF THE CITY MANAGER. 267

PARKVIEW, OHIO. 112

PARSONS, C.E. 144

PASSOW, JAMES A. 064

PAULSON, NORRIS. 432

PEACHEY, PAUL. 575

PEALY, ROBERT. 791

PEARCE, KENNETH. 525

PEARCE, ROGER. 733

PECHMAN, JOSEPH A. 523

INDEX

PEDERSON, MRS. ROBERT. 144

PELEKOUDAS, LOIS ME. 540

PENDLETON, RANDY. 238

PENJERDEL. 089, 117, 201, 244, 576, 577, 578, 579, 580, 586, 590, 742

PENNSAUKEN TOWNSHIP, NEW JERSEY. 201

PENNSYLVANIA. 002, 029, 117, 155, 184, 235, 244, 266, 375, 414, 451, 455, 470, 472, 498, 576, 577, 578, 579, 580, 581, 582, 583, 584, 585, 586, 588, 589, 590, 594, 595, 659, 712, 742, 758, 823, 824, 827, 828

PENNSYLVANIA. CONSTITUTIONAL CONVENTION, 1967-1968. 581

PENNSYLVANIA. DEPARTMENT OF COMMERCE. BUREAU OF COMMUNITY DEVELOPMENT. 582

PENNSYLVANIA. DEPARTMENT OF INTERNAL AFFAIRS. 002, 659, 823, 824

PENNSYLVANIA. METROPOLITAN STUDY COMMISSION. 583

PENNSYLVANIA. METROPOLITAN STUDY COMMISSION OF ALLEGHENY COUNTY. 584

PENNSYLVANIA. STATE UNIVERSITY. INSTITUTE OF PUBLIC ADMINISTRATION. 375, 585

PENNSYLVANIA. UNIVERSITY. FELS INSTITUTE OF LOCAL AND STATE GOVERNMENT. 029, 145, 827, 828

PENNSYLVANIA. UNIVERSITY. LAW SCHOOL. 721

PENNSYLVANIA ECONOMY LEAGUE. EASTERN DIVISION. 586

PENNSYLVANIA-NEW JERSEY-DELAWARE METROPOLITAN PROJECT, INCORPORATED. 089, 117, 201, 244, 576, 577, 578, 579, 580, 590, 742

PENSACOLA, FLORIDA. 639

PERRY, SIMON. 531

PERSICO, RICHARD. 720

PETERSON, VIRGIL. 539

PETRIS, NICHOLAS. 670

PETROLEUM COUNTY, MONTANA. 194, 195

PETTY, DAN. 238

PETTYJOHN, EARL F. 468

REFORM OF LOCAL GOVERNMENT STRUCTURES IN THE UNITED STATES: 1945-1971.

PHELAN, JAMES. 064

PHILADELPHIA, PENNSYLVANIA. 029, 155, 235, 266, 451, 455, 498, 588, 589, 827, 828

PHILADELPHIA. CHARTER COMMISSION. 588

PHILADELPHIA. STUDY COMMISSION OF THE PHILADELPHIA AREA. 589

PHILLIPS, S.D. 759

PHILLIPS, W. KEITH. 759

PHILLIPS, WALTER M. 590

PHILLIPS, WILLIAM J. 204, 468

PHOENIX, ARIZONA. 025, 266, 334, 794

PICKARD, JEROME P. 591

PICKARD, SHERMAN A. 536

PICKFORD, JAMES. 427

PICKUP, ROBERT. 791

PIERCE, DORIS S. 592

PINELLAS COUNTY, FLORIDA. 211, 212, 593

PINELLAS COUNTY, FLORIDA. GOVERNMENTAL STUDY COMMISSION. 593

PITKIN, FRANCIS. 429

PITSTICK, BILL. 238

PITTS, ROBERT B. 146

PITTSBURGH, PENNSYLVANIA. 235, 470, 583, 584

PITTSBURGH. UNIVERSITY. INSTITUTE OF LOCAL GOVERNMENT. 594, 595

PLANNING COMMISSIONS. 007, 011, 047, 048, 049, 062, 063, 073, 102, 104, 105, 113, 115, 117, 120, 128, 134, 138, 148, 152, 154, 159, 165, 174, 187, 201, 207, 222, 226, 229, 238, 240, 264, 265, 303, 305, 308, 311, 313, 314, 315, 326, 327, 336, 337, 338, 345, 349, 352, 355, 363, 366, 373, 377, 393, 406, 410, 412, 418, 422, 426, 427, 428, 429, 430, 431, 438, 440, 452, 460, 469, 471, 483, 521, 522, 524, 533, 538, 540, 541, 552, 582, 590, 610, 612, 619, 621, 623, 624, 629, 630, 637, 638, 643, 656, 658, 683, 711, 712, 719, 737, 746, 749, 781, 790, 800, 802, 807, 808, 809, 810, 834

INDEX

PLATT, GEORGE M. 010

PLATTE COUNTY, MISSOURI. 574

PLEASANT HILL, CALIFORNIA. 615

PLYMOUNT COUNTY, IOWA. 688

POCK, MAX A. 596

POCOMOKE, MARYLAND. 624

POLICY PLANNING. 007, 011, 013, 019, 045, 046, 048, 050, 053, 056, 060, 062, 063, 096, 115, 117, 125, 141, 154, 165, 168, 177, 200, 201, 204, 207, 209, 222, 233, 244, 246, 258, 271, 273, 274, 278, 279, 280, 284, 285, 286, 288, 289, 348, 355, 358, 389, 406, 433, 434, 438, 442, 450, 481, 521, 524, 534, 536, 539, 542, 561, 641, 643, 650, 685, 693, 736, 757, 810

POLITICAL LEADERSHIP. 002, 017, 031, 033, 072, 110, 168, 205, 217, 218, 247, 262, 348, 611, 662, 663, 667, 742

POLK COUNTY, OREGON. 088, 316, 317, 610

POMEROY, HUGH R. 389, 470

POMPEO, ANTHONY D. 104

PORT HURON, MICHIGAN. 099

PORTER, JOHN ROBERTSON. 601

PORTLAND, OREGON. 106, 362, 369, 554, 555, 560, 562, 566, 597, 598, 599, 600

PORTLAND, OREGON. METROPOLITAN STUDY COMMISSION. 597

PORTLAND, OREGON. METROPOLITAN STUDY COMMISSION. STATE AND LOCAL AFFAIRS COMMITTEE. 598

PORTLAND STATE COLLEGE. URBAN STUDIES CENTER. 599

PORTLAND STATE RESEARCH BUREAU. 600

POSEY, G. HAROLD. 044

POWERS, JOHN E. 767

PRAGER, ARTHUR. 378

PRAY, D.W. 798

PRESS, O. CHARLES. 602, 603, 604

REFORM OF LOCAL GOVERNMENT STRUCTURES IN THE UNITED STATES: 1945-1971.

PRICE, PAUL H. 270

PRINCE GEORGES COUNTY, MARYLAND. 235, 411, 437

PRINCE WILLIAM COUNTY, VIRGINIA. 437

PROCACCINO, MARIO. 523

PRYOR FIELD AIRPORT BOARD. 268

PUBLIC ADMINISTRATION SERVICE. 176, 178, 235, 532, 605, 606, 607, 608, 609, 610, 611, 612, 613, 614, 643

PUBLIC AFFAIRS RESEARCH (OAKLAND, CALIFORNIA). 615, 616

PUBLIC POLICY FORUM ON NEW JERSEY LOCAL GOVERNMENT. RUTGERS UNIVERSITY. 617, 618

PUBLIC RESEARCH AND MANAGEMENT (ATLANTA, GEORGIA). 619

PUFFER, NOBLE J. 222, 539

PULASKI COUNTY, ARKANSAS. 129, 206

PUTNAM COUNTY, NEW YORK. 720

QUEEN ANNE'S COUNTY, MARYLAND. 411

QUINN, KENT. 620

RAINS, ALBERT. 761

RAISSI, SHIRLEY. 797

RALEIGH, NORTH CAROLINA. 004

RAMEY, HORACE. 539

RAMOS, R. 830

RAND, EDWARD S. 104

RANNELLS, JOHN. 721

RAPID CITY, NORTH DAKOTA. 247

RAWSON, FRANCIS. 525

RAY, JIM. 238, 468

INDEX

RAY, JOSEPH M. 621, 622, 623, 624, 625

REED, DORIS D. 626, 627

REED, SAM S. 143

REED, THOMAS H. 626, 627, 760

REED CREEK, FLORIDA. 639

REGIONAL AGENCIES. 007, 011, 013, 019, 021, 029, 035, 047, 048, 049, 056, 060, 062, 063, 096, 102, 104, 113, 117, 120, 128, 134, 142, 146, 147, 148, 154, 172, 174, 180, 187, 201, 205, 209, 220, 222, 231, 238, 240, 244, 248, 256, 264, 265, 268, 271, 277, 280, 303, 305, 308, 311, 313, 315, 336, 337, 338, 345, 349, 355, 373, 377, 378, 385, 388, 393, 403, 406, 410, 412, 417, 418, 424, 426, 427, 428, 429, 430, 431, 437, 443, 451, 458, 469, 478, 479, 480, 481, 482, 483, 521, 522, 524, 532, 533, 548, 576, 577, 578, 579, 580, 581, 582, 586, 590, 591, 598, 612, 630, 638, 639, 656, 660, 667, 670, 673, 692, 707, 711, 712, 717, 720, 721, 737, 742, 743, 745, 746, 751, 757, 772, 805, 807, 808, 809, 810, 829, 834

REGIONAL PLAN ASSOCIATION. 248

REID, CHARLES. 493

REID, WILLIAM. 390

REIDY, DANIEL. 390

REILLY, GERALD. 490

REINING, HENRY. 432

REISS, ALBERT. 721

REOCK, ERNEST. 490, 617

RESEARCH AND PLANNING COUNCIL (SAN ANTONIO, TEXAS). 628

THE RESEARCH GROUP (ATLANTA, GEORGIA). 209, 629, 630

REYES, PAUL. 238

RHINELANDER, WISCONSIN. 710

RHODE ISLAND. 009, 026, 184, 225, 315, 382, 414, 472, 741, 758

RHODE ISLAND. UNIVERSITY. BUREAU OF GOVERNMENT. 741

RHODE ISLAND. UNIVERSITY. BUREAU OF GOVERNMENT RESEARCH. 009, 026

RICHARDSON, RICHARD J. 631

REFORM OF LOCAL GOVERNMENT STRUCTURES IN THE UNITED STATES: 1945-1971.

RICHMOND, VIRGINIA. 632, 832

RICHMOND, VIRGINIA. CITY COUNCIL AND HENRICO COUNTY. BOARD OF SUPERVISORS. ADVISORY COMMITTEES FOR THE CONSOLIDATION OF RICHMOND AND HENRICO COUNTY. 632

RICHMOND, VIRGINIA. CITIZENS ASSOCIATION. 832

RICHTER, A.J. 388

RIDER, DONALD C. 633

RIEGELMAN, HAROLD. 523, 634

RIGGS, FRED W. 635

RINEHART, JEFFREY C. 375

RINGGENBERG, CLAYTON L. 636

RIO GRANDE VALLEY, TEXAS. 737

RITZ, FRANCIS. 525

RIVERSIDE COUNTY, CALIFORNIA. 359

ROBBINS, PATRICK V. 804, 805

ROBERTS, GARY R. 405

ROBERTS AND RYDER. 637

ROBINSON, HOWARD. 064

ROCHESTER, NEW YORK. 126, 410, 459

ROCHESTER BUREAU OF MUNICIPAL RESEARCH. 685

ROCKEFELLER, NELSON A. 158, 389, 470, 768

ROCKVILLE, MARYLAND. 353, 437

ROGERS, J. LEE. 243

ROGIN, MICHAEL. 670

ROGOVOY, J.B. 493

ROHRENBECK, WILLIAM J. 493

ROLLINS COLLEGE, WINTER PARK, FLORIDA. CENTER FOR PRACTICAL POLITICS. 638, 639

INDEX

ROMMEL, ROSS. 238

RONAN, WILLIAM. 389

ROPCHAN, ALEXANDER. 539

ROSAMUND, EARL. 238

ROSEBURG, OREGON. 566

ROSENBERG, DR. 525

ROSENBERGER, MICHAEL F. 464

ROSS, MYRON H. 640, 641

ROSS, NATHAN. 830

ROTH, HAROLD. 493

ROWAN, THOMAS. 471

RUBIN, MAX J. 389

RUSCO, ELMER R. 642

RUTHERFORD, GEDDES W. 643

RUTHERFORD, JAMES E. 222

RYAN, JOHN W. 251

RYAN, LEO J. 231

SACRAMENTO, CALIFORNIA. 606, 646, 647, 648, 649

SACRAMENTO COUNTY, CALIFORNIA. 646, 647, 648, 649

SACRAMENTO COUNTY, CALIFORNIA. PLANNING DEPARTMENT. 647

SACRAMENTO CITY-COUNTY CHAMBER OF COMMERCE. METROPOLITAN DEVELOPMENT COMMITTEE. 646

SACRAMENTO METROPOLITAN AREA ADVISORY COMMITTEE. 648, 649

SAGOFF, SARA. 315

ST. BERNARD PARISH, LOUISIANA. 278

ST. CLAIR COUNTY, MICHIGAN. 443

REFORM OF LOCAL GOVERNMENT STRUCTURES IN THE UNITED STATES: 1945-1971.

ST. FRANCIS, WISCONSIN. 251

ST. JOHN'S UNIVERSITY. CENTER FOR THE STUDY OF LOCAL GOVERNMENT. 280

ST. JOSEPH, MICHIGAN. 608

ST. JOSEPH, MISSOURI. 454

ST. LOUIS, MISSOURI. 075, 235, 266, 339, 386, 435, 436, 450, 451, 644, 645, 662, 678

ST. LOUIS, MISSOURI. BOARD OF FREEHOLDERS. 644

ST. LOUIS COUNTY, MISSOURI. 236, 435, 436, 450, 451, 645, 678

ST. LOUIS, ST. LOUIS COUNTY, MISSOURI. METROPOLITAN BOARD OF FREEHOLDERS. 645

ST. LOUIS UNIVERSITY. SCHOOL OF LAW. 678

ST. LUCIE COUNTY, FLORIDA. 212

ST. MARY'S COUNTY, MARYLAND. 411

ST. PAUL, MINNESOTA. 018, 090, 091, 126, 142, 143, 410, 746

ST. PETERSBURG, FLORIDA. 260

SALEM, OREGON. 088, 259, 316, 317, 410, 566, 610

SALISBURY, MARYLAND. 625

SALONA BEACH, CALIFORNIA. 380

SALT LAKE CITY, UTAH. 681

SAN ANTONIO, TEXAS. 266, 733

SAN BERNADINO COUNTY, CALIFORNIA. 359

SAN DIEGO, CALIFORNIA. 266, 381, 650

SAN DIEGO. CITIZENS' CHARTER REVIEW COMMITTEE. 650

SAN DIEGO COUNTY, CALIFORNIA. 359

SAN DIEGO STATE COLLEGE. PUBLIC AFFAIRS RESEARCH INSTITUTE. 379, 380, 381,

SANFORD, TERRY. 158

SAN FRANCISCO, CALIFORNIA. 062, 063, 067, 142, 231, 311, 336, 337, 338, 419, 424, 612, 651, 652, 653, 654, 655, 656, 667, 674, 707, 743, 834

INDEX

SAN FRANCISCO. CITIZENS' CHARTER REVISION COMMITTEE. 651, 652, 653, 654, 655

SAN FRANCISCO BAY AREA, CALIFORNIA. 011, 050, 056, 062, 063, 067, 142, 143, 146, 231, 255, 311, 336, 337, 338, 417, 419, 424, 612, 656, 667, 672, 674, 707, 743, 834

SAN FRANCISCO BAY AREA AIR POLLUTION CONTROL DISTRICT. 707

SAN FRANCISCO BAY AREA RAPID TRANSIT DISTRICT. 707

SAN FRANCISCO BAY CONSERVATION AND DEVELOPMENT COMMISSION. 063, 656, 667 707, 834

SAN LUIS OBISPO, CALIFORNIA. 657

SAN LUIS OBISPO COUNTY, CALIFORNIA. 657

SAN LUIS OBISPO COUNTY, CALIFORNIA. OFFICE OF THE DISTRICT ATTORNEY. 657

SANTA CLARA COUNTY, CALIFORNIA. 359, 658

SANTA CLARA COUNTY COUNCIL ON INTERGOVERNMENTAL RELATIONS (CALIFORNIA). 658

SARPONG, M.A.B. 830

SARRATT, REED. 141

SASO, CARMEN. 032, 225

SATO, SHO. 670

SAUERS, CHARLES. 222

SAUSE, GEORGE G. 659

SAVANNAH, GEORGIA. 083, 227

SAVANNAH COUNTY, GEORGIA. 083

SCELLIE, KENNETH. 427

SCHAEFER, ROBERT. 798

SCHEIBER, WALTER A. 478, 660

SCHICK, LESTER R. 471

SCHMANDT, HENRY J. 661, 662, 663, 664, 773

SCHMID, WARREN. 143, 146

SCHNEIDER, EUGENE J. 618

SCHOENTAS, DAVID C. 525

SCHOOP, JACK. 670

SCHREIBER, WALTER A. 143

SCHRUM, JACK. 238

SCHTEN, EDWARD V. 281

SCHULMAN, S.J. 525

SCHWAN, CHARLES F. 766

SCOTT, JACK L. 490

SCOTT, MEL. 047, 204

SCOTT, STANLEY. 047, 142, 204, 231, 571, 665, 666, 667, 668, 669, 670, 671, 672, 673, 674, 743, 760, 834

SEARLES, JOHN. 761

SEATTLE, WASHINGTON. 018, 235, 321, 362, 364, 367, 370, 373, 374, 410, 433, 434, 675, 676, 803, 833

SEATTLE. METROPOLITAN COUNCIL. 675

SEATTLE. OFFICE OF EXECUTIVE DIRECTOR. 676

SEDWAY (PAUL) AND ASSOCIATES. 707, 743, 834

SELLAND, ARTHUR. 204

SENGSTOCK, FRANK S. 677, 678, 679

SERINO, GUSTAVE. 680, 759

SEROTTA, MRS. MAURICE. 759

SHANLEY, ROBERT A. 315

SHAPIRO, HARVEY. 039

SHARP, VEE J. 681

SHAUGHNESSY, HOWARD. 539

SHAW, G.N. 246

INDEX

SHAWNEE COUNTY, KANSAS. 399

SHEFELMAN, HAROLD S. 389

SHEIBER, WALTER A. 468

SHELBY COUNTY, TENNESSEE. 421, 422, 423

SHELTON, M.J. 571

SHEPOISER, LAWRENCE. 798

SHERWOOD, FRANK P. 047, 204

SHESTACK, JEROME. 721

SHOENECKER, LEE. 238

SHORE, WILLIAM. 720

SHOUP, CARL S. 523

SHULL, CHARLES W. 791

SIEGEL, JACK. 427

SIEGEL, WILLIAM. 058

SIFFIN, CATHERINE FOX. 682

SILVER SPRINGS, MARYLAND. 368, 621

SIMONETTI, FRANK. 085

SIMPSON, PHILIP G. 059

SIOUX CITY, IOWA. 217, 688, 718

SIOUXLAND. 217

SLIGER, B.F. 388

SMALL, JOSEPH F. 683

SMALL, ROBERT. 064, 065

SMALLWOOD, FRANK. 378

SMITH, CRAIG M. 685

SMITH, HARRY R. 686, 687, 688, 689

SMITH, PRESTON. 238

REFORM OF LOCAL GOVERNMENT STRUCTURES IN THE UNITED STATES: 1945-1971.

SMITH, ROBERT. 468

SMITH, STEPHEN C. 690

SMITHEE, KENNETH J. 468

SMYTH, LESLIE. 238

SNADEN, JOHN W. 691

SNOWISS, SYLVIA. 692

SO, FRANK S. 693

SOFEN, EDWARD. 694

SOKOLOW, ALVIN D. 695

SOLANO COUNTY, CALIFORNIA. 359

SOMERSET COUNTY, MARYLAND. 411

SORENSEN, ROYAL. 047, 204, 684

SOURS, JAMES K. 696

SOUTH CAROLINA. 004, 080, 081, 082, 184, 269, 352, 354, 472, 619, 627, 697, 758

SOUTH CAROLINA. OFFICE OF THE GOVERNOR. PLANNING AND GRANTS DIVISION. 619

SOUTH CAROLINA. UNIVERSITY. BUREAU OF PUBLIC ADMINISTRATION. 352, 354, 697

SOUTH DAKOTA. 074, 184, 247, 472, 698, 699, 700, 701, 702, 703, 710, 758, 804

SOUTH DAKOTA. LEGISLATIVE RESEARCH COUNCIL. 698

SOUTH DAKOTA. LOCAL GOVERNMENT STUDY COMMISSION. 699, 700, 701, 702, 703

SOUTH DAKOTA. UNIVERSITY. GOVERNMENTAL RESEARCH BUREAU. 074, 247

SOUTHEAST MICHIGAN. 096, 102, 128, 418, 431

SOUTHEAST TENNESSEE DEVELOPMENT DISTRICT. 630

SOUTHEASTERN MICHIGAN METROPOLITAN COMMUNITY RESEARCH CORPORATION. 022

SOUTHEASTERN PENNSYLVANIA. 029

SOUTHERN, DODD A. 704

SOUTHERN CALIFORNIA. 187

INDEX

SOUTHERN CALIFORNIA. UNIVERSITY. SCHOOL OF PUBLIC ADMINISTRATION. 160

SOUTHERN ILLINOIS UNIVERSITY, CARBONDALE. LOCAL GOVERNMENT CENTER. 705

SOUTHERN ILLINOIS UNIVERSITY, EDWARDSVILLE. REGIONAL AND URBAN DEVELOPMENT STUDIES AND SERVICES. 706

SOUTHERN ILLINOIS UNIVERSITY. METROPOLITAN AFFAIRS PROGRAM. 405

SOUTHERN ILLINOIS UNIVERSITY. PUBLIC AFFAIRS RESEARCH BUREAU. 279, 300

SOWERS, WESLEY. 798

SPANGLE (WILLIAM) AND ASSOCIATES. 707

SPECIAL DISTRICTS AND AUTHORITIES. 013, 016, 018, 021, 025, 026, 027, 029, 032, 034, 035, 044, 046, 050, 056, 057, 058, 060, 064, 067, 070, 073, 079, 080, 102, 103, 121, 123, 129, 133, 139, 144, 145, 147, 149, 150, 151, 155, 156, 158, 160, 181, 205, 228, 229, 231, 232, 240, 241, 242, 260, 261, 264, 283, 291, 292, 302, 303, 310, 312, 314, 315, 320, 321, 322, 331, 339, 341, 342, 354, 362, 363, 364, 366, 369, 373, 375, 377, 378, 394, 397, 398, 399, 400, 403, 410, 415, 419, 437, 445, 452, 464, 468, 473, 483, 506, 507, 511, 546, 548, 556, 557, 558, 560, 566, 568, 569, 574, 581, 595, 596, 597, 600, 602, 607, 608, 612, 657, 659, 661, 672, 673, 674, 688, 689, 700, 717, 740, 741, 747, 755, 774, 835

SPEEDWAY, INDIANA. 637

SPELLMAN, GLADYS N. 468

SPENCER, JAMES W. 390

SPENCER, JEAN E. 708

SPINDLETON RESEARCH. 313

SPOKANE, WASHINGTON. 719

SPOKANE COUNTY, WASHINGTON. 719

SPOKANE COUNTY, WASHINGTON. PLANNING COMMISSION. 719

SPRING VALLEY, CALIFORNIA. 381

SPRINGER, MARVIN R. 733

SPRINGFIELD, OREGON. 566

STALLING, JUDY E. 261

STALLINGS, E.R. 058

STANBER, RICHARD. 817

REFORM OF LOCAL GOVERNMENT STRUCTURES IN THE UNITED STATES: 1945-1971.

STANDING, WILLIAM H. 663

STANISLAUS COUNTY, CALIFORNIA. 359, 397

STARK COUNTY, OHIO. 548

STEAD, FRANK M. 743

STEINBICKER, PAUL G. 662

STEINER, GILBERT Y. 010, 116, 426, 461, 540, 709

STEINHEIMER, A.K. 238

STEMMERY, J. ANDREW. 768

STENE, EDWIN O. 710

STEVEN H. WILDER FOUNDATION. 265, 626

STIERN, RICHARD A. 065

STOCKWELL, HARLAND. 539

STODDARD, PAUL W. 144

STONEHAM, WALTER. 792

STONER, JOHN E. 711, 712

STORANDT, KENNETH M. 389

STORM, WILLIAM B. 047, 204

STOUDEMIRE, ROBERT H. 352

STOYLES, ROBERT L. 713

STRAUSS, LEO H. 231

STRAWBRIDGE, WILLIAM. 720

STREETER, CHARLES F. 144

STUART, PATRICIA. 714, 715, 716, 717

SUGARCREEK TOWNSHIP, OHIO. 130

SULLIVAN, J. JOSEPH. 231

SUNDERMANN, FREDERICK. 718

SUTTON, ROBERT P. 068

INDEX

SWANSON, K.T.W. 719

SWEENEY, JOHN. 525

SYMPOSIUM AT TARRYTOWN, WESTCHESTER COUNTY, NEW YORK, OCTOBER 16-17, 1970. 720

SYMPOSIUM ON METROPOLITAN REGIONALISM: DEVELOPING GOVERNMENTAL CONCEPTS. 721

SYRACUSE, NEW YORK. 043, 175, 722, 723

SYRACUSE, NEW YORK. CHARTER REVISION COMMITTEE. 722, 723

SYRACUSE. UNIVERSITY. MAXWELL GRADUATE SCHOOL OF CITIZENSHIP AND PUBLIC AFFAIRS. 027

TAAFFE, EDWARD J. 222

TAFT, OREGON. 565

TAKOMA PARK, MARYLAND. 437

TALBOT COUNTY, MARYLAND. 411

TALLAHASSEE, FLORIDA. 212

TAMPA, FLORIDA. 639

TARBORO, NORTH CAROLINA. 004

TARRANT, WILLIAM. 798

TARSHES, M.D. 204, 468

TAX RESEARCH ASSOCIATION OF HOUSTON AND HARRIS COUNTY (TEXAS). 724

TEGLEY, JOHN. 032

TEGNELL, GUS. G. 523

TELFORD, EDWARD T. 047, 204

TEMPLE, DAVID G. 403

TENNESSEE. 004, 033, 036, 087, 138, 143, 158, 184, 195, 198, 202, 205, 209, 235, 262, 269, 333, 339, 364, 410, 420, 421, 422, 423, 449, 465, 466, 468, 472, 531, 532, 629, 630, 639, 667, 682, 725, 726, 727, 728, 729, 736, 758, 818, 833

TENNESSEE. CHARTER. 120, 725

REFORM OF LOCAL GOVERNMENT STRUCTURES IN THE UNITED STATES: 1945-1971.

TENNESSEE. LEGISLATIVE COUNCIL COMMITTEE. 726

TENNESSEE. PLANNING COMMISSION. 728

TENNESSEE. UNIVERSITY. BUREAU OF PUBLIC ADMINISTRATION. 351, 420, 531, 682, 727

TENNESSEE. UNIVERSITY. COLLEGE OF BUSINESS ADMINISTRATION. BUREAU OF RESEARCH. 728

TENNESSEE MUNICIPAL LEAGUE. 531

TENNESSEE TAXPAYERS ASSOCIATION. 729

TENNESSEE VALLEY AUTHORITY. 728

TERHUNE, GEORGE A. 373

TERRE HAUTE, INDIANA. 371

TEXAS. 019, 039, 098, 109, 155, 173, 184, 219, 228, 235, 238, 243, 258, 266, 269, 364, 386, 396, 414, 472, 724, 730, 731, 732, 733, 734, 735, 736, 737, 740, 758, 804

TEXAS. LEGISLATIVE COUNCIL. 730

TEXAS. LEGISLATIVE COUNCIL. STUDY COMMITTEE ON COUNTY GOVERNMENT. 731

TEXAS. OFFICE OF THE GOVERNOR. DIVISION OF PLANNING COORDINATION. 238

TEXAS. UNIVERSITY. INSTITUTE OF PUBLIC AFFAIRS. 019, 228, 396, 732, 733, 740

TEXAS CONFERENCE ON METROPOLITAN PROBLEMS, 1958. 733

TEXAS RESEARCH LEAGUE. 734, 735, 736, 737

THARP, CLAUDE R. 738, 739

THOLIN, A.L. 427

THOMPSON, C.C. 733

THROMBLEY, WOODWORTH G. 733, 740

TIBBITTS, WALTER. 238

TOLEDO, OHIO. 548

TOMPKINS, PATRICK A. 144

TOOMEY, JOHN. 104

INDEX

TOPEKA, KANSAS. 399

TORGOVNIK, EFRAIM. 741

TORONTO, CANADA. 127, 143, 145, 155, 235, 362, 364, 373, 374, 432, 444, 445, 470, 532, 638, 639, 667, 803, 818, 830, 833

TOSCANO, JAMES V. 742

TOWNSEND, HAROLD. 238

TRAVIS COUNTY, TEXAS. 228

TRENTON, NEW JERSEY. 744

TRENTON, NEW JERSEY. CHARTER COMMISSION. 744

TRI-CITIES, WASHINGTON. 464

TRI-STATE REGION (NEW YORK, NEW JERSEY, CONNECTICUT). 172, 248, 378

TROWER, RALPH K. 743

TUCSON, ARIZONA. 025

TUCSON. COUNCIL. 334

TUDOR, WILLIAM. 706

TULSA, OKLAHOMA. 745

TULSA METROPOLITAN AREA PLANNING COMMISSION. 745

TUSCALOOSA COUNTY, ALABAMA. 268

TWIN CITIES AREA, MINNESOTA. 142

TWIN CITIES METROPOLITAN PLANNING COMMISSION (MINNESOTA). 746

UNITED STATES. ADVISORY COMMISSION ON INTERGOVERNMENTAL RELATIONS. 216, 255, 406, 747, 748, 749, 750, 751, 752, 753, 754, 755, 756, 757

UNITED STATES. BUREAU OF THE CENSUS. 758

UNITED STATES. CONGRESS. HOUSE. COMMITTEE ON GOVERNMENT OPERATIONS. 759, 760, 761, 762, 763

UNITED STATES. CONGRESS. JOINT COMMITTEE ON WASHINGTON METROPOLITAN PROGRAMS. 764

UNITED STATES. CONGRESS. SENATE. COMMITTEE ON GOVERNMENT OPERATIONS. SUBCOMMITTEE ON INTERGOVERNMENTAL RELATIONS. 766, 767, 768

REFORM OF LOCAL GOVERNMENT STRUCTURES IN THE UNITED STATES: 1945-1971.

UNITED STATES. CONGRESS. SENATE. COMMITTEE ON GOVERNMENT OPERATIONS. SUBCOMMITTEE ON REORGANIZATION AND INTERNATIONAL ORGANIZATIONS. 765

UNITED STATES. DEPARTMENT OF AGRICULTURE. ECONOMIC RESEARCH SERVICE. 039, 603, 712

UNITED STATES. DEPARTMENT OF HOUSING AND URBAN DEVELOPMENT. 769

UNITED STATES. HOUSING AND HOME FINANCE AGENCY. 410

UNITED STATES. OFFICE OF ECONOMIC OPPORTUNITY. 770

UNITED STATES CONFERENCE OF MAYORS. COMMUNITY RELATIONS SERVICE. 771

UPPER PENINSULA, MICHIGAN. 695

THE URBAN INSTITUTE. 456, 457, 458

URBAN LAND INSTITUTE. 591

URBAN POLICY CONFERENCE, 5TH, UNIVERSITY OF IOWA, 1968. 773

URBANA, ILLINOIS. 461

URSTADT, CHARLES. 720

UTAH. 184, 472, 681, 758, 774, 775, 776

UTAH. LEGISLATIVE COUNCIL. 681

UTAH. LOCAL GOVERNMENT SURVEY COMMISSION. 774

UTAH. UNIVERSITY. CENTER FOR ECONOMIC AND COMMUNITY DEVELOPMENT. 775, 776

UTHE, ZELDE M. 390

VALPARAISO, INDIANA. 004

VANLANDINGHAM, KENNETH. 777

VAN LARE, FRANK E. 390

VAN METER, RALPH A. 144

VAN WALSUM, G.E. 830

VAUGHAN, DONALD S. 273

VELLA, IGNAZIO A. 142

INDEX

VENABLES, VANCE V. 058

VENTURA COUNTY, CALIFORNIA. 359

VER BERG, KENNETH. 778, 779

VERMONT. 184, 225, 315, 382, 413, 472, 546, 758

VERMONT. UNIVERSITY. GOVERNMENT RESEARCH CENTER. 546

VERNON, RAYMOND. 765

VICKREY, WILLIAM. 523

VIGO COUNTY, INDIANA. 371

VIRGINIA. 012, 013, 040, 155, 184, 194, 207, 208, 219, 226, 227, 235, 236, 269, 361, 364, 403, 437, 472, 611, 632, 643, 758, 780, 781, 782, 783, 784, 785, 786, 792, 799, 832

VIRGINIA. ADVISORY LEGISLATIVE COUNCIL. 780

VIRGINIA. METROPOLITAN AREAS STUDY COMMISSION. 781, 782

VIRGINIA. METROPOLITAN AREAS STUDY COMMISSION. COMMITTEE ON GOVERNMENTAL STRUCTURE. 783

VIRGINIA. UNIVERSITY. BUREAU OF PUBLIC ADMINISTRATION. 226, 784, 785, 792

VIRGINIA. UNIVERSITY. INSTITUTE OF GOVERNMENT. 012, 013, 403, 786

VIRGINIA MUNICIPAL LEAGUE. 792

VOGEL, JOSHUA H. 321

VOLUSIA COUNTY, FLORIDA. 212

WAALAND, THOMAS. 390

WABASH, INDIANA. 004

WADE, DAVID. 238

WAGNER, ROBERT F. 761, 768, 830

WAKEFIELD, GEORGE W. 060

WALDO, DWIGHT. 670

WALDRON, ELLIS. 772

REFORM OF LOCAL GOVERNMENT STRUCTURES IN THE UNITED STATES: 1945-1971.

WALKER, HARVEY. 760

WALKER, JACK. 427

WALKER, MABEL. 389, 721

WALKER COUNTY, GEORGIA. 629, 630

WALL, HUGO. 798

WALLA WALLA, WASHINGTON. 789

WALLA WALLA COUNTY, WASHINGTON. 789

WALSH, DONALD. 525

WARREN, ROBERT O. 787

WARREN WOODS, MICHIGAN. 103

WARWICK, VIRGINIA. 235, 784

WASHINGTON. 018, 069, 070, 098, 140, 143, 184, 235, 321, 322, 350, 362, 364, 367, 370, 373, 374, 410, 433, 434, 464, 472, 675, 676, 719, 758, 788, 789, 790, 803, 833

WASHINGTON (STATE). LEGISLATURE. JOINT COMMITTEE ON URBAN AREA GOVERNMENT. CITIZENS ADVISORY COMMITTEE. 788

WASHINGTON (STATE). PLANNING AND COMMUNITY AFFAIRS AGENCY. 143

WASHINGTON (STATE). RESEARCH COUNCIL. 789

WASHINGTON. STATE UNIVERSITY. DIVISION OF GOVERNMENTAL STUDIES AND SERVICES. 140

WASHINGTON. UNIVERSITY. BUREAU OF GOVERNMENTAL RESEARCH AND SERVICES. 069, 321, 322, 350, 790

WASHINGTON, D.C. 205, 235, 255, 256, 265, 410, 417, 437, 498, 643, 764

WASHINGTON CENTER FOR METROPOLITAN STUDIES. 014, 256, 575

WASHINGTON COUNTY, MARYLAND. 411

WASHINGTON COUNTY, OREGON. 362, 562, 597, 599

WASHINGTON SUBURBAN SANITARY COMMISSION. 621

WASTENAW COUNTY, MICHIGAN. 096, 443

WATT, PAUL C. 733

INDEX

WAYNE COUNTY, MICHIGAN. 096, 443

WAYNE STATE UNIVERSITY. DEPARTMENT OF POLITICAL SCIENCE. 791

WAYNE STATE UNIVERSITY CITIZEN LEADER CONFERENCE, 1961. 791

WEAVER, ROBERT C. 469, 767, 830

WEBB, WILFRED. 733

WEBSTER, DONALD H. 321

WEEKS, J. DEVEREUX. 792, 814, 815, 816, 818

WEIFORD, DOUGLAS G. 819, 820

WEINBERG, ROBERT F. 720

WELCH, LEWIS P. 175

WELDON, JOHN D. 468

WENDEL, GEORGE D. 662

WENTZ, JOHN B. 793

WENUM, JOHN D. 794

WESCHLER, LOUIS F. 108

WEST, BEN. 765

WEST VIRGINIA. 004, 184, 203, 372, 404, 472, 691, 758

WEST VIRGINIA. UNIVERSITY. BUREAU FOR GOVERNMENT RESEARCH. 203, 404

WESTCHESTER COUNTY, NEW YORK. 720

WESTERN GOVERNMENTAL RESEARCH ASSOCIATION, 17TH, LONG BEACH, CALIFORNIA, 1957. 795

WESTERN MISSOURI. 453

WETMORE, LOUIS B. 426, 428

WETMORE, RUTH Y. 796

WETTERLING, CATHERINE. 493

WHALEN, ROBERT P. 508

WHEATON, WILLIAM L.C. 760, 761

REFORM OF LOCAL GOVERNMENT STRUCTURES IN THE UNITED STATES: 1945-1971.

WHITE, ERSKINE N. 104

WHITE, GILBERT. 428

WHITE, JAMES. 733

WHITE, MAX R. 797

WHITE, MELVIN. 523

WHITMORE, HOWARD. 104

WICHITA, KANSAS. 798

WICHITA. UNIVERSITY. 696

WICHITA REGIONAL CONFERENCE ON LOCAL GOVERNMENT PROBLEMS AND POLICIES. 798

WICHITA STATE UNIVERSITY. CENTER FOR URBAN STUDIES. 798

WICKER, WARREN J. 536

WICKSTEAD, GEORGE W. 222, 428

WICOMICO COUNTY, MARYLAND. 625

WIEBOLT, ROBERT. 720

WILDAVSKY, AARON. 670

WILES, WALTER. 427

WILL, ARTHUR G. 060, 068, 158

WILL, PHILIP. 222

WILLBERN, YORK. 027, 206

WILLIAM AND MARY COLLEGE. RICHMOND PROFESSIONAL INSTITUTE. 832

WILLIAMS, G. MENNEN. 470

WILLIAMS, HARRISON A. 765

WILLIAMS, J.D. 774

WILLIAMS, ROBERT R. 539

WILLIAMSBURG, VIRGINIA. 013, 799

WILLIAMSBURG-JAMES CITY COUNTY JOINT CONSOLIDATION STUDY COMMISSION. 799

INDEX

WILLMOTT, JOHN. 733

WILLOUGHBY, THOMAS H. 061

WILSON, S. LEIGH. 536

WINGFIELD, CLYDE J. 175

WINGFIELD, J.D. 720

WINSTON-SALEM, NORTH CAROLINA. 004

WINTER, ARTHUR BRUCE. 397

WINTER, RICHARD. 432

WINTERS, JOHN M. 800, 801

WISCONSIN. 040, 184, 185, 186, 195, 230, 235, 251, 252, 281, 408, 472, 573, 661, 710, 711, 712, 758, 802, 803, 804, 805, 806, 807, 808, 809, 810, 811, 812, 813, 814, 815, 816, 817, 818, 819, 820, 821, 822

WISCONSIN. LEGISLATIVE COUNCIL. 803

WISCONSIN. LEGISLATIVE REFERENCE BUREAU. 804, 805

WISCONSIN. LEGISLATIVE REFERENCE LIBRARY. 806

WISCONSIN. LEGISLATURE. INTERIM URBAN PROBLEMS COMMITTEE. 802

WISCONSIN. METROPOLITAN STUDY COMMISSION. 807, 808, 809, 810, 811, 812

WISCONSIN. METROPOLITAN STUDY COMMISSION. REVENUE SOURCES AND DISTRIBUTION COMMITTEE. 813

WISCONSIN. TASK FORCE ON LOCAL GOVERNMENT FINANCE AND ORGANIZATION. 815, 816, 817, 818, 819, 820

WISCONSIN. TASK FORCE ON LOCAL GOVERNMENT FINANCE AND REORGANIZATION. 814

WISCONSIN. UNIVERSITY. BUREAU OF GOVERNMENT. 185, 251, 252, 281, 573, 664, 821, 822

WISCONSIN. UNIVERSITY. INSTITUTE OF GOVERNMENTAL AFFAIRS. 186

WISE, HAROLD F. 469

WISE, SIDNEY. 823, 824

WITHERSPOON, JOHN V. 468

WITTE, ARNOLD. 523

REFORM OF LOCAL GOVERNMENT STRUCTURES IN THE UNITED STATES: 1945-1971.

WITTELS, HERBERT G. 525

WOLFE, THOMAS W. 767

WOLFF, REINHOLD P. 825

WOLIN, SHELDON. 670

WOOD, C. RAYMOND. 068, 204

WOOD, ROBERT C. 478, 760, 826

WOOD, SAMUEL E. 427

WOODBURY, COLEMA. 760

WOODBURY COUNTY, IOWA. 688

WORCESTER COUNTY, MARYLAND. 411, 624

WORKSHOP ON METROPOLITAN AREA PROBLEMS. UNIVERSITY OF PENNSYLVANIA. 827, 828

WORKSHOP ON VOLUNTARY MULTI-PURPOSE REGIONAL ORGANIZATIONS, SEATTLE, 1961. 829

WORLD CONFERENCE OF LOCAL GOVERNMENTS, WASHINGTON, D.C. 1961. 830

WORLD HEALTH ORGANIZATION. EXPERT COMMITTEE ON "HEALTH AND SANITARY ASPECTS OF METROPOLITAN PLANNING, HOUSING AND INDUSTRIALIZATION". 200

WRIGHT, J. WARD. 468

WURSTER, CATHERINE B. 760

WYANDOTTE, MICHIGAN. 094

WYANDOTTE COUNTY, KANSAS. 398

WYOMING. 184, 472, 758

YAMHILL COUNTY, OREGON. 610

YEE, ROBERT. 350

YERBY, RICHARD D. 183

YERKES, WILLIAM. 238

INDEX

YLVISAKER, PAUL N. 222, 571

YOSHIDA, M. 830

YOUNGER, J. ARTHUR. 761

YUVAPURNA, C. 830

ZEIDLER, FRANK P. 765

ZEIGLER, FRANK W. 831

ZETZMAN, MARION. 238

ZIMMER, KENNETH. 832

ZIMMERMAN, JOSEPH F. 277, 833

ZION, WILLIAM R. 834, 835, 836

Z
7165
U5
M448

SEP 21 1978